Praise for *Unguarded*

"A master class in settling scores, or creating new ones."

—*The New York Times*

"The Chicago Bulls stalwart tells all—and then some. Pippen also writes evenhandedly of the world outside basketball: 'No matter how many championships I have won, and millions I have earned, I never forget the color of my skin and that some people in this world hate me just because of that.' Closely observed and uncommonly modest."

—*Kirkus*

"Pippen offers an intriguing take on one of the NBA's greatest dynasties, [his] youth as the youngest of 12 children in a family ripped by tragedy, and his unlikely ascent to basketball greatness. Expect all the sports talking heads to be in full cry when this much-hyped memoir hits the shelves."

—*Booklist*

UNGUARDED

SCOTTIE PIPPEN

WITH MICHAEL ARKUSH

ATRIA PAPERBACK
New York London Toronto Sydney New Delhi

ATRIA
PAPERBACK

An Imprint of Simon & Schuster, Inc.
1230 Avenue of the Americas
New York, NY 10020

First Atria Books paperback edition October 2022

ATRIA PAPERBACK and colophon are trademarks of Simon & Schuster, Inc.

For information about special discounts for bulk purchases, please contact Simon & Schuster Special Sales at 1-866-506-1949 or business@simonandschuster.com.

The Simon & Schuster Speakers Bureau can bring authors to your live event. For more information, or to book an event, contact the Simon & Schuster Speakers Bureau at 1-866-248-3049 or visit our website at www.simonspeakers.com.

Interior design by Silverglass

Manufactured in the United States of America

1 3 5 7 9 10 8 6 4 2

Library of Congress Control Number: 2021946494

ISBN 978-1-9821-6519-2
ISBN 978-1-9821-6520-8 (pbk)
ISBN 978-1-9821-6521-5 (ebook)

To my children, who inspire me to be my best self and live a meaningful life:
Antron, Taylor, Sierra, Scotty Jr., Preston, Justin, and Sophia

CONTENTS

PROLOGUE

May 19, 2020, 6:31 p.m.

The text was from Michael. He didn't reach out very often.

What's up dude? I'm getting word that you're upset with me. Love to talk about it if you have time.

My schedule was packed that evening and I knew the conversation would take a while.

I hit him back an hour and a half later:

Let's talk tomorrow.

Michael was right. I was upset with him. It was because of *The Last Dance*, the ten-part ESPN documentary about the Chicago Bulls' final championship season (1997–98), which millions of people watched during the early weeks of the pandemic.

With no live sports on TV, *The Last Dance*, for five straight Sunday nights starting in mid-April, provided a much-needed distraction from the new normal we suddenly found ourselves in. There was only so much news about hot spots and hospitalizations and deaths anyone could absorb.

The final two episodes aired on May 17. Similar to the previous eight, they glorified Michael Jordan while not giving nearly enough praise to me and my proud teammates. Michael deserved a large portion of the blame. The producers had granted him editorial control of the final product. The doc couldn't have been released otherwise. He was the leading man *and* the director.

I had expected much more. When I was first told about it over a year earlier, I couldn't wait to tune in, knowing it would feature rare footage.

My years in Chicago, beginning as a rookie in the fall of 1987, were the most rewarding of my career: twelve men coming together as one, fulfilling the dreams we had as kids in playgrounds across the land when all we needed was a ball, a basket, and our imagination. To be a member of the Bulls during the 1990s was to be part of something magical. For our times and for all time.

Except Michael was determined to prove to the current generation of fans that he was larger-than-life during his day—and still larger than LeBron James, the player many consider his equal, if not superior. So Michael presented his story, not the story of the "Last Dance," as our coach, Phil Jackson, billed the 1997–98 season once it became obvious the two Jerrys (owner Jerry Reinsdorf and general manager Jerry Krause) were intent on breaking up the gang no matter what happened.

As Krause told Phil in the fall of '97: You can go 82-0 and it won't make a difference. This will be your last season as the coach of the Chicago Bulls.

ESPN sent me links to the first eight episodes a couple of weeks in advance. As I watched the doc at home in Southern California with my three teenage boys, I couldn't believe my eyes.

Among the scenes in the first episode:

- Michael, a freshman at the University of North Carolina, hitting the game-winning jump shot against the Georgetown Hoyas in the 1982 NCAA title game.

- Michael, drafted third by the Bulls in 1984 behind Hakeem Ola-juwon (Houston) and Sam Bowie (Portland), talking about his hopes of turning the franchise around.
- Michael leading the Bulls to a comeback triumph over the Mil-waukee Bucks in just his third game.

On and on it went, the spotlight shining on number 23.

Even in the second episode, which focused for a while on my difficult upbringing and unlikely path to the NBA, the narrative returned to MJ and his determination to win. I was nothing more than a prop. His "best teammate of all time," he called me. He couldn't have been more condescending if he tried.

On second thought, I could believe my eyes. I spent a lot of time around the man. I knew what made him tick. How naïve I was to expect anything else.

Each episode was the same: Michael on a pedestal, his teammates secondary, smaller, the message no different from when he referred to us back then as his "supporting cast." From one season to the next, we received little or no credit whenever we won but the bulk of the criticism when we lost. Michael could shoot 6 for 24 from the field, commit 5 turnovers, and he was still, in the minds of the adoring press and public, the Errorless Jordan.

Now here I was, in my midfifties, sixteen years since my final game, watching us being demeaned once again. Living through it the first time was insulting enough.

Over the next few weeks, I spoke to a number of my former teammates who each felt as disrespected as I did. How dare Michael treat us that way after everything we did for him and his precious brand. Michael Jordan would never have been Michael Jordan with-out me, Horace Grant, Toni Kukoc, John Paxson, Steve Kerr, Den-nis Rodman, Bill Cartwright, Ron Harper, B. J. Armstrong, Luc

Longley, Will Perdue, and Bill Wennington. I apologize to anyone I've left out.

I'm not suggesting Michael wouldn't have been a superstar wherever he ended up. He was that spectacular. Just that he relied on the success we attained as a team—six titles in eight years—to propel him to a level of fame throughout the world no other athlete, except for Muhammad Ali, has reached in modern times.

To make things worse, Michael received $10 million for his role in the doc while my teammates and I didn't earn a dime, another reminder of the pecking order from the old days. For an entire season, we allowed cameras into the sanctity of our locker rooms, our practices, our hotels, our huddles . . . our *lives*.

Michael wasn't the only former teammate to reach out that week. Two days later, I received a text from John Paxson, the starting point guard from our first two championships, who later became the Bulls' general manager and then vice president of basketball operations. I heard from Paxson less often than from Michael.

Hey, Pip . . . its Pax.

Michael Reinsdorf [Jerry's son, who runs the franchise] *gave me your number. Just want you to know I respected everything about you as a teammate. Fucking narratives can be told but I rely on my real experiences. Watched you grow from a rook . . . to a pro. Dont let others, including the media, define you. You are successful and valued and I have always felt lucky to be your teammate.*

Was receiving texts from Michael and Paxson only two days apart a coincidence? I think not.

Both were aware of how angry I was about the doc. They were checking in to make sure I wouldn't cause any trouble: to the Bulls, who still paid Paxson as an adviser; or to Michael's legacy, always a major concern.

Paxson and I hadn't gotten along in years. In the summer of

2003, I turned down an offer from the Memphis Grizzlies to sign a two-year contract with the Bulls, where I would be a mentor to young players such as Eddy Curry, Tyson Chandler, Jamal Crawford, and Kirk Hinrich, while working closely with the coach, Bill Cartwright. I played with Bill from 1988 through 1994. We used to call him Teach. He didn't say much. When he did say something, he made you think.

"Pip, I want you to help Bill out," Paxson said, "to sort of be a coach from the sidelines."

Why not? A new challenge was exactly what I needed. At thirty-eight, my career was winding down. There was a lot I could offer, on and off the court, and I felt confident the experience would pave the way for me to be a coach myself one day, perhaps with the Bulls.

It didn't quite work out that way. Bill was fired after 14 games, replaced by Scott Skiles.

I played in only 23 games before retiring in October of 2004. My body was shot after seventeen years in the league—more like nineteen and a half years, if you count the 208 playoff games. Paxson felt I had let him, and the franchise, down. Which might explain why, after my career was over, he didn't seek my opinion about personnel matters even though he knew how much I wanted to have a say in the team's future.

In 2010, when I was finally put on the Bulls' payroll, I was nothing more than a mascot, trotted out a few times every year for "appearances." I signed autographs and met with season-ticket holders, hired for mainly one purpose, to serve as a link to the glory days.

At last, in early 2014, it appeared I would play a more meaningful role. The Bulls sent me to about a dozen college games to do some scouting. One of the trips was to Cameron Indoor Stadium in Durham, North Carolina, to see No. 5 Duke host No. 1 Syracuse. I had watched many Duke games on TV. What a scene it was: the students, their faces painted in blue, standing up the whole game to root for their beloved Blue Devils and rattle their poor opponents.

Duke, led by freshman forward Jabari Parker, defeated Syracuse, 66–60.

I couldn't believe how loud it was. Louder even than Chicago Stadium, where we played for many years. I was excited to be involved with the basketball operations. For the Bulls to benefit from my expertise instead of exploiting my name.

After filing the scouting reports, I waited to hear back from Paxson and other members of the organization. What would they want me to do next?

I didn't hear a word.

Nor did the Bulls invite me to any meetings or workouts with prospects in the weeks leading up to the 2014 NBA draft. It dawned on me they'd been humoring me from the start.

On May 22, 2020, the day after Paxson sent his text, the two of us spoke for a few minutes over the phone. He got right to the point:

"Pip, I hated how things turned out when you came back to Chicago. This organization has always treated you poorly, and I want you to know that I think it's not right."

I was glad to hear Paxson admit a wrong I had known forever. Which didn't mean I was willing to forgive him. If that, indeed, was what he was looking for. It was too late for that.

"John," I said, "that is all fine and dandy, but you worked in the front office for the Bulls for almost twenty years. You had a chance to change that and you didn't."

He began to cry. Not knowing how to respond, I waited for him to stop. Why he was crying, I couldn't be sure, and honestly, I didn't care.

Before long, our chat was, mercifully, over.

■ ■ ■ ■

There is a great deal in the ESPN documentary that has no business being in there. And a great deal that should be in has been left out.

Bottom line: the doc fails to give my Hall of Fame career the treatment it deserves.

Coming from someone who was my teammate and, supposedly, my friend, there is no excuse. It was almost as if Michael felt the need to put me down to lift himself up. Given everything he has accomplished, in and out of basketball, one would assume he'd feel more secure.

Apparently not.

Take, for starters, what happened in Game 6 of the 1992 NBA Finals against Clyde Drexler and the Portland Trail Blazers. Leading three games to two, we were trying to close them out to capture our second straight championship, and first in front of our beloved fans. They had waited decades for this moment.

It wasn't going according to plan.

Heading into the fourth quarter, the Blazers were ahead by 15 points. Jerome Kersey, their small forward, and Terry Porter, their point guard, were playing extremely well.

Michael, meanwhile, was trying to do too much and it was backfiring.

"You have to get him out of there," Tex Winter, one of our assistant coaches, pleaded to Phil. "He's holding the ball too long, destroying the action."

No one broke the game down quite like Tex. He wasn't shy about criticizing anyone, including Michael, whenever that player deviated from the triple-post offense he ran at Kansas State in the 1960s. The triangle, as it came to be known, with its emphasis on ball and player movement, meant everything to Tex and was critical to our success.

A Game 7 seemed inevitable. Anything can happen in a Game 7. An injury. A poor call from the officials. A miracle shot. Anything.

Beginning the fourth quarter with the second unit and myself on the floor—Michael stayed on the bench—we turned the game around. Bobby Hansen, a guard we acquired from the Sacramento Kings early in the season, hit a huge three-pointer to launch a 14–2 run. Others reserves, such as Stacey King and Scott Williams, made one key play after another on both ends of the court. The fans were going crazy.

The score was 81–78 in favor of the Blazers when Michael came back in with about eight and a half minutes remaining. Phil had kept him on the bench a few minutes longer than usual.

The Blazers were done. The final: 97–93.

I can think of no better illustration of what the game of basketball is about: the team, not any one individual. Except not a word about the comeback was in the documentary, as if it never happened. The only footage of Game 6 was showing the final seconds ticking off.

Why not? The answer is obvious.

It wouldn't have enhanced Michael's legacy to show his "supporting cast" being the difference in a game of such magnitude. The Bulls would likely have lost that game if Phil had put Michael back in earlier in the fourth quarter. Tex was right. Michael wasn't moving the ball.

The footage from the 1992 Finals instead focused on Game 1 and how determined Michael was to prove that Clyde, who finished second in the MVP race that season, wasn't his equal. This was a recurring theme in the doc: Michael coming up with a villain, real or imaginary, to motivate himself. I always wondered: Wasn't the goal of winning a championship motivation enough?

Another glaring omission has to do with what took place on Sunday, June 1, 1997, in Game 1 of the Finals against the Utah Jazz. With 9.2 seconds to go, the score tied at 82, their star power forward, Karl Malone, aka the Mailman, was awarded two free throws.

While Karl was on the line, I told him, "The mailman doesn't deliver on Sunday."

Karl, a 76 percent free throw shooter, missed both attempts.

On the next possession, Michael hit a jump shot at the buzzer to win the game. We went on to beat the Jazz in six for our fifth championship.

What I said to Karl should have been in the documentary. You can bet that if MJ had uttered those words, the moment would have received the full treatment, the point being: Michael Jordan wasn't just a great basketball player. He was a master at gamesmanship.

In Game 6 of the same series, I deflected an inbounds pass in the closing seconds when the Jazz had a chance to tie the game or take the lead.

The steal *was* in the doc. Only no emphasis was given to who actually made it. The focus was on how unselfish Michael was by throwing the ball to Steve Kerr, who hit the winning jumper, just as Michael kept passing it to Paxson down the stretch in Game 5 of the 1991 Finals against the Lakers, when we captured our first championship.

There was nothing heroic about what Michael did. Finding the open man was what Phil and Tex drilled into us from day one.

Meanwhile, the few occasions where I didn't come off particularly well were examined with more scrutiny than the twenty-six-second Zapruder film of the JFK assassination.

Exhibit A: The final 1.8 seconds of the Bulls-Knicks playoff game in May 1994 when I took myself out of the lineup after Phil called for Toni Kukoc to have the last shot and me to throw the ball in bounds. I played in 1,386 games, regular season and playoffs combined. Those 1.8 seconds are, by far, what people ask me about the most.

Why did you sit out? Do you have any regrets? Would you behave differently if given a second chance?

They are fair questions, indeed (and ones I'll address later on). Except the incident had nothing to do with The Last Dance and therefore didn't belong in the doc. Why then did Michael feel it necessary to bring it up again? Did he consider for a moment how it might affect me and my legacy? Besides, he wasn't on the team in 1994. He was playing baseball.

I understand, on the other hand, why my decision to postpone foot surgery until October 1997 was in the doc. Same for my demand that fall to be traded. Both *were* during The Last Dance.

Even so, how dare Michael call me "selfish."

You want to know what selfish is? Selfish is retiring right before the start of training camp when it is too late for the organization to sign free agents. When Michael put the Bulls in that position in 1993, Jerry Krause was forced to bring in a journeyman, Pete Myers, who had most recently played for a team in Italy.

That wasn't the only example of Michael's hypocrisy. He called out Horace Grant for, supposedly, having been a source for Sam Smith's 1991 bestseller, *The Jordan Rules*, which revealed what went on behind closed doors in the months leading up to our first championship. Yet in the documentary, Michael mentioned that, as a rookie, he witnessed his teammates one day in the hotel using coke and smoking weed.

Horace put it best in a radio interview last year:

"If you want to call somebody a snitch, that's a damn snitch right there."

Michael could be incredibly insensitive.

In one episode, he recalled how upset he was with Dennis Rodman for being kicked out of a game during the '97–98 season. I was still recovering from foot surgery. Michael blamed Dennis for leaving "me out there by myself."

By myself? That doesn't say much for the other professionals who were on the court, does it?

I could go on and on, listing the subtle and not-so-subtle slights toward myself and my teammates. What would be the point? The ratings confirmed America is as much in love with Michael Jordan today as it was in the eighties and nineties. That's never going to change and I can live with that.

All I could control was how I would respond to *The Last Dance*. With silence.

That meant not appearing on *The Jump*, the daily hoops show on

ESPN hosted by my friend Rachel Nichols, where I'd been a regular guest in recent years. If I had come on, Rachel would have expected me to weigh in on what America was seeing every Sunday night. Nor did I accept any of the dozens of media requests that flooded in.

I didn't keep quiet on the matter entirely. I couldn't. I was too angry. As the episodes rolled out, I reached out to former teammates such as Ron Harper, Randy Brown, B. J. Armstrong, and Steve Kerr. The bond between us remains as tight as it was during our playing days.

In the doc, Michael attempted to justify the occasions in which he berated a teammate in front of the group. He felt these guys needed to develop the toughness to get past the NBA's more physical teams. Seeing again how poorly Michael treated his teammates, I cringed, as I did back then.

Michael was wrong. We didn't win six championships because he got on guys. We won in spite of his getting on guys.

We won because we played team basketball, which hadn't been the case my first two seasons, when Doug Collins was our coach. That's what was special about playing for the Bulls: the camaraderie we established with one another, not that we felt blessed to be on the same team with the immortal Michael Jordan.

I was a much better teammate than Michael ever was. Ask anyone who played with the two of us. I was always there with a pat on the back or an encouraging word, especially after he put someone down for one reason or another. I helped the others to believe in and stop doubting themselves. Every player doubts himself at some point. The key is how you deal with those doubts.

Michael and I aren't close and never have been. Whenever I call or text him, he usually gets back to me in a timely fashion, but I don't check in just to see how he's doing. Nor does he do the same. Many people might find that hard to believe given how smoothly we connected on the court.

Away from the court, we are two very different people who have led two very different lives. I was from the country: Hamburg, Arkansas, population about 3,000; he was from the city: Wilmington, North Carolina.

When I came out of high school, no one recruited me. Everyone recruited him.

Once the season ended, whether we celebrated with champagne or not, the two of us rarely said a word to each other until training camp in October. Michael had his circle of friends and I had mine. No one was to blame. You can't force intimacy between two individuals. Either it's there or it isn't.

Yet as the years wore on, each of us developed a deeper appreciation for the other, especially once we both retired for good.

Perhaps the sport had been too small for our big egos, he seeing me as his sidekick—God, I hated that term and being referred to as Robin to his Batman—someone he felt he needed to pull along to approach every game and practice as intensely as he did; me, a team-oriented purist, offended when he tried to win games by himself.

. . . .

Michael and I caught up two days after he sent the text. I didn't hold back:

"I was disappointed in the documentary. It didn't shine a good light on me. You were promoting *The Last Dance* but switched it to the Michael Jordan documentary. I don't know what you are selling. Was I great or was I a villain?"

I asked why he had allowed the 1.8-seconds game to make the final cut. He didn't say much other than to apologize and acknowledge that if it were him, he, too, would be upset. I didn't press any further. I knew it would do no good. After we hung up, Michael and I were in the same place we were before we spoke, cordial toward each other, even warm, but I also felt the distance between us that has always been there.

When Ron Harper signed with the Bulls as a free agent in September of 1994, he asked me what every new player who came to Chicago asked:

"What's your relationship like with Michael?"

"It's a great question. I don't have a great answer."

Nearly a quarter century has passed since Michael and I played together, and I still don't have a great answer. I don't usually allow our lack of closeness to bother me. I have plenty of friends. Yet there are occasions, and watching the doc was definitely one, when I think about the relationship I wish the two of us had, and it hurts. It hurts a lot.

By no means am I an innocent party here. I missed some openings that might have made a difference, and I have to live with that.

When I was a rookie in 1987, Michael gave me a set of Wilson golf clubs. He was inviting me into his sanctuary away from basketball. Except I was too naïve to realize it. It didn't help that I was having serious problems with my back. My doctor didn't mince words:

"Don't play golf if you want to have a basketball career."

Another opportunity, if you can call it that, came during the summer of 1993, and I feel horrible every time I think about it. Michael's father, James Jordan, had been murdered. The two were inseparable.

When I heard the news, I should have reached out to Michael right away. Instead, I went through the Bulls' PR department, and once they told me no one from the organization had been in contact with him, I gave up. Having lost my own dad three years before, I might have been able to offer Michael some comfort. To this day, he and I haven't spoken about his father's death.

People told me I shouldn't be disappointed with *The Last Dance*. That it cast me as an endearing figure who failed to receive the respect from the Bulls I deserved and showed fans too young to have seen us play how indispensable I was to our success.

Michael himself gave me credit. "Whenever they speak Michael Jordan," he said, "they should speak Scottie Pippen."

I deeply appreciated what he said and the similar kind words I received in the spring of 2020 from friends, ex-teammates, and fans. Even so, as I watched one episode after another, it dawned on me that my story had yet to be told.

Some of that is my fault—I could have been more assertive—and some is the fault of a press and public who have long been seduced by Michael Jeffrey Jordan. Everyone became so enamored of his acrobatic moves that they overlooked the intangibles that don't show up in the box score or the highlights on *SportsCenter*: taking a charge, boxing out your man, setting a pick. The list is endless. I executed those fundamentals as well, if not better, than Michael did.

Nonetheless, he was the superstar in everyone's mind, not Scottie Pippen. Never Scottie Pippen.

That was only because he was there first, three years before I came into the league. With him established, I was expected to remain the No. 2 guy no matter how rapidly I was developing on both ends of the court. Truth is, after three or four years, I was as valuable to the Chicago Bulls as he was, and I don't care how many scoring titles he won. People didn't realize how valuable until Michael retired in 1993.

In our first year without him, the Bulls won 55 games and advanced to the second round of the playoffs. If not for a horrible call by a ref in the closing seconds of Game 5 against the New York Knicks, we might have won another championship.

Michael Jordan was 1-9 in the playoffs before I joined the team. In the postseason he missed, the Bulls went 6-4.

The Last Dance was Michael's chance to tell his story.

This is mine.

CHAPTER 1: HAMBURG

I wish I experienced one of the idyllic childhoods so common in the small-town America of the late 1960s and early 1970s.

But I didn't.

I don't recall the day when everything changed in our corner of the universe. All I know was that for the longest time my brother Ronnie, thirteen, wasn't around to play anymore. He was in the hospital after being seriously injured in gym class. Attacked was more like it. I was three years old when it happened, the youngest of twelve.

Ronnie was waiting for class to start when, out of nowhere, this bully delivered a sucker punch in the middle of his back. He fell to the floor and was unable to get up. My sister Sharon, two years younger than Ronnie, rushed to his side when she found out, but the authorities quickly cleared the gym and didn't allow anyone near him. The bully had been pushing Ronnie around in school for some time. Sharon urged him to fight back. He wouldn't. That wasn't who Ronnie was. I have never known a more gentle soul.

One day, after months in the hospital, he finally came home.

I remember feeling as if I were meeting my brother for the very first time. He was paralyzed from the neck down and would never walk again. Not until many years later did I learn the whole story of how my mother, Ethel Pippen, got Ronnie out of the hospital.

The hospital was a few hours from Hamburg. My parents visited him on the weekends. Mom had her hands full raising everyone, while my father, Preston Pippen, a veteran of World War II, cut logs at the Georgia-Pacific paper mill in Crossett, fifteen miles away, where they made toilet paper, tissues, and paper towels. Everyone knew someone who worked at the mill. The mill had a distinct odor you could smell from anywhere in Hamburg. I can't describe what the odor was like. Trust me, it was putrid.

Anyway, one Sunday when they arrived at the hospital, Mom and Dad were told they couldn't see Ronnie. The doctors had put him in a new program and were concerned that if my parents continued to coddle him, Ronnie wouldn't make any progress.

There is nothing wrong with your son's back, the doctors told them. The problem is in his head. That is why he's not walking.

The doctors had moved Ronnie from his bed in the main section of the hospital to the mental ward. Knowing Mom, who was tougher than any of the Bad Boys (the Detroit Pistons) from the late 1980s and early 1990s, I can easily imagine the look she gave the doctors when she found out what they had done. I saw that look many times growing up. It was scary.

"I'm not leaving the hospital without seeing my son," she insisted.

"If we let you see him," they warned her, "you will have to take him with you. We won't want him anymore."

No problem. Mom was more than happy to take Ronnie where he belonged. Home.

"Go ahead," they finally agreed. "We don't care. He is going to die anyway."

"If he's going to die anyway," she said, "he's going to die with me."

My mother hardly ever brought up that day in the hospital. Whenever she did, she broke down. I wonder if a part of her might have feared the doctors were telling the truth.

Once Ronnie had been home for a while, we began to get a clearer picture of what they did to him at the hospital. No wonder he had nightmares for months.

Not from the accident itself. From how he was treated.

Every night, before going to sleep, we knew the nightmares were coming. We just didn't know when. Ronnie would wake up in a sweat and start to scream. Mom along with my brothers and sisters did everything they could to get him to stop.

"You'll never have to go back to that place," they assured Ronnie.

After my brother calmed down, for the time being, Mom turned her attention to the rest of us. A number of my siblings had already moved out. Even so, there was still a lot of work to get done.

"You need to go back to sleep," she would tell us. "You have got to get up early in the morning."

No one woke up earlier than her. Lots of mornings, after I was five or six, she took off to clean other people's houses. Every dime made a difference.

I only wish we had the money back then to go after the people who caused my poor brother so much harm. That includes the school, which should have disciplined the bully long before he attacked Ronnie. They did nothing.

The nurses at the hospital would leave a tray of food next to Ronnie's bed, telling him he could feed himself whenever he wanted.

He couldn't feed himself. He couldn't move. He just lay there, helpless, hungry.

Ronnie was terrified of the dark. We had to keep the light on before he went to bed, turning it off once we were certain he had fallen asleep. After about a month, he grew secure enough to close his eyes with a small desk lamp on instead of requiring the light from the ceiling. His back was filled with ugly bedsores. Our task was to get them off and clean up the bed whenever he soiled himself.

Day by day, with a lot of effort and a lot of love, we all nursed him back to health—and I mean all of us.

We bathed him. We fed him. We helped him exercise. It took years, but we got Ronnie to where he could move around with two canes, earning the nickname Walking Cane. He learned how to ride to the grocery store on a specially fitted bicycle.

Now in his midsixties, Ronnie still lives in Hamburg on the same plot of land where he grew up. My sister Kim takes care of him. The nightmares are long gone. I see him as often as I can. He has inspired me like no one else. Ronnie had every right to give up, to curse the fate he was handed. He didn't. He fought hard to build a productive and happy life. I'm not the biggest success story in the Pippen family. He is.

Ronnie kept believing in himself no matter what the obstacles were. He has spent many evenings on his precious CB radio, speaking for hours to truck drivers across America. That's his bridge to the outside world.

I should probably hate the bully who did Ronnie and our family so much damage. I don't. He was a kid, and kids do horrible things to one another. At the same time, I don't understand why he or anyone in his family didn't apologize to my brother or parents. Last year, the bully, who is still hanging around the area, reached out to see if he could visit Ronnie.

My brother wasn't interested. I didn't blame him. Too late to apologize now.

I have never asked Ronnie about the day in gym class or what they did to him in the hospital. I see no point in rehashing those painful times. For him, and for us.

■ ■ ■ ■

Roughly ten years after Ronnie was attacked, my family was dealt another shock. That day I remember. All too well.

Dad was sitting on the sofa, enjoying his dinner. He liked nothing better than to watch a baseball game on television. He was a heck of a player in his day. By this time, Dad, who was about sixty, was on disability from the mill due to arthritis. The arthritis bothered him so much he would sit in his truck in the parking lot instead of on the bleachers when he showed up at my Little League baseball games.

On this particular night, Mom was at church down the block, rehearsing for a revival. Her faith meant the world to her.

All of a sudden, Dad dropped his plate and slumped toward the edge of the sofa. A deranged look was in his eyes and he was throwing up, food coming out of his nostrils. I didn't know what to do. Kim, who had brought him his dinner, ran out to have a neighbor go to the church to find Mom, who made it home before the ambulance arrived.

Dad was having a stroke on the right side of his body. Somehow I assumed he would be fine. I was too young to understand what a stroke can do to a person. He would never be able to walk, or really speak again. He could say yes or no, but he couldn't put together a full sentence, except, strangely enough, this one: "You know what I mean." We never understood why that sentence and no others. He was aware of what had happened to him, and that had to be the cruelest part. I can't imagine the despair and frustration he must have felt, day after day, a prisoner in his own body, no hope of escape.

Once again, everyone came together to help out in any way he or she could. Such is one of the countless blessings of belonging to a large, loving family.

We fed Dad, we carried him into the shower, and because he couldn't control his bodily functions, we cleaned up his messes. Another brother lifted him as I slid a diaper underneath or vice versa. I wondered years later whether the back problems I suffered my first season in Chicago were from lifting weights or picking up Dad and Ronnie. Both were heavy.

Mom, as usual, knew how to handle the situation. She made sure Dad never felt left out of any gathering. He sat in his wheelchair with the rest of us at the dinner table, having learned how to feed himself. At times I almost forgot about his disabilities.

The strength Mom showed was remarkable. Her faith had a lot to do with it. Never once did she feel sorry for herself.

What good would that have done?

Her mother, Emma Harris, was even tougher. The word on the street was Grandma could work as hard as any man. I believed it. She, too, didn't engage in self-pity. Perhaps it was from growing up in an era when black folks in the South didn't complain about their fate. They simply accepted whatever the Good Lord gave them and did their best to improve their circumstances, one day at a time.

Mom grew up in Louisiana, picking cotton with her mama when she was a little girl. At the end of each year's harvest, the owner of the farm was supposed to reward the workers with a bonus. One year, the bonus didn't come, and they got by, barely, by eating food from their own garden.

In 1940, when she was sixteen, a hurricane caused flooding in much of the Southeast. Mom moved with her family to Arkansas. As a kid, I used to visit the relatives who stayed behind. I was always amazed that three families lived on one plantation. Our race had come a long way by the late sixties and early seventies, with desegregation, the Civil Rights Act, and the Voting Rights Act. We still had a long way to go.

I was in ninth grade when Dad suffered his stroke. From then on, he could never be the father I needed him to be or show me what is required to be a man—a black man, especially, in a white world.

With guidance from my older brothers, I found my way, though the void I felt would remain no matter how hard I tried to fill it over the years with older men, black and white, whom I held in high regard. That included my basketball coaches in high school and college. I didn't see them necessarily as father figures. Though, from each person, I picked up values that would mean so much to me for the rest of my life.

Also missing was the freedom other boys my age experienced.

Most days, when they returned home from school, they went out to play, to explore, to be . . . kids. There was no agenda other than having a good time. When I got home, I went to work, ready for whatever chore Mom or one of my brothers or sisters might have in store for me. Even my homework would often come in a distant second.

By any standard, we were poor. Our house when I was born in September of 1965 had only four bedrooms, and for many years we shared one bathroom. One of us might be at the sink, another in the tub, another on the toilet. No one gave it a second thought. For the longest time we didn't have a phone. People would call Grandma, who lived next door, and she would come get us.

In spite of everything, I never felt poor. I felt blessed.

There was plenty of food on the table. We grew squash and corn and other vegetables in the garden and raised hogs and chickens. There was no shortage of love, either. Many black kids never had a father in their lives or a mother as devoted as Ethel Pippen was to her children.

Unlike many boys I knew, I stayed out of trouble. Mom made sure of it. When I wanted to go outside to play, I asked her first, and if one of the youngsters she saw me with mixed with the wrong crowd, I was told in no uncertain terms to avoid that kid from then on. Disobeying her was not an option.

Nor was missing curfew. When Mom locked the door to go to sleep, it would remain locked for the night. With another long day ahead, she wasn't about to tolerate someone waking her up because the person failed to follow the rules. Sleep was the only break Mom got, and it never lasted long enough.

She was stricter with me than she was with my brothers and sisters. They didn't have to go to Sunday school and church as I did. I resented it at times, feeling as if I were being punished by having to sing hymns and listen to sermons I didn't understand while my friends were out playing. Looking back, I couldn't be more grateful. The Lord is a powerful presence in my life today, and that's because of her.

She wasn't the only person who kept me in line. So did my brothers and sisters, and so did our neighbors. Someone's eyes were always on me. If you screwed up in any way, the news of your mistake would beat you home. As the folks down the block used to tell me:

"You do that again and I'm going to tell your mama."

I felt a wonderful sense of community in Hamburg. Everyone was always willing to help one another. When a friend needed a couple of bucks, I gave it to him and vice versa. Regardless of whether it was the only money either of us had.

Back then, people pretty much left you alone. If you didn't bother them, they didn't bother you.

With one exception that remains fresh in my mind more than forty years later.

It was June 1, 1979. Charles Singleton, twenty, a guy I knew from the neighborhood, was walking down the street in front of our house. I thought nothing of it. I used to run into Charles all the time. I would say hello and he would say hello back.

Charles was on his way to York's Grocery Store, a half block away. I shopped at York's just about every day. Mrs. York was a nice lady who let my family buy supplies on credit. She lived in a small house in back of the store.

Mrs. York was stabbed twice in the neck. She died in the hospital. Before she did, she told the police Charles was responsible. It blew me away to realize I had seen him only moments before he took the life of another human being.

Once word got around town, the police searched everywhere for Charles. Hamburg is a small place. He wouldn't be able to hide for long.

Singleton was incarcerated for twenty-four years before he was executed in 2004.

While Charles was still at large, my brother Jimmy headed toward our front door. Jimmy had a light complexion, and in keeping with the times, had an Afro similar to Charles Singleton's.

"Son, I don't think you need to be going out there, because you're looking like Charles Singleton," Dad said. This was about a year before the stroke.

The key to avoiding trouble for someone of my color was simple: stay on your side of the tracks.

Yes, it's a cliché. It also happened to be true.

In the cafeteria at our grade school, with few exceptions blacks sat with blacks, whites with whites—whites making up roughly two-thirds of the school population. It seemed normal to me.

My parents, you see, never sat me down for a long discussion on race in America. Nothing had to be said. It was understood.

No matter how many championships I have won, and millions I have earned, I never forget the color of my skin and that some people in this world hate me just because of that.

■ ■ ■ ■

For a long time, I didn't reflect on how my upbringing shaped me to be the person I am today. I focused on the future, not the past.

My approach these days is different. Being in my midfifties, I want to take a deeper look at why I made the decisions I did and what that might mean for me going forward.

Take the decision to sign the five-year, $18 million extension with the Bulls in June of 1991, a week or so before the franchise won its first championship. The ESPN documentary made me seem naïve given how much more money players would eventually earn under the revised collective bargaining agreement with the owners.

Do I wish I hadn't signed the extension?

Of course.

It cost me millions of dollars and had a negative effect on my relationship with Jerry Reinsdorf and Jerry Krause for the rest of my time in Chicago. My mindset would have been entirely different. Who knows? I might have played my entire career with the Bulls.

That doesn't mean I have any regrets. I made the decision with the information I was presented with at the time. I have no doubt it was the right decision for me.

I wasn't like other players, white and black, who came from stable backgrounds. Because of what happened to my brother and father, I learned early on how everything in your life can be taken away without the slightest warning. I couldn't afford the risk I would get injured and end up with nothing.

If I needed any reminders, I had only to consider the fate of former NFL wide receiver Darryl Stingley, who often sat behind our bench at Chicago Stadium.

Darryl, the first-round draft choice of the New England Patriots in 1973, was living his dream. Until he wasn't. During an exhibition game in 1978 against the Oakland Raiders, he was hit by defensive back Jack Tatum, one of the most ferocious tacklers in pro football.

One hit is sometimes all it takes. Darryl would never walk again.

He and I became friendly in the early nineties. After games, we'd meet for dinner or a drink. He wanted to feel he was one of the guys in spite of his limitations. How well he adapted to his circumstances was more inspiring than anything he accomplished on the field. Darryl reminded me of my brother. I admired him tremendously and was deeply saddened when he passed away in 2007.

What I endured in my childhood also affected how open I was with other people. I could never be certain they wouldn't leave me, whether they meant to or not. Developing trust takes time. Which explains why, except for my brothers and sisters, my best friends have always been my teammates. If I could count on them on the court, I could count on them in the areas of life that truly matter.

A basketball team is no different from a family, each person assigned a specific role. Failing to fulfill that role will have an adverse effect on everyone else. That was true in the Pippen household and on every team I played for in high school, college, and the pros. I could tell, almost instinctively, growing up in a different group of twelve, what each teammate needed at any moment. Just as I sensed what any of my brothers or sisters needed.

Maybe a pass to a shooter in his favorite spot to rebuild his confidence after missing a few.

Or a compliment after a coach, or Michael, was too hard on them for committing a turnover or failing to box out.

Or simply taking the time to listen to someone vent about one slight or another.

The interest in helping others went far beyond the basketball court. As I grew older, I found myself bonding with those who required the most nurturing.

One example is Amy Jones, the daughter of Arch Jones, one of my assistant coaches in college. When Amy was two, she bumped her head, which caused a blood clot on the frontal lobe of her brain. The doctors removed the clot, although it would lead to Amy's being developmentally disabled for the rest of her life.

I met her when she was eleven. Whenever I was around Amy, I

didn't see a girl who was limited in any way. I saw a girl to joke with, to embrace, to treat as normal as anyone else. The way she treated me. The two of us became friends.

Believe me, I'm not trying to come across as a saint. By helping Amy, I was helping myself. I was better able to understand what I went through as a child. To this day, the rush I get when I can be there for someone who has faced tremendous hardships is more fulfilling than anything else, and, yes, that includes winning an NBA championship.

Seeing the smile on Amy's face lifted my spirits for the rest of the day. I feel the same whenever I spend time with Ronnie. Not for a moment do I treat him differently because he's confined to a wheelchair. I make fun of him and he makes fun of me.

Neither of us would want it any other way.

CHAPTER 2: **I GOT GAME**

Down the block from our house were the courts on Pine Street. The courts were so close that in the evenings, when there was little or no traffic, I could hear every dribble, every ball hitting the rim, every player calling for a foul. I can close my eyes this very moment and still hear those beautiful sounds. Those sounds remind me of my youth.

I was seven years old when the Pine Street courts were being built. The timing couldn't have been any better.

If not for those courts, I wouldn't have learned the game at such a formative age. No other courts were near our neighborhood. You can practice for hours and hours by yourself on your own court, however smooth it might be, but only when you stack up your game against that of your peers day after day do you find out whether you have what it takes. Better to find out sooner than later.

The Pine Street courts featured nylon nets—not the unattractive chain nets, thank goodness—and the ground was concrete, the ball bouncing true. There was more than enough room for a kid to dream.

I dreamed I was Julius Erving, who played for the NBA's Philadelphia 76ers. Dr. J, as he was called, glided through the air as if he were from some other galaxy. It took him forever to come down. When he did rejoin the rest of the human race, he would typically finish with a spectacular dunk or gorgeous underhanded floater in the lane.

Talk about charisma. There has been no one in the sport like Dr. J ever since. Sorry, MJ. Sorry, Magic. Sorry, LeBron. Whenever one of Dr. J's games was on TV, I couldn't take my eyes off him.

Yet ask anyone who knew me back then which player my game resembled, and I guarantee Dr. J won't be their answer. They will bring up his teammate Maurice "Mo" Cheeks, the Hall of Fame point guard who played in the league for fifteen years.

"I'll take Mo Cheeks," kids would say in pickup games on the playground.

I couldn't have asked for a more flattering compliment.

My middle name, ironically, is Maurice, and the man himself, toward the end of my career, coached me for a couple of seasons in Portland. I retired 3 steals shy of his total of 2,310. He's sixth on the all-time list; I'm seventh.

"You ain't ever going to catch me," he tells me whenever I see him.

Mo was a point guard from an era that, sadly, is gone, probably for good. He thought of passing first, scoring second, and while I was considered a small forward in the NBA, during my entire career I saw myself more as a point guard—some called me a point forward—who tried to emulate Mo and other unselfish guards like him. Only six foot one, he was on the small side for a professional basketball player. Being about five foot nine when I was in high school, I could pretend I was him and it didn't seem as far-fetched as pretending I was the six-foot-seven Dr J.

Mo seemed to come from *this* galaxy.

I hung out in my teenage years with a friend, Ronnie Martin, whom I met in grade school. Ronnie and I competed against each other in Pop Warner football and Little League baseball.

We were usually the first ones at the Pine Street courts every Saturday and Sunday evening, and on weekdays in the summer, normally no later than about 2:00 p.m. While waiting for others to show up, we played a half-court game of one-on-one called 21.

The winner was the first to 21 points, each basket worth two points, while free throws counted as one.

Ronnie was skinny. I weighed even less, 110 pounds at the most. He was able to push me around without too much difficulty.

I didn't enjoy physical contact in those days. I was more of a finesse player, using my long arms and dribbling skills to get off high-percentage shots. I won my share. So did he.

One of us, or both, we told each other, was going to make it big in this game someday. We told each other a lot of things.

We worked hard on every aspect of the game. Ronnie had a cousin who taught us how to shoot the ball off the glass from any position on the floor, including the top of the key, and, surprisingly, with no arc. As long as you hit the square in the middle of the backboard, his cousin told us, you can throw the ball as hard as you want, and in nearly every case it will fall in the basket. I practiced shooting off the glass so frequently it became my go-to shot, and that would remain the case my whole career.

Around four o'clock, the other players would begin to show up. Some were fresh out of high school, some much older, in their thirties or forties. Quite a few of came directly from their shift at the mill. You could tell by the smell. These guys could ball. I couldn't believe how strong they were.

And, man, they could jump. To as high as the moon, it seemed.

"You better learn how to shoot the ball really high," they would tell us, "or we are going to keep blocking your shots."

They weren't kidding.

The games were intense. No matter if nothing was on the line except our pride. That was plenty.

Win and you kept playing. Lose and it could be three or four games before you got back out there, if at all. Whenever the team I played on got to 19 points, one basket from victory, I was double-teamed. Which was perfect training for the double-teams ahead.

This being the South, the only drawback was the unbelievably oppressive heat. Guys would sometimes wait until it cooled down before showing up and then not hesitate to kick us off the court. There was nothing we could do. They were bigger than us.

Without there being any refs, players called their own fouls. Did they ever. Some guys, and I know there are a few in every playground in America, called for a foul whenever someone had the nerve to breathe on them. It is no different in the NBA, where certain individuals—and the other players know who they are—believe they are fouled every time they miss a shot. In my day, it was Adrian Dantley, the outstanding small forward best known for his years with the Pistons.

"I didn't foul you," a defender would argue at Pine Street. "We'll shoot for it."

"No, I'm not shooting for it," the other guy would respond. "You fouled me and it's our ball."

"I didn't foul you."

On and on it went, no one close to giving in.

To keep the game moving—otherwise, we would still be out there—the aggrieved player took one shot from the top of the key. If he made it, his team maintained possession; if he missed, the ball was given to the opponent.

Lots of times, Ronnie and I stuck around after everyone else left. We played H-O-R-S-E over and over. That's the game where players receive a letter whenever they can't match the shot the other guy made. When it got dark, we could see the basket thanks to the streetlights. Every so often, we went out for a burger afterward. Just one, which we cut in half. That's what we could afford.

If the Pine Street courts weren't available, I practiced on a court a cousin of mine put up in Grandma's yard.

The court was filled with dirt, the rim attached to an old, rickety light pole, the backboard made out of plywood. Some days, there were no nets. Others, the nets were barely attached to the rim by a string or two. Someone would have to climb on a ladder and tie them back up. I miss those days.

I could be out there for hours, pretending I was Mo Cheeks or Dr. J—sometimes Larry Bird, the Boston Celtics star—taking the final shot in Game 7 of the NBA Finals. Always making it, of course. I even practiced Kareem Abdul-Jabbar's signature skyhook and became darn good at it.

Some mornings, I got to the dirt court very early. There were more shots to make, more moves to refine, more dreams to imagine.

Too early, in Grandma's opinion.

"Put that ball down and go home!" she would yell. "Do you have any idea what time it is?"

Grandma scared me when she raised her voice, and I suspect others were just as terrified. In those days, folks in our neighborhood walked through one another's yards without giving it a second thought. That bothered her to no end.

"If you come through my yard one more time," Grandma told them, "I swear I am going to shoot you."

It wouldn't have shocked me one bit.

. . . .

Despite the hours and hours I spent at the courts on Pine Street and in Grandma's backyard, basketball wasn't my favorite sport growing up. Football was. In the South, football was, and still is, a religion. I played wide receiver in seventh and eighth grade and was certainly talented enough to have made the starting lineup in high school. I was fast, possessed excellent hands, and ran precise routes.

Except there was an obstacle I couldn't overcome.

The kid competing against me was the mayor's nephew.

Many in my position would probably have walked away at that

point. Not me. I became one of the team's managers. That's how much I loved the sport. I washed uniforms, handed out water bottles, and traveled on the bus with the players and the coaches to road games. I felt as if I were a member of the team.

There was another reason I stuck around.

Football gave me an excuse to spend more time away from the house. Away from the trips to the grocery store and cleaning diapers. I wouldn't get home from practice until about six o'clock, just in time for supper. Most of the chores to help out with Ronnie or Dad had been done by then. I loved my family. They meant the world to me. I was just tired of our house feeling more like a hospital than a home.

Everything was going pretty well until early in my junior year, when Coach Wayne said he needed to talk to me.

Coach Wayne—his first name was Donald—was in charge of the basketball team and was one of the assistant football coaches. He had the reputation of being a tough guy. It was well deserved. If a player was caught talking in class or showed up late to practice, Coach Wayne didn't hesitate to discipline you. Corporal punishment was still around when I was in high school, and I don't recall parents raising any objections.

"When are you going to quit being the manager and join us for the off-season workouts?" he asked me.

"I will come in after football season is over," I answered, rather nonchalantly.

I saw no reason to work out. None.

Besides, it dawned on me that a half dozen other guys on the basketball team competed in both sports and Coach Wayne didn't expect them to lift weights while the football season was still going on. What made me any different?

Wrong answer. Coach Wayne kicked me off the basketball team.

I never felt so low. I wasn't even permitted to come to the gym to shoot baskets on my own. This went on for weeks. I was sure my basketball career was over.

Just then, someone came to the rescue.

Michael Ireland was Coach Wayne's assistant. He was my basketball coach in junior high. He saw something in me Coach Wayne didn't.

Every few days, Coach Ireland pleaded with Coach Wayne to let me back on the team.

The answer was no. Coach Wayne's rules were in place for a reason, and he wasn't about to make an exception. He had kicked out plenty of others for not lifting weights and didn't give it a second thought. There was always another kid who could take his place. I realized how much I was missing out by Dad not being the man he used to be. He would have stood up to Coach Wayne and it might have made a difference. My brother Billy pleaded my case. Bless his heart, he tried. Only, Billy wasn't my father.

One day, out of nowhere, Coach Wayne decided to let me back in.

I have Coach Ireland to thank. Without him speaking up, I doubt Coach Wayne would have changed his mind, and I would probably never have had the life I did. Like some of the kids I grew up with, I might still be in Hamburg, maybe even working at the paper mill, none of my dreams coming true.

Coach Wayne demanded something in return. Not only would I have to take part in the workouts, he made me run up and down the stairs in the bleachers after practice every single day.

How many stairs? Beats me. I lost count.

He was trying to find out how committed I was to the game of basketball, and to my future. Good question.

I hated to run those bleachers, but I believe someone told me, or perhaps I knew it deep in my gut, that if I stopped running, I would be kicked off the team for good.

Yet, on one occasion, I nearly did.

The weather was hot and humid and I had just practiced for an hour, if not longer.

Coach Wayne could kick me off the team, get me expelled, ship me off to a military school up North, I didn't give a damn. Anything would be better than running up and down one more freakin' stair. Fortunately, a couple of my teammates wandered by and noticed I wasn't running. They knew what the penalty would be and how devastated I would feel if I gave up.

Perhaps not that day, or the next day, or the day after that. But for the rest of my life.

"Come on, Pip," they shouted. Everyone called me Pip. "You can do it."

That was all the encouragement I needed. I ran the bleachers that afternoon and every afternoon from then on. I never again came close to giving up.

I still felt I was being unfairly punished. Only what could I do? This was the South. I was black, Coach Wayne was white, and although I never thought of him as a racist, it was impossible to ignore who we were and where we were and the times we lived in.

Back then, I thought he was trying to hold me back. I couldn't have been more mistaken. He was hoping to instill in me a purpose, a sense of right and wrong, which no one, except for my mom, had ever bothered to teach me. I was too young and full of myself to realize it.

One day I woke up. Thank God it wasn't too late.

Coach Wayne asked me to come to his office for another chat. *What did I do wrong now?* Could be almost anything.

"What do you want to do in life?" he asked me.

I was taken aback. No one had ever asked a question like that. In the Pippen household, there wasn't time to talk about what career I might be interested in. As for going to college, give me a break. The subject never came up.

"I want to play professional basketball," I told him without the slightest hesitation.

There, I said it.

He didn't seem surprised in the least. I was pretty sure I wasn't the first player he ever coached to be sharing this particular dream.

"Then, son, you better get those grades together," he said. "If you don't, you're not going anywhere."

Coach Wayne was right. If I didn't get serious about my grades, and a heck of a lot more than that, I wasn't going anywhere. The clock was ticking. High school, one of the final stops before joining the real world, would soon be coming to an end.

My whole mindset changed. I started to approach the bleachers as a friend, not an enemy. *My legs will become stronger,* I told myself. *I will jump higher. I will have stamina at the end of the game while everyone else is running out of gas.* Day after day, I worked on my shooting, defense, and ballhandling. I was on a mission to become a star. Not just in high school. In college and, one day, I hoped, the NBA.

The work didn't pay off. Not yet.

In junior year, Coach Wayne started Ronnie Martin, my best friend, over me. Nothing against Ronnie—he was a fine player— but I was better in every phase of the game. I was better than some of the seniors. Whenever we were getting our butts kicked, I sat on the bench thinking that we wouldn't be in this predicament if I were leading the offense. I didn't let it drag me down. I realized how fortunate I was to be on the team at all. It could easily have gone the other way.

Soon, the season was over. For me, the hard work was just beginning.

During the summer between my junior and senior years, I spent countless hours on the court and in the weight room. I practiced with Myron Jackson, who had just graduated and would be playing in the fall for the University of Arkansas at Little Rock. Myron, a distant cousin, proved there was, indeed, a way out of Hamburg.

I don't recall every game from senior year. That was a long time ago and there have been many games since. I do recall that the Hamburg Lions were quite a team. Coach Ireland and Coach Wayne complemented each other perfectly. Coach Ireland focused on the defense, while Coach Wayne was a fabulous X's-and-O's guy.

In a typical two-hour practice, we worked for forty-five minutes on defense. On zone, man-to-man, half-court press, full-court press, you name it. To Coach Ireland, everything was about angles and moving faster than the basketball. We forced opponents to throw the ball over the top. By the time it came down, we were in an ideal defensive posture. It's how you come up with the deflections and steals that often spell the difference between winning and losing. If you couldn't play defense on our team, you couldn't play, period.

I thought we spent too much time on defense. Everyone did. Stopping the other team wasn't nearly as much fun as putting the ball in the basket.

How wrong I was. The time spent was worth every second and would benefit me in ways I never anticipated.

Take the Bulls' first appearance in the NBA Finals, against the Lakers in 1991. Phil put me on Magic Johnson early in Game 2 after Michael picked up his second foul. Michael couldn't contain Magic in Game 1, and that's one of the reasons we lost. I tried to keep the ball out of Magic's right hand, where he was most dangerous. How I did that came from the techniques I first learned from Coach Ireland. We beat the Lakers handily that day and took the series in five games.

One moment from senior year stands out. We were playing McGehee, a school about an hour from Hamburg.

I raced toward the basket after catching the ball from Ronnie. No one was anywhere near me. Normally, I would have gone in for a routine layup. That was one of the fundamentals drilled into us from day one.

Not this time.

The ham in me, and he is liable to come out at any moment, decided, *Forget the fundamentals.*

Flying down the lane in my finest Dr. J impression, I jumped as high as I possibly could and slammed it home. My teammates flew off the bench and didn't take a seat for the longest time. Unless I am mistaken, the official gave us a technical. No one cared. We could have received ten technicals and still beaten McGehee. For the rest of the season, I went for a dunk at every opportunity I could.

We finished the regular season 23-3, going undefeated in our conference. At one point we were ranked, in our class, by the *Arkansas Gazette* as the No. 1 team in the state.

Our big men, Ira Tucker and Steven White, scored inside and controlled the boards, while Ronnie and I ran the offense. At six foot one, I was the point guard, although depending on the matchups, I could play any position, including center. By observing the game from different vantage points, I learned a lot at both ends of the floor. I was excited to be named to the All-District team.

Other lessons I learned were just as vital—none more profound, or enduring, than the lessons dealing with race. I saw how the color of your skin factored into basketball.

Coach Wayne sometimes put in inferior white kids over blacks vying for the same position. I don't mean to single him out. That was happening all over the South, and if he didn't put the white boys in, the school would find a coach who would.

There was nothing we could do. To keep our spirits up, we used to tell ourselves, *Wait your turn.*

Eventually, in most cases, talent would win out.

One white kid transferred to Hamburg High from a private school prior to senior year. Some thought he would start over me. I beat him out. Just as I beat out the kid who had gotten the nod over me in football. It wouldn't have mattered if he'd been Governor Bill Clinton's nephew. That's how much better I was.

Being black meant never forgetting who you were and where you were. A bunch of us used to go on occasion to Coach Ireland's house for a bite to eat or to hang out. Coach Ireland was black.

We didn't go to Coach Wayne's house. Nothing against Coach Wayne personally. It was just that with him being white, he lived in a white neighborhood.

Stay on your side of the tracks.

. . . .

As the No. 1 seed in the regionals, we felt good about our chances to win the state.

We didn't come close.

In our first game, Stamps, a school a couple of hours to the west, beat us, 45–43. What hurt our cause, besides missing shots, was foul trouble. I was as guilty as anyone else. I fouled out with about a minute to go. Just like that, my high school career was over.

Once I got over the disappointment, I realized how much I had to be thankful for. I proved to myself that if I put in the work, I could play the game I loved at a high level.

Only now what?

The top colleges in the region had already signed the players they wanted. I spoke on the phone to assistant coaches from Southern Arkansas in Magnolia and the University of Arkansas in Monticello, though, to the best of my knowledge, no college head coaches ever came to see me play. It was as if I didn't exist.

Coach Wayne came through again, asking me, "What are your plans now?"

"I want to play college ball."

"How are you going to do that? You're just a puny kid."

Gee, Coach, please tell me how you really feel.

All kidding aside, he saw a lot of potential in me, as Coach Ireland had from the beginning, and vowed to help in any way he could.

He was a man of his word.

Coach Wayne reached out to Don Dyer, the well-regarded coach at the University of Central Arkansas in Conway, two and a half hours from Hamburg. Coach Wayne had played for him at Henderson State in the 1960s.

"He's a little small and needs to lift weights, but this kid can definitely play," Coach Wayne told him. "Can you take a look?"

Sure, Coach Dyer said, bring him over here.

Before I knew it, my brother Billy and I were on our way to Conway. When we got to the gym, Coach Dyer rounded up a couple of guys and told me to show him what I could do.

Nothing was on the line. Nothing except my future.

I wasn't on the court for long, twenty minutes tops. The best coaches don't need a lot of time to determine whether somebody has what it takes.

The other players were much bigger than I was. I weighed roughly 150 pounds. Coach Wayne was right. I was puny.

Even so, I felt confident afterward that I had more than held my own and Coach Dyer would be impressed.

Then again, what did I know?

He could tell Coach Wayne he had done what he'd been asked but I wasn't a good fit for his team. That would be the end of it. No college coach has a spot for every player who tries out.

"Coach Dyer wants to see you in his office," someone said.

I knocked on his door.

He got right to the point. "You looked pretty good out there. What do you have going on?" He was referring to my options for college.

"Coach, I have nothing going on."

He made me an offer. Sort of:

"We have signed our players for the upcoming season, but I can get you into a work-study program. You won't be allowed to play in any games, but you'll be able to work out with the rest of the team. How does that sound?"

I don't recall him saying, "Take it or leave it," though that was clearly the impression I was getting.

I took it.

No, it wasn't a scholarship, but here was someone who wanted me, Scottie Maurice Pippen, from Hamburg, Arkansas.

No one else wanted me.

I would, naturally, have to prove myself when the opportunity came, if it came, but that I could do, just as I did for Coach Wayne. My brother and I got in the car and headed home. I don't remember a thing about the drive. My mind was a million miles away.

I couldn't have been more excited. I was going to college.

CHAPTER 3: BIGGER MAN ON CAMPUS

I spent the summer of 1983 lifting weights and putting up a million shots from every spot on the floor, going for the bank—and the square in the middle—as much as possible. Ronnie still kicked my butt every so often in one-on-one at Pine Street. Which was fine with me. Losing made me better, hungrier. That was true my entire career.

After a couple of months, summer was over and I was on my way to Conway. To a new life.

I was anxious, to say the least. A new life meant becoming acquainted with a new group of people, and that was never easy for me. Except for road trips to games in high school, and the occasional visit to my mom's relatives in Louisiana, I didn't take one step outside the city limits of Hamburg. A whole world was out there that I knew nothing about.

From my first day on campus, the focus was basketball. Basketball was my ticket to the future, nothing else. I spent every day at the gym, which was a short walk from the dorm. My goal was to show Coach Dyer and his staff a different player from the frail youngster they saw in the spring.

Mission accomplished.

I still had a long way to go. Every other player on the floor was on scholarship except me.

No problem, I told myself. I would wait for my turn. A few weeks later, it came, sooner than I imagined.

Two students left the program, and suddenly there was a scholarship with my name on it. With Coach Dyer, as I would later discover, guys were constantly coming or going. He would never stop searching for the unknown gem who had somehow slipped by everyone else. That player was out there. Somewhere. He just had to find him.

Once when the team was on the road, having dinner at McDonald's after a game, Coach Dyer spotted a kid standing in line who was six foot five, maybe taller.

Coach immediately stopped what he was doing and approached him. "How old are you? Do you have any eligibility left?"

The kid must have thought the man was off his rocker.

I can't overstate how much it meant to be on scholarship. College wasn't cheap, and even though I didn't see myself as being poor, I most definitely was.

My expenses were less than other students' because I was in a work-study program and the recipient of a Pell Grant. Still, they were substantial enough. I was always looking for a way to save a few bucks. After finishing supper in the cafeteria, I would go back in line to stuff a couple of ham-and-cheese or turkey sandwiches in my backpack. I'd stick them in the microwave before going to bed. I ate four meals a day, not three.

To me, the scholarship was about much more than receiving financial support. I was now truly part of the team. I hadn't felt that way before. Being part of the team meant having to give what Don Dyer expected from his players. A lot. And I thought Coach Wayne was demanding. You know the saying "my way or the highway"? Coach Dyer said it so often you might think he invented it.

He made us practice constantly—once, I kid you not, on Christmas. On some occasions, if we had just been beaten pretty decisively on the road, he would have everyone stay for a walk-around practice when we arrived back in Conway. No matter how late it might be.

Like my teammates, I did whatever he wanted. I hadn't forgotten what happened the last time I didn't listen to my coach.

To a point, that is.

One time, when he was working us right to the edge, if not over the edge, I walked off the court. I didn't care if practice wasn't over.

"Fuck this, my feet are killing me," I said. "I'm out of here."

If anyone else had pulled a stunt like that, Coach Dyer would have booted him off the team right then and there. Except, by this point, I was our best player and one of the best in the Arkansas Intercollegiate Conference. He couldn't afford to get rid of me.

"We're done," he said. "See you all tomorrow."

Coach wasn't always that lenient with me.

We lost one game because I went for the dunk in the closing seconds instead of trying to tip it in. The ball bounced off the back of the rim. Coach Dyer was beside himself. In his view, I had committed a mortal sin, an affront to the basketball gods. In the locker room afterward, he said I needed to apologize to the whole team.

Fat chance.

"We aren't going anywhere then," he said. "Come and get me when Scottie is ready. I don't care how long we have to wait."

I stood my ground for a half hour, maybe longer.

Apologize? For what? I wanted to win as badly as anyone else. I just made a mistake. Sue me. Besides, if anyone needed to apologize, it was Coach Dyer for keeping us here this long.

My teammates were on my side. On the other hand, they also wanted to go home. It had been a long day.

"Pip, we know it wasn't your fault," they said. "Just tell him you're sorry so we can get the hell out of here."

"Go get him."

When Coach Dyer arrived, I said what he wanted to hear. I couldn't have been more insincere.

"See you tomorrow," he told everyone.

Then there was the time I missed the bus—literally. I was taking a class that started at one o'clock. The bus was scheduled to leave from our facility, the Farris Center, at two to take us to Magnolia for a game that evening. I knew I would be cutting it close but figured if I could sneak out a couple of minutes early, I'd make it in time. The Farris Center wasn't far away. Besides, if I was a little late, no sweat. I was an AA (All-American), as I used to tell everyone. They wouldn't dare leave me behind.

So much for being an AA.

Luckily, I was bailed out by a gentleman named David Lee, who ran Chick-a-Dilly, a restaurant on campus the team visited regularly. Mr. Lee was a big booster of the basketball program and a friend of Coach Dyer's. When I ran into Mr. Lee an hour or two later and explained what had happened, he practically threw me into his Cadillac. He must have been going close to eighty the whole way to Magnolia.

When I got to the gym, about seven minutes remained in the first half. Everyone was surprised to see me.

Including Coach Dyer, who didn't call my number until about six minutes had gone by in the second half. I assumed he was punishing me. Only he couldn't punish me for long. We trailed by 3 when I checked in. I scored 11 points the rest of the way, and we won by 6.

I never missed the bus again.

Coach often kept us at practice past six o'clock. Guys hated that. The cafeteria closed at six. Someone would call over there to tell them we were running late and ask if they could keep it open for a few extra minutes. The answer was usually yes. If they couldn't, Mr. Lee was more than happy to feed us.

I will say this about Don Dyer, who passed away earlier this year. He went over every aspect of the game as thoroughly as any coach I ever played for, and that includes Phil Jackson. He won more than 600 games and ended up in the National Association of Intercollegiate Athletics (NAIA) Hall of Fame.

Like a mathematician working on a new theory, he was constantly drawing up a new play on the board in his office.

"Do you think this will work?" he would ask anyone who stopped by.

Yet no individual had a more profound, and lasting, impact on the team than Arch Jones, our assistant coach. While Coach Dyer focused on the plays, Coach Jones—or Coach J, as we fondly called him—focused on the people. He helped us think of the lives we would be living long after we were finished with basketball. Or basketball was finished with us.

What kind of fathers would we be? What kind of husbands? What kind of citizens?

Coach J was raised by his mom. His dad died before he was born. When he was in high school, his basketball coach cared for him deeply. I believe that was why he went into the coaching business, to guide those youngsters who needed a role model, just as his coach was there for him.

Whenever Coach Dyer got on a player's case, Coach J would wait for the right moment and assure the kid that what he did, or did not do, wasn't as horrible as what he was led to believe. There's no telling how many young men Coach J kept from losing their confidence.

I could talk to him for hours. We talked about a lot more than basketball. We talked about life. I wasn't that open with anyone else outside my family. In addition to Amy, his sweet daughter who was developmentally disabled, I got to know his other two children and his remarkable wife, Artie. Her strength in coping with Amy's accident reminded me a lot of my own mom.

Coach J was there for me in other ways, too.

When I needed money for gas or other basic necessities, he gave me a ten-spot or a twenty without any hesitation. That added up to a couple of thousand, easy. Looking back, I'm sure that violated NCAA rules. Truth is, I wouldn't have made it through all four years without his help. To ask my family for another dime was simply out of the question.

Many college athletes today find themselves in the same situation. Which is why I agree with those who call for them to be compensated, and with this year's Supreme Court decision, we are headed in that direction. Don't give me any of that holier-than-thou student-athlete nonsense. These young men—and women—are athletes first, not students, and make up the labor that generates fortunes for their schools.

They are, for lack of a better term, slaves.

. . . .

During my freshman year, I averaged only 4.3 points and 3 rebounds. No matter. I came to Central Arkansas, remember, as a walk-on, assuming I would sit out the whole year. Instead, I played in 20 games. That was more games than the freshmen who were recruited and on scholarship from day one.

Off the court, to my pleasant surprise, I made plenty of friends and discovered I could survive just fine on my own. I felt so comfortable on campus I stuck around the summer after freshman year and the next two summers, as well.

Conway was where my life was now. Not Hamburg.

The schedule I kept in the summer between my job and basketball was insane. From 11:00 p.m. to 7:00 a.m., I worked the graveyard shift at Virco, a welding plant that built home and office furniture.

The work was extremely dangerous. Fall into a batch of acid and you might not make it out alive. I suffered my share of burns, leaving some nasty scars I still have on my shoulders. My job was to dig into boxes to take out the legs, two at a time, and put them on the chairs using a four-pedal automatic machine. The welded metal was unbelievably hot. You needed to wear two pairs of gloves. Even that didn't necessarily protect you.

It was worth the risk. The money was tremendous. The company paid you depending on how many chairs you put together in each shift. I could usually assemble about three hundred, unless it got too hot. Some days the temperature inside the plant was well over one hundred degrees. I earned about $750 a week, saving close to $5,000 that first summer. To someone from my background, it was like winning the lottery.

When my shift ended, I drove home for a short workout, caught six or seven hours of sleep, then got right back in the car, heading to Little Rock, about a half hour away, to compete in what was known as the Dunbar Summer League. Some of the top players from around the state participated. We used to tell ourselves, "No scrubs allowed."

Among the regulars was Pete Myers, a future teammate of mine with the Bulls. Pete was about to start his junior season at the University of Arkansas at Little Rock after transferring from a community college in Alabama. I more than held my own against Pete and the others. Around 9:00 p.m. I would drive back to Conway, take a shower, grab a quick bite, and be back at the plant by eleven.

Insane, I tell you.

And productive. I was ready to take my game to a whole new level.

Something else happened in the summer of 1984, and it would change everything.

I grew.

I had wondered for quite some time why I wasn't as tall as my brothers, who each stood well over six feet. I started to worry I might not grow another inch.

Then it happened.

I grew four inches to six foot five and wasn't done yet. I would eventually end up around six foot seven. Anyone who hadn't seen me for a while, the first thing they usually brought up was my height:

"Man, you're getting up there."

The added size would serve me well.

I already possessed the passing skills of a point guard. Now I could employ those skills against smaller defenders. If guys doubled me, I would be able to see above them and easily spot the open man. The only negative was that, because I didn't have to shoot much from the outside to be effective, that element of my game didn't improve and would need some fine-tuning in the NBA.

I couldn't wait to show off to Coach Dyer and Coach Jones in practice and see how this new and improved version of myself would perform in the games themselves.

Unfortunately, I would have to wait.

In the fall of '84, I was placed on academic suspension. I had no one to blame but myself. The semester before, being on my own, I was so eager to find out what I had been missing that I had neglected my studies. Now it was time to pay the price. I don't recall what the minimum grade point average was at Central Arkansas. Safe to say, I was not anywhere near it.

I approached the problem the way I approached running the bleachers in high school: make academics my friend, not my enemy. I received help from tutors and classmates and went to the library for the first time. I was no Einstein, but by the end of the fall semester, my grades were decent enough. I was cleared to play.

And play I did.

I led the conference in scoring (18.5 points) and rebounds (9.2), and with the guys we had returning, and the arrival of guard Jimmy McClain, a transfer from the University of Arkansas at Monticello, the expectations would be high come junior year.

Consider them met.

We captured our first outright conference title since 1965 with a record of 23-5, though one of those losses came in the district championship game against the Boll Weevils from UA-Monticello. The team messed up at the end.

Correction: *I* messed up at the end.

On the first possession of overtime, I missed a dunk. That was upsetting enough. On the final possession, with three seconds to go, I missed a layup that would have tied the game, the ball going around the rim and out. I had played well up to that point, with 19 points, 10 rebounds, 4 steals, and 2 blocked shots. Big deal. I failed in the clutch and that's what mattered.

As a result, the Boll Weevils, and not the Central Arkansas Bears, were headed to the NAIA's national tournament in Kansas City. I felt awful for the rest of the guys, the seniors primarily, and for myself. Gone was the opportunity to appear on a national stage, and there was no guarantee I would get another.

I craved the stage so much that even before my sophomore year had ended, I looked into the possibility of transferring to the University of Arkansas in Fayetteville.

Nothing was bigger in the state of Arkansas than being a Razorback, and I wouldn't have cared if they had offered me a scholarship or not. Just let me put on a uniform and work out with everyone else and I'd find a way to make it as a walk-on, as I'd made it in Conway. The Razorbacks had a new head coach, Nolan Richardson, who had turned the program around at Tulsa, winning the NIT in 1981. He possessed one of the brightest basketball minds in America and would be the first black man to lead a major school in the South. To play for Coach Richardson would be a privilege.

When Arch Jones found out I was exploring the idea, he tracked me down right away. I was ready for him.

"This isn't working out," I said. "I need to play somewhere else."

I was a Division I talent trapped in what was, essentially, a Division II school, afraid I would never be discovered. This was long before the internet. Today, if a player is any good, he won't stay under the radar for long.

By going to U of A, I told Coach J, I would be seen by NBA scouts and have an opportunity to hone my skills by competing against the top players.

And in all likelihood, I would experience the thrill of March Madness. As a kid, I watched the NCAA basketball tournament year after year. Like millions of others, I couldn't keep my eyes off the screen when Larry Bird (Indiana State) and Magic Johnson (Michigan State) went at each other in the spring of 1979. College basketball would never be the same.

Coach J waited for me to finish, then made his pitch:

"The opportunity will be there, I promise. I will call scouts and make sure people find you."

I appreciated how he treated me as a human being and not as a commodity. Coach J sincerely believed I would be happier in Conway, and in the end he was right. With the talent level as deep as it was, I might easily have been lost in Fayetteville or another Division I school.

Remaining in Conway, I kept getting better and better. The same could be said of the team itself.

In senior year, Ronnie Martin was our point guard and Robbie Davis our best shooter. I rotated from one position to the next, depending on the size and speed of our opponents. Coach Dyer was his usual demanding self. Having been around the guy for three seasons, I knew what to expect.

We won our conference again, but came up short once more in the NAIA District 17 tournament.

I thought the loss to Monticello the year before was heartbreaking. That loss was nothing compared to the game against the Harding Bisons, who beat us in the semifinals, 88–87. We should never have lost that game. I repeat: never! A month earlier, we destroyed them 84–54, and that was in their building.

This game was in our building. How can that happen?

I'll tell you. They had a five-foot-eight senior guard by the name of Tim Smallwood—I swear I'm not making that name up—who went out of his mind, hitting 7 of 11 threes, while a freshman, Corey Camper (another name out of central casting), nailed a three from 23 feet with five seconds remaining to put the Bisons on top by 1. Camper found himself wide open on the right wing. His coach was screaming for a time-out. Just our luck that this kid didn't hear him and proceeded to hit the shot of his life.

We still had one last chance to pull it out. After we called time, I drove the length of the court to about ten feet from the basket but took too long and was unable to get a shot off before the buzzer sounded.

I scored 39 points and pulled down 12 rebounds. One of my best games, right?

Wrong. How could it be? I failed again to lead my team to victory. I was 8 for 15 from the line, and that killed us. If I had made just two more free throws, we would have moved on.

As soon as the horn sounded, I fell to the floor and cried. I don't know how long I was on my knees. It felt like an eternity. My college career was over.

Gone, as well, was my last opportunity to go to Kansas City for the NAIA Tournament. March Madness? Perhaps not. Scouts from the NBA would be there, nonetheless. The year before, a player from another NAIA school, Southeastern Oklahoma State, scored 46 points and had 32 rebounds in one of those games. That player would be drafted in the second round by the Detroit Pistons.

His name: Dennis Rodman.

Though I led the conference in points (23.2) and rebounds (10) for the third year in a row, while finishing second in assists, I felt the same as I did after finishing high school.

Now what?

My personal life was also up in the air.

During junior year, a friend introduced me to Karen McCollum. Karen became my first girlfriend. That's how shy I was around the opposite sex, dating back to junior high.

Before long, Karen and I fell in love. I could see the two of us settling down one day and having a family. Except there was another love in my life, basketball.

That was bound to be a problem.

CHAPTER 4: MY KIND OF TOWN

Coach J did what he'd promised when I told him I wanted to leave Central Arkansas. He made sure someone saw me play. He couldn't have found anyone better. That man was Marty Blake, the NBA's director of scouting.

No one spent more time searching for players with the potential to make it at the next level than Blake, and he didn't only go to the big-name schools. He went to every college basketball gym in America, or so it seemed. One of his discoveries was Rodman. So what if Blake knew little about a player, except for what some overzealous coach or sports information director might have told him? That did not mean they were wrong.

How Coach J got Blake to show up in Conway was an example of how good fortune—and tragedy, I suppose—can play a huge role in one's destiny. In 1961, when Blake was the general manager of the NBA's St. Louis Hawks, he was intrigued by J. P. Lovelady, a guard at Arkansas Tech. J.P. could shoot and played tough defense. On February 10, J.P. had a big night against one of Arkansas Tech's conference rivals: 23 points, 14 rebounds. A couple of days later, he got in a car accident, which, eventually, claimed his life. Blake attended the funeral, where he met one of J.P.'s teammates, Arch Jones.

Fast-forward to my senior season in Conway. Coach J called Blake, reminded him of how the two met, and suggested he attend one of my games. Coach J must have been awfully persuasive.

On December 13, 1986, Blake showed up at Southern Miss in Hattiesburg. The Golden Eagles were a much better team—they would win the NIT that season—beating us, 95–82. I played well, scoring 24 points. More important, I scored points with Marty Blake. He was impressed I could play all five positions. I don't suspect he saw that kind of versatility often.

Blake spread the word to teams around the league: You should come see this kid. He's got a real future.

No thanks, every general manager decided.

Every general manager except the Bulls' Jerry Krause. Jerry sent Billy McKinney, who had played for seven seasons in the league and was the team's lone scout.

Jerry, who passed away in 2017, received a ton of criticism over the years, including from yours truly. There isn't one word I wish I could take back. At the same time, give the man his due. He could spot talent where others couldn't and, like Blake, felt no place in this vast country was too remote. Exhibit A: Earl "the Pearl" Monroe from Winston-Salem State University in North Carolina.

The Baltimore Bullets drafted Monroe in the sixties when Jerry was a scout. He was one of the first to identify Monroe's rare skills. Monroe, a guard, went on to become a Hall of Famer and one of the most exciting players the game has ever seen.

McKinney came to Conway in late February of 1987 to see the Bears take on Henderson State. I didn't know he was going to be there, and that was probably a good thing. If I had known, I might have pressed a bit and not played my normal game. You can never be certain when your next audition will come. *If* it will come. I finished with 29 points, 14 rebounds, and 5 steals. McKinney was impressed but not convinced of my potential just yet.

Was I this good, or was the competition this weak?

That's why the 1-point loss a month later to Harding, and missing out for the second straight year on the NAIA Tournament in Kansas City, felt like a tremendous blow. Here was a golden opportunity to prove to McKinney, and other scouts who might show up, I could come through in the biggest games against the better teams.

Anyone can get on a roll for a game or two. The top players bring it night after night. Year after year.

When I think of Marty Blake and what he did for me, I'm reminded once again of how blessed I have been. Wherever I went, someone believed in me, fought for me, gave me a chance as long as I did my part. Coach Ireland. Coach Wayne. Coach Dyer. Coach Jones. And now Marty Blake. I was a kid from a small town in southern Arkansas with nothing but a dream. None of them were obligated to help me. Yet they did.

Not only did Blake urge teams in the NBA to check me out. He made sure I was invited to participate in the Portsmouth Invitational Tournament in Portsmouth, Virginia. That's how much clout he had. The event, which had been held every year since 1953, included many of the premier college players in the land. Among those who have participated are John Stockton, Dave Cowens, Rick Barry, and Earl Monroe, each with his name on a plaque in Springfield. I was excited beyond belief.

I was also nervous. Here was another new group of people to get acquainted with. They all seemed to know one another, having played in tournaments together since high school. I didn't know a soul. What if I didn't fit in?

And what if I wasn't as good as I thought I was? What then?

At Portsmouth, there were sixty-four players, eight on each team. One who stood out was Muggsy Bogues, a five-foot-three guard from Wake Forest. Kids today have probably never heard of Muggsy. That's their loss. He was remarkable. Despite his size, he could see the floor and finish better at the basket than any other point guard I ever played with. Muggsy was similar to Mo Cheeks. He thought pass first, score second, and would play in the league for fourteen years.

The two of us were quite a pair in Portsmouth. Darting down the lane, causing havoc, having a blast. Being ourselves, young and fearless. Both of us were named to the all-tournament team.

A number of scouts and general managers went up to Blake in the stands to thank him for getting me invited. Among those impressed was Jerry Krause, who believed he had discovered the missing piece to help Michael Jordan bring a championship to Chicago. The Bulls would own the No. 8 and No. 10 picks in the upcoming NBA draft.

Jerry, who missed his true calling—he was so secretive he should have gone into the spy business—tried, according to some reports, to keep me from taking part in any more pre-draft tournaments. He was afraid other general managers would come to the same conclusion he had. One report indicated he had been willing to pay for me to go on a vacation instead. I can't confirm a thing, although knowing Jerry, I wouldn't be a bit surprised.

To stop auditioning at this point wasn't an option. The more I played, the better my chances were of going higher in the draft. Prior to Portsmouth, the speculation was I would be selected in the later rounds. There were seven rounds back then, as opposed to the two rounds today. If my stock continued to rise, I could go as high as the second round, perhaps the first. Anything was possible.

The next stop was the Aloha Classic in Hawaii. I wasn't on the list at first. The way I performed in Virginia changed that in a hurry.

The competition in Hawaii was fierce, many players projected to go in the first round. My attitude was the same as always: bring it on. If anything, I played better. I was named to the all-tournament team again and won the slam dunk contest. The prize was a boom box I brought back to Arkansas. Along with more confidence than ever.

So much for Jerry's hopes of keeping me under the radar. Not that he didn't try. He wouldn't be Jerry Krause if he didn't.

One day in Hawaii, Fred Slaughter, an agent and friend of Jerry's, took me for a long trip around the Big Island. Why, I thought to myself, does this man think I might be the least bit interested in doing any sightseeing? I was here to play basketball, nothing else. Then it dawned on me what the true purpose of the "tour" was: to keep me from speaking to representatives from any team other than the Chicago Bulls.

The scheme didn't work. I was interviewed by a number of general managers and scouts during my stay.

At one point, Marty Blake summed up my appeal:

Can play point and off guard and point forward . . . great 3 pt college range . . . can handle ball . . . has ability to become a star if he can handle the pressure . . . has a variety of big-time skills.

After Hawaii, I wasn't done yet.

Shortly before the draft, the top players got together one last time in Chicago, for what was known as the Chicago combine.

I was looking forward to being back in the Windy City. The previous summer, I had spent about a month there visiting my oldest sister, Barbara, and a few relatives. I was blown away.

Chicago was everything Hamburg and Conway were not: large, glamorous, unpredictable. And being in Chicago, even for such a short time, sure beat building chairs—and hoping not to get burned—at the furniture factory.

I felt a connection to the city from having watched Cubs games on WGN, their legendary play-by-play broadcaster, Harry Caray, firing up the crowd at Wrigley with "Take Me Out to the Ball Game" during the seventh-inning stretch. So what if the Cubs weren't very good?

Dad and I watched as often as we could. Those were some of our best times together.

When visiting my sister, I spent many evenings on the courts at Sixty-Third and Lake Shore Drive.

A cousin who worked for the hospital picked me up when he got off work. We would be out there for hours. The games reminded me of Pine Street: guys unwinding after another hard day of work. One of the regulars was Dwyane Wade Sr., the father of the future NBA star. The dude could play. Could he have made it in the league? That's difficult to say. There is a vast difference between street ball and the pros.

At the combine, I could sense something was different. Everyone was paying closer attention to me than they had in Portsmouth and Hawaii.

I was approached by one agent after another. In the end, I signed with Kyle Rote Jr., the soccer player, and his partner, Jimmy Sexton. The two would represent me for most of my career. I was comfortable with them, both living in Memphis, a few hours from Hamburg. I appreciated their down-to-earth, Southern hospitality and that they were men of faith. I could trust them.

Each day, I met again with representatives from different teams. They wanted to know who I was as a human being, not just as a basketball player. Each team invests a lot of time and money in the player they pick. If they pick the wrong player, especially near the top of the draft, it can set a franchise back years.

Case in point: Len Bias.

In 1986, Bias, a supremely gifted six-foot-eight power forward from the University of Maryland, was the No. 2 overall pick by the Boston Celtics, who had just won another championship. Bias would fit in perfectly on a team that had Larry Bird, Kevin McHale, and Robert Parish. The future was set.

Not exactly. Bias died of a cocaine overdose two days later.

In mid-June, I visited some of the cities with the highest picks in the draft. That's how much my stock had gone up since Portsmouth. Jimmy, my agent, went with me. I didn't feel comfortable meeting everyone on my own.

One visit was to Phoenix. The Suns owned the No. 2 pick, which was as high as I could go. (The San Antonio Spurs, choosing first, were set on the star center from Navy, David Robinson.) I met with the Suns' general manager, Jerry Colangelo, and the former (and future) coach, Cotton Fitzsimmons, who was working in the front office. They asked the same questions everyone was asking:

"Have you ever used drugs?"

"Has anyone in your family ever used drugs?"

"What do you do with your free time?"

No one would have asked those questions if it hadn't been for what happened to Len Bias.

The next stop was Chicago.

The Bulls put me through a rigorous workout with Al Vermeil, their strength and conditioning coach, and brother of Dick, the ex–football coach for UCLA and the Philadelphia Eagles. In one drill, they put basketballs in different spots close to the foul circle. To determine my speed and agility, I was given thirty seconds to dunk as many balls as I could. I dunked quite a few.

Being on the court for two hours, if not longer, I was starting to get pretty gassed. Which was one of their goals from the beginning. Teams want to find out where your breaking point might be. If you quit in a workout, you are liable to quit when things get really tough, and believe me, in the NBA, they will. Better they know that sooner than later. Before it's their turn on draft night.

I didn't quit. That's not who I was.

I was burned-out, that's for sure. I had been playing basketball without any significant time off for months. I told my agents:

Please, no more workouts. If that means a team might hesitate to choose me, so be it.

• • • •

On June 22, 1987, the big day arrived.

The site was the Felt Forum, a theater located inside Madison Square Garden.

This was my first time in the Big Apple. I was in shock. I thought Chicago was big. New York was Chicago on steroids. After being stuck in cabs that seemed to barely move, I realized the fastest way to get around this city was to walk. I walked everywhere.

I can't believe how naïve I was in those days. Having never watched an entire draft on television, I wasn't sure if they would show just the first round or every round. Nor, as the moment approached, did I have a clue of which team would pick me. I thought the chances were decent I would be taken by the Suns, who needed a forward. The New Jersey Nets, at No. 3, and the Sacramento Kings, at No. 6, were other possibilities.

In any case, it wouldn't be long now. Jimmy Sexton and I were about to leave the hotel when the phone rang. On the line was Jerry Krause, as secretive as ever.

"You can't tell anyone," Jerry said, "but I have made a trade and you will be playing for the Chicago Bulls."

The trade had the Bulls agreeing, in principle, to send the rights to the No. 8 pick and a second-rounder in 1988 and the option to trade spots in the 1988 or 1989 draft, to the Seattle SuperSonics for the No. 5 pick.

I was excited. Chicago was my first choice.

Only I didn't let myself get too excited. Nothing was official, and lots of deals fall apart at the last minute. This one, I didn't know at the time, depended on Reggie Williams, the small forward from Georgetown, being off the board. If Williams was still available at No. 5, Seattle would take him, and the Bulls would be out of luck.

Jimmy and I arrived at the Felt Forum in the early evening. I was dressed in a brown suit that must have cost more than $1,000. I had never spent that kind of money on a suit. On anything.

The commissioner of the NBA, David Stern, stepped to the podium.

Robinson went first, followed by University of Nevada–Las Vegas forward Armen Gilliam. The Suns picking Gilliam was no surprise. He played for one of the top programs in America. I didn't. The Nets then chose Ohio State guard Dennis Hopson, with Williams going fourth to the Los Angeles Clippers.

Then it came:

"The Seattle SuperSonics," the commissioner said, "select Scott Pippen of Central Arkansas."

There were no loud cheers or boos. Only confusion. Who, many in the Felt Forum—and around the nation—must have wondered, is Scott Pippen? By the way, that might be the last time anyone referred to me as *Scott* Pippen.

Before I knew it, I was being interviewed on national TV. Some guy (he called me Scottie) asked about the prospect of playing in the back-court on a team that already had Xavier McDaniel and Tom Chambers as their starting forwards. I answered without letting on that it was a moot point. Jerry Krause wasn't the only one who could keep a secret.

The deal soon became official. I wouldn't have to pretend for another second. I exchanged my Seattle hat for a Chicago hat and called home. One of my brothers told me Dad cried when he heard the commissioner call my name. Dad never saw me play basketball in person, which sad-dens me to this day. At least he saw the moment my dream came true.

Now I could get excited. To a point.

To be drafted by a team in the NBA was a huge step. Except it was just that, a step. With, hopefully, many more to come. Lots of players who get drafted never make an impact. I was determined not to be one of those players.

I was a long way from where I needed to be, physically and mentally. That's what pushed me to work hard on my craft in high school and college, and I wasn't about to stop now. The moment you stop working hard and become satisfied with what you've accomplished is the moment you begin to fall behind. There is no guarantee you will ever catch up.

The next morning, I flew to Chicago, where I was formally introduced with the player chosen at No. 10, a power forward from Clemson, Horace Grant.

Horace and I met for the first time at the hotel the day before the draft. The two of us had a great deal in common, both from small towns in the South—Horace growing up in Mitchell, Georgia, which had fewer people than Hamburg. I didn't think that was possible. I saw in him the same hunger I had in me, the same work ethic. God gives us the talent. We have to do the rest.

Our friendship would be critical in those early days. Both of us had entered a new world we knew nothing about:

A more physical style of play. Back-to-back games. Long plane rides. Reporters ready to pounce on your slightest mistake. Etc., etc. There was so much to get used to about life in the NBA.

As we grew closer, Horace and I would often greet each other by repeating: "Nineteen eighty-seven, nineteen eighty-seven."

The year our lives changed forever.

CHAPTER 5: STARTING OVER

I remember the first time Michael spoke to me.

Okay, he didn't actually speak *to* me. He spoke *about* me, and he didn't have much to say.

It was at the Multiplex, the facility in the suburb of Deerfield where the Bulls worked out for years. I had just walked into the gym with our coach, Doug Collins.

"Hey, guys," Doug told everyone, "here's our rookie. He just wants to say hello."

Michael was working out with two teammates, Pete Myers and Sedale Threatt. Pete, whom I knew from the Dunbar Summer League in Little Rock, had been drafted by the Bulls in the sixth round the year before. He surprised the coaches by making the roster. I wasn't surprised one bit. I knew how driven and talented he was.

All of a sudden, I heard a voice I recognized, a voice I would hear for years to come. Probably even in my dreams.

"Oh, shit, we got ourselves another one of those Arkansas boys," Michael said.

He didn't look at me when he said it. He kept shooting. I don't recall what I said in response, if anything. Knowing how reserved I was in those days, it couldn't have been clever. No matter. How I responded on the court would be the surest way to get Michael's attention, and that would be the case my whole time in Chicago.

I got his attention, all right, the first time we played against each other.

He was guarding me as if it were Game 7 of the NBA Finals. I weaved into the lane and slammed it home with authority. I knew I couldn't allow Michael Jordan to intimidate me.

As the details of my contract were being ironed out, I wasn't allowed to participate in any formal practices. I was frustrated beyond belief. Looking back, the delay was the first—and by no means the last—sign of how cheap the Bulls organization could be. Jerry Krause was trying to get me to sign for the money the eighth pick in the draft normally earns, not the fifth. The man didn't miss a trick.

I worked out on my own for hours every day. Which wasn't the same as being on the floor with others, trying to impose your will on them, and vice versa. With each practice I missed (nine in the end), I fell further behind in my battle with Brad Sellers for who would be the starting small forward on opening night.

Brad, in his second season, from Ohio State, was a lanky seven-footer who could shoot. He would be tough to beat.

I finally signed for about $5 million over six years, four of the years guaranteed.

Maybe not exactly the deal I was looking for. A deal, nonetheless, and I couldn't have felt more blessed.

This was my opportunity to play with, and against, the best players in the world. To live my dream. The money was more than enough. I would be able to buy almost anything I wanted, including a new house for Mom and Dad. They worked so hard for the twelve of us to have a better life. Mom, especially. To be there for Dad and Ronnie, and everyone else, the way she was, day after day, year after year, the woman was a saint.

In any case, the Bulls would take care of me the next time.

Or so I assumed.

• • • •

I was the second player to show up at the next practice. That's how anxious I was to make up lost ground. The start of the 1987–88 season was only a few weeks away.

Two days later, we played our first preseason game, against the Utah Jazz at Chicago Stadium.

When I went on the floor to warm up, I was blown away. More than fifteen thousand fans were in the building. I'd never seen anywhere near that many people in one place. The most we drew at Central Arkansas was a couple thousand, tops, and the crowds on the road were even smaller.

Football was a big deal in Conway. Not basketball.

This was also the first NBA game I ever attended. The closest franchise to Hamburg was in New Orleans, where the Jazz played until the late 1970s, and that was roughly three hundred miles from us. Might as well have been *three thousand* miles, as far away as it seemed.

I checked in with about four minutes to go in the opening quarter. We were already up by double digits.

The first basket the Bulls scored, if I'm not mistaken, with me on the floor was a dunk by you-know-who. I had a feeling I would see a few more of these from Michael before I was done. Though, to be honest, prior to joining the Bulls, I hadn't watched many of Michael's games, in college or the pros. I was a fan, no doubt about it, and vividly recalled the jumper he hit in 1982 against Georgetown to win the national championship. It's just that I was consumed with my own game and what I needed to work on.

Michael was where he wanted to be. I was not.

I ended up with 17 points in twenty-three minutes, having success both inside and outside.

In the next game, also against the Jazz, I followed up with another 17 points, as well as 7 rebounds, 5 assists, and 4 steals—the kind of all-around performance I would later pride myself on.

As Phil Jackson and one of his assistant coaches, Jim Cleamons, would tell me over and over, "Scottie, you don't need to score the basketball to be effective."

The battle, meanwhile, was on with Brad. He and I were bringing out the best in each other. That was bound to benefit the whole team no matter who got the nod.

The battle was especially intense during practice.

Practice is your best chance to make an impression with the coaching staff. In games, depending on matchups and how the refs call the action—whether they let guys be physical or blow the whistle whenever there's the slightest contact—a player can never be certain how many minutes he will receive. That's not the case in practice, where just about everyone participates.

Before I knew it, opening night at the Stadium was here. I was eager to show the fans the Bulls knew what they were doing when they made the trade with Seattle.

Our opponent was the Philadelphia 76ers.

I was sorry to miss Dr. J, who had retired after the previous season at the age of thirty-seven. The Sixers were still very competitive, with Mo Cheeks, Andrew Toney, who could score from anywhere, and a young star in power forward Charles Barkley. How fitting it was that Mo, who everyone on the playground used to call me, was on the court for my first regular season game.

The Bulls prevailed, 104–94. I played a key role with 10 points, 4 assists, and 2 steals. One of the steals was from Barkley, and it led to a Michael dunk late in the game to seal it after we had squandered a 23-point lead.

From there, the team took off, capturing 12 of its first 15 games to post the best record in the league. Coming off the bench—Brad had won the starting job—I reached double figures in ten of those games and picked up my share of rebounds and steals.

One of the victories came at Boston Garden. The Bulls hadn't beaten the Celtics in almost two years.

My numbers that night: 20 points, 7 rebounds, 6 steals. I was most pleased with how I came through in the clutch. With us down by 3 points with less than five minutes to go, I stole the ball from their All-Star center, Robert Parish, and made a basket. I scored again on a fast break in the next possession to put us on top for good.

However, I was still a rookie, which meant a few of my teammates assumed they could push me around. Charles Oakley, our six-foot-eight power forward, took advantage more than anyone else. Who was I to tell him to stop?

On the court, Oak had my back. Oak had everyone's back.

Whenever a player from the other team got too physical, Oak was in his face right away, and we greatly appreciated it, Michael most of all. He often got hacked when he went in the lane. Oak was Michael's protector.

Off the court was another matter entirely.

Oak knew everyone in Chicago and went out of his way to make sure I got to know them, as well. That would pay off in more ways than I could ever anticipate. Basketball, and this privileged life I was lucky to lead, would not last forever. The more people I knew in other fields, such as business and entertainment, the better.

Meanwhile, as the months dragged on, Horace and I were becoming closer and closer. The two of us called each other five or six times a day and lived only a few hundred yards apart in the city's North Shore. We were the best man at each other's wedding, shopped for clothes together, went on vacations together, shared the same agent, and bought the same car, a Mercedes 500 SEL. Mine was black, his white.

For the team yearbook, the Bulls asked, "Who would you take with you if you had to go to the moon?"

I said the first person I thought of, Horace Grant.

I don't know how I would have made it through my rookie year without him. Whenever I had a bad game, and there were more than a few, he assured me it was just that, a bad game, and that everyone has bad games. Even MJ. Bad game or not, I was the same player I was the day before.

Having Doug Collins as my coach didn't make it any easier.

Doug was demanding of rookies. With Donald Wayne and Don Dyer, I was used to demanding coaches. They were exactly what I needed to help me get the most out of my talent. Except, unlike those two, Doug was critical of me and my teammates in front of the fans.

Like every rookie, I was bound to make my share of mistakes: forget to box out, throw an ill-advised pass, allow my man to get open, take a low-percentage shot with plenty of time left on the shot clock.

The list was endless.

The best coaches are critical in a constructive manner. They don't humiliate their players. They nurture them. They patiently explain, one-on-one, during a time-out or at the next best opportunity, what the guy did wrong.

Not Doug. Never Doug.

One night, against the Milwaukee Bucks, he became so agitated with me he sounded like a fan.

"You don't deserve your paycheck, the way you're playing!" he shouted.

Everyone on the team could hear him. Every man, woman, and child in the arena could hear him.

I could take it, that wasn't the point.

It was about respect. Doug, whether he was my coach or not, needed to respect me as I needed to respect him. I knew better than anybody else when I made a mistake. I didn't need him to point it out to the rest of the world. For someone who was supposed to be on my side, he sure had a funny way of showing it.

He was way too animated. A coach in the NBA shouldn't be running up and down the sidelines. In the locker room after the game, his shirt and jacket were drenched with sweat as if he, too, had been playing. None of the assistant coaches, and that included Phil, who was in his first season with the Bulls, challenged Doug. Which was unfortunate.

My biggest complaint was how much Doug was in love with Michael. He was more of a fan than a coach. Whenever a reporter wrote anything remotely negative about Michael, and granted, it wasn't often, Doug grew defensive, as if someone had insulted his girlfriend.

I'll never forget the quarrel the two lovebirds staged after Michael walked out of practice, claiming that Doug had given the wrong score of a scrimmage. MJ insisted it was 4–4, while Doug said it was 4–3 in favor of Michael's opponent.

No one hated to lose more than Michael Jordan.

They made up before long, Michael kissing Doug on the cheek in front of the cameras. I thought it was disgusting for two grown men to act like that.

"Pip, how low will Doug go?" Horace once asked me.

I wish I knew.

Here's the saddest part: Doug Collins knew the game as well as anyone.

Of all the former coaches and players who moved on to TV, he was perhaps the most incisive. I wasn't surprised. When he put his mind to it, he taught me how to penetrate to the hoop and put defenders on their heels. He was an outstanding guard in the league before a knee injury ended his career at the age of thirty.

For someone so smart, he could say the stupidest things.

When my production slipped in January of my rookie season, mostly due to back problems, Doug questioned whether I had what it took to play in pain.

I played plenty of times in pain, in high school and college. In college, I was diagnosed with a hairline fracture near my thigh. One doctor suggested I sit out the whole year. I didn't give it a second thought. I just kept playing.

Besides, Doug had no idea how badly I was hurting.

The pain was so excruciating that during the nearly two-hour drive from my home in the North Shore to the Stadium downtown, I had to pull over several times and get out of the car. I would get this tingling sensation running down my leg to where I couldn't feel my foot hitting the gas pedal or the brake. Nor could I sit up straight in a chair. I was scared, and this went on for months. Some nights, as I sat on the bench, my back bothered me so much I prayed Doug wouldn't call my number.

Leave Brad in. He's doing just fine.

I began to wonder if the pain would ever go away and whether my career was in jeopardy. When I told our trainer, Mark Pfeil, what I was going through, he didn't take me seriously.

Worse yet, he spread the word it was my fault, that I wasn't doing enough stretching.

Nonsense. I was stretching as much as anyone else.

The Bulls could not have been more inept. The only diagnosis they came up with was: muscle spasms. *Muscle spasms?* It didn't make sense. I knew what a muscle spasm was. This wasn't it.

About a month after the season ended, I decided to seek a second opinion from Dr. Michael Schafer, the physician for the Cubs. His diagnosis *did* make sense: a herniated disc. The way the Bulls treated my back situation was the second time—the first being the contract talks in training camp—when I wondered whether Chicago might not be the best place for me, after all.

I wasn't thrilled when Dr. Schafer told me the news. At least now I knew what I was dealing with.

"I've been saying there's something wrong with my back the whole time," I told Pfeil and Jerry Krause. "You guys didn't listen to me."

They didn't say much. What could they say?

My biggest regret was that I didn't see Dr. Schafer much sooner. That is why I can't state emphatically enough how imperative is that players coping with what could be a major injury seek a second opinion and not blindly accept the word of the team doctor.

The team doctor is looking out for just that, the team. Not the player and not his long-term future.

Due to the disc problem, I was at 70 percent during much of my rookie season, maybe less. Some nights, I felt as if I was twenty-two years old; others, forty-two. I was taking my meds (a mix of muscle-relaxing and painkilling drugs), but when you are playing four games in five nights, the meds can't possibly keep up, and in our day the league was a lot more physical than it is now.

For the life of me, I don't recall when I first hurt my back. My guess is it took place while I was lifting weights, though lifting my dad and brother when I was in high school couldn't have done those muscles any good. If teams had been more cautious in the late 1980s, as they are these days—the way, in 2019, the New Orleans Pelicans

protected their rookie sensation, Zion Williamson—I would probably have missed a good portion of the season.

No one in my circle ever suggested something to the effect of
"Hey, why don't we just take some time off to allow this to heal?"
I wish they had.

. . . .

Doug kept me coming off the bench, game after game, and it had little
to do with how Brad Sellers or I was playing. It was personal.

He was upset Horace and I were spending so much time off the
court with Sedale Threatt, a backup guard the Bulls acquired from the
Sixers in the middle of the '86–87 season.

Doug didn't mince words: "If you guys want to be in this league for
a long time and save your career, then you better not run around with
Sedale. That man burns the candle at both ends."

Sedale enjoyed a drink or two, everyone knew that. You could
sometimes smell the alcohol on his breath when he showed up at
practice. Yet he was one heck of a player. He could go from club
to club the night before and still give you 15 points and guard his
man as if there were no tomorrow. Sedale would get so excited
about going into a game he used to hyperventilate the first few
minutes.

That, ladies and gentlemen, is known as passion, and I was lucky to
have him as a teammate.

I learned so much during my time with Sedale. He and another
veteran guard, Rory Sparrow, taught me how to slide my feet to stay
in front of my man. They were masters at that technique. Sedale was
committed to his craft. That's how he, similar to Pete Myers, made it
in the league after being a sixth-round pick.

Doug didn't know what he was talking about. He assumed that
because Horace and I hung out with Sedale it meant we must be

drinking, as well. I would have told him that wasn't the case . . . if he had ever bothered to ask.

The other guys saw what was going on between Doug and us. One simple truth I discovered early on about life in the NBA: there are few secrets.

"Did you stay out all night again?" Michael joked to Sedale during practice. "Now you got Pip and Horace hanging out with you, too?"

Kidding around was common. And essential.

Except Doug and Jerry didn't see it as an innocent joke. They saw it as a sign Michael didn't approve of Sedale's behavior, and keeping Michael happy was always a priority.

Doug believed he should be able to control how I spent my free time. He couldn't have been more mistaken. I learned after my father's stroke to make my own decisions. Those decisions included the people I chose to hang out with. I wasn't about to change now. Doug wasn't wrong to be concerned. The list is long of athletes who have squandered their God-given talents with terrible judgment and lived to regret it.

Doug was wrong in the way he shared those concerns. Horace and I were grown men. No one had the right to speak to us like that. Not even our coach.

I knew my body, and mind, better than anyone else. When to rest and when to go out. It would have done me, and the Bulls, no good to stay in every night.

With Doug, it always came down to the double standard he set: one set of rules for Michael, one for everyone else.

He would never have told Michael whom he shouldn't be hanging out with during his free time. Doug deferred to him in every situation, on or off the court. It would make me want to vomit.

Doug used to tell Mark Pfeil: "Go ask Michael what he wants to do." What *he* wants to do? Are you kidding me? I felt like chiming in,

"Doug, you are the freakin' head coach of the Chicago Bulls. You decide what we should do. Not Michael Jeffrey Jordan!"

Michael, recognizing the power he possessed, took full advantage. If he had a commercial to shoot or a tee time to make, practice would be set around his narrow window. If practice was running too long, Doug would simply excuse him.

The worst was what occasionally took place at practice the day after a game.

"Michael, you got off today," Doug would say. "Go take a shower. Everyone else, I want you on the floor right away."

His rationale for giving Michael a break was that he had expended a lot of energy in scoring 30 points or whatever the total might be. What Doug failed to take into account was that Horace and I had played nearly as many minutes as Michael did and would benefit from the time off, as well. It also didn't occur to Doug that Michael was flawed, like everyone else. On some nights, he needed to take 30 shots, or more, to get those 30 points. Spending a little extra time on his shooting couldn't hurt.

Guys lose trust in a coach when he places one player over the rest of the team. I don't care who that player is. All of us were stars in high school and college. We didn't make it this far by accident. To now suddenly feel we were second-rate was incredibly insulting.

To Doug, it wasn't just about winning. It was about giving the people the show they had come to see. The Michael Jordan Show. No doubt some fans preferred that Michael score 50 points in a loss rather than 20 points in a victory. They could brag to their buddies by the watercooler the next day they had seen the one-and-only Michael Jordan at his best.

A more secure coach would never have given in like that to his star player. Can you imagine Pat Riley allowing Patrick Ewing to do whatever he wanted? Or Gregg Popovich constantly deferring to Tim Duncan? Please.

By favoring Michael, Doug stunted the growth of everyone else, including me.

I was fortunate. Over time, I was able to develop, mostly due to Phil and Tex and a strong work ethic. What about the guys who weren't as fortunate? Would their careers, and lives, have turned out differently? We'll never know.

* * * *

In March of 1988, I went through a stretch in which I missed 11 of 12 free throws. I was far from automatic from the line in the best of times. This, however, was inexcusable. No one could figure out what was wrong.

I was to blame, needless to say. Although not entirely. Doug and Michael were also partly responsible.

In many games I barely touched the basketball. As a result, I couldn't sustain any rhythm. Horace and I used to talk about how we would run up and down the court like deer in headlights, with no purpose to what we were doing. Why bother? The ball wasn't coming to either of us. Only to Michael.

I'm not suggesting I needed 15 or 20 shots a game. I wasn't a scorer. Not yet.

What I needed were *touches*. When I had the ball in my hands, for even two or three seconds, I felt I was part of the game in a way I didn't feel when I watched Michael throw up one shot after another.

I should have taken a seat with the other spectators.

So when the ball did—stop the presses—come to me and I was fouled, I wasn't nearly as confident as I should have been when I stepped to the line.

I finished the regular season averaging only 7.9 points and 3.8 rebounds a game and failed to make the All-Rookie team.

Was I disappointed? You bet.

Discouraged? No way.

Not when Doug kept me out of the starting lineup. Not when my back flared up. Not when MJ acted as if it were one against five.

Never.

When I came to the Chicago Bulls in the fall of 1987, I couldn't have been more naïve. I thought being a professional basketball player meant you practiced for two hours and got the rest of the day off. Since then, I had learned so much. That if you are truly dedicated to your craft, two hours is nothing. You need to remain in the gym long after practice has ended. To work on the parts of your game that need work. And the parts that don't.

Even when you don't feel like it. Especially when you don't feel like it.

The key is to constantly remind yourself that at this point in your life, nothing in this world is more important than basketball.

That means making sacrifices, some small, some large, almost all painful. That's why they are called sacrifices and why most players don't dig deep enough. They might play in the league for fifteen years and even be an All-Star. Yet by not digging deep enough, they will never know how good they could have been. I didn't want that happening to me.

That meant letting go of Karen, who had become my wife, and a son, Antron, who was born that past November. I still adored Karen as much as ever and was thrilled to have a son. I just didn't have the time to be a good husband or a good father, and the sooner she and I realized that, the better. The divorce would become final in 1990.

I made a commitment to another family, my teammates. For which I have no regrets.

We spent a lot of time together, on the road especially. For me and Horace, being rookies, this was the first time in our lives we had our freedom and the money to take advantage of it. That can be a very good—or very dangerous—combination. In our case, it was very good, and a lot of that was from being surrounded by veterans who enjoyed themselves yet never crossed the line.

In *The Last Dance*, the players Michael said he saw doing coke and smoking weed were gone by the time I arrived. Jerry Krause made sure of it. A couple ended up in rehab.

Even Michael didn't drink in the early days. He didn't begin drinking until he returned from his first retirement, in 1995. As for drugs, I didn't see any, I swear. This being the late 1980s, when drugs were rampant in the NBA, and the culture at large, that said a lot about the men in our locker room.

Gambling was another matter.

We loved playing cards. On the bus. On the plane. At the airport. In the hotel. Everywhere. The game we played most of the time is called tonk. The key to tonk, as it is with gin rummy, is to dispose of your cards as quickly as possible.

There were two leagues: the majors and minors.

MJ, it should come as no shock, was in the majors. He was always trying to bring in more guys to increase the size of the pot so he could break everyone. Oak also played in the majors. I went back and forth. Even in the majors, the most you would lose in any one game was a few hundred bucks, maybe a grand.

In any case, it was never about the money. It was about ribbing each other and having fun. We needed to blow off steam.

"You know I'm about to get you," a player would say.

"No, you're not."

"Oh, yes, I am."

Playing cards was also an opportunity for Michael to get away from people who might otherwise approach him in the airport for an autograph or photo. You can't imagine how many requests there were, and that was before he became even more popular in the midnineties.

Michael and I got along well enough, though I could tell even then we were never going to be close. Maybe if we had played golf together, with the Wilson clubs he gave me rookie year, it would have been different. I doubt it. He lived in a different world from the rest of us. It occurred to me on more than a few occasions:

If this is what fame looks like, I don't want any part of it.

Everyone (the folks at Nike, Gatorade, NBC's Ahmad Rashad, etc., etc.) fussed over Michael as if he were the king of Siam. He was a basketball player.

I made a conscious decision at the time and not once did I regret it. I wasn't going to be one of those people desperately trying to get Michael Jordan to like me. Only by charting my own course, and not relying on him for validation, would I reach my potential as a player and, more important, as a human being.

Being surrounded for as long as I could remember by eleven brothers and sisters who loved me unconditionally, I never felt the need to win someone over.

They were my best friends then and always will be.

CHAPTER 6

THE FIRST HURDLE

We peaked at the perfect time in the '87–88 season, capturing 10 of our final 13 games. With a record of 50-32, we tied the Atlanta Hawks for second place in the Central Division, only four games behind the Pistons. Seven of those last 10 victories were on the road, which was encouraging. The road hadn't always been friendly to us.

One reason for our success was the play of Sam Vincent, the point guard acquired from Seattle shortly before the trade deadline. While Sam could score, his job was to get the ball to Michael, and he did that very well. In 29 games with the Bulls, he averaged more than 8 assists. To obtain Sam, we had to get rid of Sedale. No one was surprised. I felt a little disappointed to see him go, though the two of us were never as tight as Doug believed.

Our opponent in the opening round of the playoffs was the sixth-seeded Cleveland Cavaliers.

The Cavs were extremely talented. They had a young center to build around in Brad Daugherty, the No. 1 overall selection in the 1986 draft, along with forwards Larry Nance and Hot Rod Williams, and guards Mark Price, Ron Harper, and Craig Ehlo. Their coach was Lenny Wilkens, who led the Sonics to a title in 1979.

Magic Johnson would dub the Cavs the "team of the nineties." Magic was a man of many gifts. Being able to see the future wasn't one of them.

We jumped out to a 2–0 lead at the Stadium, with Michael doing his best imitation of Wilt Chamberlain: 50 points in Game 1, followed by 55 in Game 2. (Of course, he took 80 shots in the two games combined. The rest of the team took 118.)

The Cavs took the next two in Cleveland, *holding* Michael to 82 points, to set up a deciding Game 5 in Chicago. The first round in those days was a best three out of five.

While warming up, I got myself prepared for when Doug would summon me from the bench. Pretty early, I figured. Except for Game 3, Brad Sellers had not been having an especially productive series. Over the first four games, I averaged about twenty-five minutes. That's a lot of minutes for a backup.

Only I would be a backup no longer.

Roughly a half hour before the opening tip, Doug told me I would start instead of Brad.

He's got to be kidding, I thought to myself. I didn't start a game the whole year, and not once in the three days since Game 4 did he give the slightest indication a change might be coming.

I was ready for the challenge, don't get me wrong, although the logic escaped me then and still does. Why now, after I had come off the bench for 79 regular season games and 4 playoff games, was Doug having me take on a new role in what was, to that point, the most important game of my life?

Doug never explained his logic. He didn't have to. He was the coach. I was a player. I did what I was told. I believe he was concerned that, my being a rookie, the moment might be too big for me if I knew a day or two ahead of time.

If that, indeed, was his reasoning, he couldn't have been more mistaken. Keeping me in the dark was another sign of how little he respected me. I wasn't some punk from the local Y. I played four years of college basketball and had been a starter since my sophomore season.

No moment was too big for me.

Being a starter requires a different mindset from coming off the bench. Memo to Doug: it would have been helpful to have a day—heck, a few hours—to put myself in that mindset.

As it turned out, I fared quite well, scoring 24 points to match my high for the year. I went 10 of 20 from the field and finished with 6 rebounds, 5 assists, and 3 steals. Most important, we won the game, 107–101, to extend our season.

We dug ourselves a huge hole in the first quarter, trailing by 18 points. Then Michael, despite hurting his knee, got hot in the second quarter to cut into that deficit. We seized our first lead of the game late in the third after I stole the ball from Ron Harper and went in for a layup. The Cavs made a run down the stretch, until Michael, who finished with 39 points, hit two free throws to put it away.

The fans in Chicago finally had something to celebrate. The Bulls hadn't won a playoff series in seven years.

It was just the beginning.

On a personal level, I felt vindicated. I should have been starting ahead of Brad from day one.

Anyway, it was on to Detroit for the Eastern Conference semifinals.

The Pistons were the clear favorites. In Game 1, they played like it, holding us to 82 points; they scored 93. Their center, Bill Laimbeer, was outstanding: 16 points and 14 rebounds. I was not: 2 points and 3 rebounds. We earned a split by winning Game 2, 105–95, thanks to 36 points from Michael and 31 from Sam Vincent. Oak added 10 points and 12 boards.

Everything went downhill from there.

In Chicago, we couldn't manage to score 80 points in either game. The Pistons took Game 3, 101–79, and Game 4, 96–77. They put us out of our misery in Game 5. The final: 102–95. The only positive from the season coming to an end was that I could give my back a much-needed rest. The Pistons, as physical as they were—*vicious* might be a more accurate way to put it—were the worst possible team to play if you're not at 100 percent. Every drive down the lane, every scramble for a loose ball, felt more like rugby than basketball.

Friedrich Nietzsche, the nineteenth-century German philosopher, said that if it doesn't kill you, it makes you stronger. Mr. Nietzsche never met Bill Laimbeer. The guy was a thug.

Unfortunately, the rest did my back more harm than good.

That's what led to my seeking the second opinion from Dr. Schafer and the diagnosis of a herniated disc. I would need to have surgery. I was scared. What if the operation went poorly? I was warned by family and friends you should never let someone cut you open; the risk of permanent damage being too great. I had come so far since Coach Wayne kicked me off the team in high school that I began to wonder, Had the basketball gods been toying with me all along, setting me up for the cruelest of fates?

That my career in the NBA—my dream—would be one and done?

In July 1988, I put any fears aside and went through with the surgery. I was willing to do anything to get rid of the pain. The pain that was running my life.

The operation went smoothly, according to the doctors, who were optimistic I would make a full recovery. I wasn't so sure, especially in the first couple of weeks when I couldn't move my right leg and the pain in my back remained constant and sharp. They assured me this was a normal response to the procedure.

Easy for them to say. My future was on the line, not theirs.

I thought of Ronnie and Dad and how they spent day after day trapped in a wheelchair. Would that happen to me?

The feeling slowly began to come back in my leg. I was never so relieved. Every day, I went for a stroll around the neighborhood. One area, known as Picardy Circle, had a beautiful pond in the back. I walked around the circle over and over. I began to know it better than my own house. For six weeks, the walk was my only exercise. I wasn't allowed to sit in a car until I went to see Dr. Schafer for a checkup. Doug and Jerry reached out every so often, which I appreciated, while my brother Jimmy kept me company until I could manage on my own.

As I look back, the operation was a godsend.

Not just because it alleviated the pain and allowed me to resume my career, but because it set me on a new training regimen I would adhere to from then on.

"If you want to play this game for a long time," Dr. Schafer said, "you are going to have to work on your back and keep it strong."

Every summer, whether my back was hurting or not, I underwent therapy for two months before heading to training camp. I kept my hamstrings loose and worked on the small muscles around the spine that are often ignored.

The operation served as a reminder. For a professional athlete, there can never be too many:

Take care of your body. If you do not, it will not take care of you.

Even so, the Bulls would have to start the 1988–89 season without me. I wasn't the only one missing. So was Charles Oakley, shipped to the New York Knicks for center Bill Cartwright the day before the draft.

I knew how the NBA worked—teams demanding loyalty from their players while rarely showing it themselves in return—and there had been rumors Oak was on the trading block. I was stunned nonetheless. Oak was the first player traded whom I was close to. The fans see us as nothing more than pawns on a giant chessboard, never giving any thought to the tight relationships we are forced to give up when we are sent, without our consent, to another city. That doesn't usually happen in other professions.

Imagine how you would feel if you showed up at work one day and your boss said, "Hey, Johnny, I hate to break it to you like this, but the company has decided to transfer you to Buffalo. Your flight leaves at eight. Have a nice life."

I called Oak right away: "Hey, man, I'm sorry. I can't believe they traded you."

He couldn't believe it, either.

Trading Sedale was one thing. He was a backup. Backups, with all due respect, are expendable. Oak wasn't a backup. He was one of the cornerstones of the franchise.

As Michael, who had lost his closest friend on the team, put it, "We're giving up the best rebounder in the league. How are we going to replace that?"

Good question.

Rebounding wasn't the only thing we were losing. Oak was a leader in a way MJ could never be. Every team needs a Charles Oakley. Someone who would die for you. On his way out the door, Oak criticized the organization for not giving him the proper respect. I knew exactly how he felt.

On the other hand, we had to give Jerry Krause the benefit of the doubt. He wasn't the NBA Executive of the Year in 1988 for nothing.

We sorely needed scoring from the low post. The center position meant something in those days with such outstanding bigs as Hakeem Olajuwon, Moses Malone, Robert Parish, Patrick Ewing, and, of course, Kareem, who was still a threat at age forty-one.

Our center was Dave Corzine. God bless him, but Dave was not a threat.

In the 1987–88 season, Dave averaged just over 10 points, and a good portion of the points came from the outside. The problem was more glaring than ever in the Detroit series. Over the five games, Dave scored only 25 points.

In all likelihood, Bill would be a significant upgrade. He had averaged more than 20 points a game in each of his first two seasons with the Knicks. Our top pick in the 1988 draft, Will Perdue, from Vanderbilt, played the position, as well. Meanwhile, Horace was developing into a superb rebounder and defender. He was more than ready to take over for Oak.

The question regarding Bill was his durability. He missed the entire 1984–85 season because of a foot injury and appeared in just 2 games the following year and 58 games the year after that.

■ ■ ■ ■

We didn't get off to a good start in fall of 1988, losing by 13 on opening night to the Pistons in Chicago. Horace finished with only 2 rebounds. Over the first two weeks, our record was 4-4. The Pistons were 7-0. Bill, to put it mildly, didn't appear to be the answer to our problems in the post. He had bad hands, couldn't spot open teammates when he was double-teamed, and was unable to keep up with our speed, the best in the league.

Michael wasn't pleased. That also is putting it mildly.

He told the rest of us to stop passing the ball to Bill in the last few minutes of a game. Bill was a smart guy. He saw what was going on. He was ready to kill Michael, and I didn't blame him.

"That motherfucker," Bill said one day when Michael wasn't around. "I don't care what that fucker says. Just get me the fucking ball."

"You got it," I told him.

Meanwhile, the word was that I wouldn't return to the lineup until early December.

It had to be sooner. I couldn't afford to fall behind Brad for the second year in a row and spend more time on the bench. I had spent too much time there already.

I came back on November 18, against the Atlanta Hawks at the

Stadium. With us about to embark on a long road trip, it made sense to see how my back would hold up. If I was still in pain afterward, I could continue my rehab at our facility in Deerfield and join the team later on the trip or wait until it returned. I checked in with roughly four minutes to go in the first quarter. I felt like a rookie again.

The jitters. The sense of wonder. The desire to prove I belonged. All of it.

I thought I would be on the court for fifteen, maybe twenty, minutes. Make it thirty-five. Doug asked me a few times if I was tired. I was not. I was energized. With every possession, every touch, I became more comfortable, almost as if I had never been away. My numbers for the evening: 15 points, 9 rebounds, 5 assists.

And one huge steal.

The team was trailing by 3 points with around thirty seconds to go when I stripped the ball from Moses Malone as he was driving to the hoop. We scored to cut the lead to 1 and ended up winning in OT.

I approached this game like any other, focusing on the fundamentals—setting a screen, boxing out my man, taking a charge, etc.—though every so often, when play stopped, I found myself thinking about the days after the operation, when my fears got the best, or worst, of me. I felt incredible joy to run up and down the court without any pain shooting through my spine.

In late December, when we took on the Knicks at the Stadium, I hit the game winner, a jumper from near the free-throw line. Michael had driven to the hoop, but his shot was blocked by Ewing, and after Horace missed the follow-up, I found myself in the right place at the right time. By this point, I was in the starting lineup, replacing Brad for good. He would be traded to Seattle in June of 1989.

Even with the victory, we were only 14-12, sitting in fifth place in the Central Division. A season filled with high hopes was slipping away.

I don't mean to place too much blame on Doug Collins. We were the ones missing shots and missing assignments, not him.

Yet he was the same old Doug, harder on us than he needed to be, and that didn't help. When a team struggles, the coach has to be patient, making sure the players keep believing in themselves. Regardless of how many losses pile up. The key is to emerge from those struggles before it ruins the whole season.

We made it safely to the other side, all right, winning 6 straight in January, 5 straight a month later.

Those wins, however, would prove to be misleading. The underlying problems that had plagued the team since training camp hadn't suddenly gone away. Doug continued to defer to Michael, who kept throwing up too many shots. That didn't sit well with Tex.

You could make the most acrobatic move in the world and dunk the basketball like Dr. J, and Tex would be fuming you didn't make another pass. He preferred a great pass to a great move. Anything else, in his opinion, was "showboating."

Every day, he would tell us, "Don't be a horse's ass."

Translation: make the right play.

Just because you beat your man off the dribble doesn't mean your shot is the best shot. The best shot might be the guy who is standing in the corner or cutting in the lane.

Except Doug wasn't listening to Tex.

That was another big mistake. Think about it: Here was someone, in Tex Winter, who had been around the game of basketball for more than forty years as a coach and teacher, and you're not interested in soaking up every ounce of knowledge he has? In what world, please tell me, does that make any sense? Tex, we used to say, has forgotten more about the game than we could ever learn. To top it off, this was only Doug's third season as a head coach in the NBA. As a head coach, period.

The conflict between these two strong-willed personalities was never resolved. Which didn't just harm their personal relationship. It harmed the whole team.

To Doug, the No. 1 overall pick in the 1973 draft, and an outstanding one-on-one player with the Sixers, basketball was an individual game. To Tex, who never played in the NBA, it was a team game.

Doug wanted Michael to do whatever suited him on any possession. Tex wanted Michael to pass the fucking ball.

Doug, in front of the whole team, would put Tex down in ways you wouldn't believe.

"Do you think Tex is here with us today?" Doug would say.

Tex was sitting right there.

I felt awful for him. In addition to possessing a brilliant basketball mind, he possessed a gentle soul. He didn't deserve to be treated that way. No one does.

It got to the point where Tex wasn't allowed to sit on the bench during games. At practices, he stood by himself in the corner of the gym, taking notes. How humiliating. Sometimes it took every ounce of self-restraint for me not to punch Doug in the mouth. That is one fine I would have been happy to pay.

Tex, on the other hand, showed up at practice day after day as if nothing were going on between the two of them. I don't know how he did it.

Why, you may wonder, didn't Jerry Krause do something about the way Doug was treating Tex? Jerry idolized Tex Winter. He was the one who brought him here. Nothing escaped Jerry's attention, on or off the court.

I don't have a good answer. Though, in the end, Jerry did do something about Doug Collins.

Something quite drastic.

Phil, meanwhile, was gaining respect with each passing day. Joining the team the same time I did, Phil started at the bottom, behind Tex and Johnny Bach, another assistant coach. He wouldn't stay there for long. He was too knowledgeable. Everyone could see that.

He possessed one skill Doug couldn't master in a million years. Phil could communicate.

What impressed me the most were the scouting reports he gave on upcoming opponents. Phil took the teams that were far from Chicago, while Tex and Johnny, both a lot older, went on shorter trips.

Phil's reports were filled with tons of details, large and small:

Which side of the floor players preferred to operate from. Which hand they liked to dribble with. Where any of them might be a little soft on the defensive end. Which plays the opposing coach would usually run at different stages in the game.

On and on it went. The only detail Phil didn't share with us was what the other team ate for breakfast. I'm sure he knew.

Doug felt threatened by Phil. With good reason.

Jerry wouldn't have brought in someone with Phil's credentials—he won a title coaching the Albany Patroons in the CBA, which used to be pro basketball's minor league, and two as a player with the Knicks—to be an assistant coach forever.

One night in mid-December of 1988, Doug was kicked out of a game against the Bucks in Milwaukee.

Phil took over and ran a full-court press, and let the guys have more freedom on offense instead of going with the plays Doug preferred. Doug was always coming up with a new play for everyone to learn at practice, in many cases copying ones that had worked against us the night before.

Having Phil in charge was a refreshing change. We outscored the Bucks in the second half, 66–38, to win going away.

When Doug found out that Phil's wife, June, had sent next to Jerry and his wife, Thelma, at the game, he was beside himself. He was insecure enough as it was.

He went to see Phil. They talked for hours. Doug was concerned with how tight Phil and Jerry were becoming. Jerry, as it turned out, had been meeting with Phil every so often to get a better sense of how Doug was coping with the pressures of the job.

"How did it go with him today?" Jerry would ask Phil. "How did he take the loss?"

Not very well, I suspect.

Once, on the bus after a tough loss, Doug told the driver to stop. "Let me out. I'll see you guys back at the hotel."

During the 1988–89 season, Jerry called Phil while he was on a scouting trip in Miami. Jerry worried Doug's temperament might worsen if Phil wasn't around to defuse the situation.

"I don't want you to ever be that far away from the team," Jerry told Phil. "If you have to do any scouting, it has to be on your day off."

. . . .

We dropped 8 of our last 10 heading into the playoffs to finish 47-35. That wasn't exactly the momentum we were looking for.

Our health was partly to blame. Horace was having trouble with his wrist, while Brad, Michael, John Paxson, and I were dealing with one aggravating injury or another. Craig Hodges, the shooting guard we had acquired from the Phoenix Suns in December, was also at less than 100 percent.

Two of those eight losses were to the Pistons, one to the Cavaliers, who, for the second year in a row, would be our opponent in the opening round.

The Cavs were vastly improved. They won 57 games, 15 more than the year before, including each of the six meetings with us. Brad

Daugherty was developing nicely, while Mark Price and Ron Harper were among the best guard tandems in the league.

Magic predicted the Cavs would be the team of the nineties. Maybe the nineties had arrived ahead of schedule.

Maybe not.

We took Game 1 in Cleveland, 95–88, Michael leading the way with 31 points. I chipped in with 22, while Horace finished with 13 points and 13 boards.

To win a playoff game on the road was a huge step for us. During the regular season, our record away from the Stadium was an abysmal 17-24. On the road, you need to be smart with the rock, take high-percentage shots, avoid unnecessary fouls, and outhustle your opponent for the all-important fifty-fifty balls. Check, check, check, and check. It helped that Price was out with a strained hamstring.

With him returning to the lineup, the Cavs held serve in Game 2, 95–88. Harper was sensational: 31 points, 11 rebounds, 5 steals. The teams split the next two games in Chicago.

The Game 4 loss was tough to digest.

With nine seconds to go, Michael was on the free throw line with a chance to extend the lead to 3 points. He made the first but missed the second. The Cavs tied it with two free throws from Daugherty and won in overtime to set up a deciding Game 5 in Cleveland.

What happened at the end of that game, I probably don't have to tell you.

Here it goes, anyway:

With 3 seconds left, Brad Sellers throws the ball in bounds to Michael, who has finally broken free. Craig Ehlo is guarding him. Michael takes two dribbles toward the foul line. Then rises in the air, double clutches, and fires away from about 18 feet.

Nailed it!

A game, and series, is won. A legend is made.

I have nothing against "The Shot." How could I? Whenever they show it on TV, it brings back the most wonderful memories. Given the circumstances and what was at stake, I can't think of another player in the history of our sport who would've done what Michael did.

That's how incredible that moment was—and always will be.

Yet when I think about that series, I don't focus on Michael's heroics. I think about what the Chicago Bulls accomplished as a group, it being the first hurdle we cleared to put us on the path to, eventually, winning a championship. Every team on the rise, to reach the promised land, needs to come through in a defining moment. When you no longer believe you are destined for greatness, you know it.

In the next series, we knocked off the Knicks in six. Another hurdle, for sure.

Then, in Game 1 of the Eastern Conference Finals, we shocked the Pistons, 94–88, in their building. A third hurdle?

Hardly.

Laimbeer and the other thugs rebounded to win Game 2, then grabbed two of the next three to go up in the series, 3–2. Not once did we crack the 100-point barrier. Their strategy was the same as it had been for the last year or so: the famous "Jordan Rules." Chuck Daly, the Detroit coach, came up with the rules after Michael embarrassed the Bad Boys in April of 1988 by scoring 59 points in a game on national TV.

The rules were fairly straightforward:

Put two or three guys on Michael whenever he comes into the lane. Knock his butt to the floor. Throw him in front of a train if need be.

Bottom line: do whatever it takes to keep him from going airborne. Once he does that, forget it. In their judgment, and they weren't wrong, one man, as dangerous as he might be, can't possibly beat five men. Maybe in one game. Maybe two. Not over a seven-game series.

Michael wasn't the only victim. In Game 6, moments after Isiah Thomas, their star point guard, made a jumper for a 2–0 lead, I caught an elbow in the right eye from Laimbeer underneath the basket.

It was an accident . . . I think. One could never be sure with that guy.

I was knocked unconscious. After sitting on the bench for a few minutes to clear my head, I wanted to go back in. The doctor said no. Jerry Krause didn't object. I was taken to the hospital with a mild concussion and missed the rest of the game.

Even without me in the lineup, we rallied from 10 down early in the fourth quarter to narrow the deficit to 81–79. In the end, Thomas couldn't be contained. He scored 33 points, 17 in the fourth, the Pistons prevailing, 103–94. Their bench came through, as usual, which included 9 points and 15 rebounds from Dennis Rodman.

Were we frustrated?

Not entirely. We knew we weren't at their level. Not yet.

The talent was there, no question. What the Pistons possessed, and we did not, was a sense of when to be patient and when to attack. You don't acquire that wisdom just from listening to your coaches or reading the scouting reports. You acquire it on your own, from playing in the big games. From losing the big games.

• • • •

Once the season was over, the guys went their separate ways. To get a break from the game, and from one another. From the first week of October to the first week of June, we had spent more time with our teammates than our families.

I took off for Hamburg. I was overseeing the new home that was being built for my parents. Mom wasn't too keen about moving, so instead I had some landscaping done to put in a larger, ranch-style house, along with a new park and homes for other family members.

In early July came big news from Chicago:

Doug Collins was out.

I'd gotten used to teammates being traded. Getting rid of a coach was something else entirely. A coach who, whatever one thought of him, had just taken his team to the Eastern Conference Finals. Could this really be happening?

Oh, yes, it could, and the more I thought about it, the more it occurred to me: What took them so long?

The catering to Michael. The criticism of players in front of the fans. The running up and down the sidelines. This wasn't how to unite a group of twelve men with twelve distinct personalities into a unit ready to compete for a championship. That we would start the upcoming season with three rookies drafted in the first round— Stacey King (No. 6), B. J. Armstrong (No. 18), and Jeff Sanders (No. 20)—might also have factored into the decision. Doug wasn't exactly the nurturing type.

Even so, I harbor no ill feelings toward Doug. Whenever I ran into him over the years, I wished him well.

He just wasn't the right man to take the Chicago Bulls to the next level. That man was Phil Jackson. I wasn't surprised when Jerry Reinsdorf and Jerry Krause handed the job to Phil. I don't believe anyone was.

I can't remember what Phil said to everyone when we got together at training camp in the fall of 1989. I can definitely remember how I felt.

That everything would be different.

That the Chicago Bulls would be a team. And no longer the Michael Jordan Show.

CHAPTER 7

PHIL IN THE VOID

Phil wasn't a star in his playing days. Not even close.

From 1967 through 1980 he appeared in 807 regular season games, almost entirely with the Knicks, coming off the bench in the vast majority of them. Phil was what we refer to as a role player. On the Knicks, his role was to throw his wiry frame around and scrap for every loose ball. He scooped up more than his share, his body still paying the price.

New York had plenty of guys who could put the ball in the basket, such as Willis Reed, Walt Frazier, and Earl Monroe. That wasn't enough. Like any franchise hoping to make a serious run at a championship, the Knicks needed to impose their will physically. Which was what Phil and Dave DeBusschere, their rugged power forward, did nightly.

The Knicks, who won it all in 1970 and 1973, defeating the Lakers on both occasions, were known for their unselfishness. No team over the last fifty years has passed the ball with as much purpose. It was a clinic in how the game should be played. Their individual and team defense was another sight to behold.

Phil saw absolutely no reason why the Bulls couldn't be like those Knicks teams.

Heading into the 1989–90 season, something had to be done. As good as we were, we weren't good enough to beat the Pistons. Fortunately, having been an assistant coach for two years and seeing where Doug had gone wrong (fill in the blank), Phil knew precisely which changes to implement from day one.

The most important change was to convince Michael he needed to score less for us to succeed. That would be like asking Picasso to paint fewer portraits.

Michael was the most prolific scorer the game had ever seen, with the exception of Wilt Chamberlain. To suggest Michael wasn't enamored with the idea would be a massive understatement. He was concerned that changing the offense would keep him from being . . . Michael Jordan. He had led the league in scoring the previous three seasons, averaging 37.1, 35.0, and 32.5 points per game.

Many of those points came with him in isolation, or on a fast break, the rest of us in as much awe as the fans.

Now he would have to score in a system that would require a word that wasn't in his vocabulary: *trust.* He would have to trust his teammates to get him the ball where he wanted it. And he would have to trust them to come through when he was double-teamed and they ended up with open looks. The problem, as he saw it, was they hadn't done enough to earn that trust.

Take Bill Cartwright. A year had gone by since Michael told us to stop throwing the ball to Bill in crunch time, and it didn't appear anything had taken place to change his mind.

If Michael's goal was to win championships like Magic Johnson and Larry Bird, the main two players he measured himself against, he would have to trust his teammates. He might win a ton of games—as well as more scoring titles and MVPs (he had one so far, from the 1987–88 season)—by taking around 25 shots every night.

He wouldn't win a ring.

From day one, Tex had wanted us to run the triangle offense. Only Doug wasn't a believer. Phil couldn't have been more of a believer, as was Jerry Krause.

It wouldn't surprise me if Phil, in those occasional private meetings with Jerry, had given him the impression that he would run the triangle if he was put in charge. The offense was similar to how the Knicks shared the ball under Phil's former coach and mentor, Red Holzman.

So what, exactly, is the triangle?

To begin with, the name comes from the triangle that is formed when three players line up on the strong side of the floor. The strong side is where the ball is presently located.

The system is complicated, at first. No wonder it took us a year and a half to get it down pat. Some players never get it.

It wasn't like the offense we were used to running, that's for sure, where someone, usually the point guard, calls out a set play. Instead, the triangle is an offense that reacts to the way the defense is set up.

If the defense, for example, takes away a pass to the corner or a dribble penetration, that will automatically open up other options. Your job is to understand, almost instinctively, what those other options are, and that's where it gets confusing. You are luring the defense into a trap. To put it in boxing terms, the triangle, known for years as the triple-post offense, is the perfect counterpunch.

The triangle deviated so fundamentally from how each of us learned how to play the game that, for the longest time, Michael wasn't the only one who had doubts it could work. Why, if it was so ingenious, were no other teams running it?

In the past, players focused only on where they, themselves, were on the court. Now they would have to keep track of where everyone else was, and that's a big difference.

Whoever has the ball in the triangle is like a quarterback in football, who must quickly read the defense and spot open receivers. The goal is for every player on the court to read the defense the same way. You can see where that would be a problem if one man reads it differently from the rest and makes the wrong pass or moves to the wrong spot. The shot clock will wind down, usually resulting in a low-percentage shot.

Now for the upside: once you get it down, the triangle will create excellent scoring opportunities. In every game, the goal is to get as many uncontested shots as you can. We used to tell ourselves that, after the third pass during any possession, the defense will begin to break down.

Our poor grasp of the system was obvious from the start. Guys had trouble getting used to the idea they didn't have to dribble after catching the ball. When they threw a pass, the defense read where the ball was going as if it had an informer on the inside.

We were driving a car with a flat tire and there was no spare.

In the first half hour of practice, Tex went over one fundamental after another. I felt as if I were back in high school.

Two-hand chest passes. Bounce passes. Passes to the post. Passes to the elbow.

During some practices he didn't allow us to put the ball on the floor. He wanted to see ball movement and player movement and nothing else. Tex believed in what he referred to as the "four pass." That meant making a minimum of four passes in every possession before someone could take a shot.

Were we a professional basketball team or appearing in a remake of *Hoosiers*?

I kept waiting for Gene Hackman to show up.

We practiced throwing passes from every spot on the floor, knowing one of us might get stuck there in a game and not know what to do next.

In a typical forty-eight-minute game, Tex explained, the most any player, including MJ, would have the ball in his hands would be about four and a half minutes. Given so little time to operate, it would be natural to assume Michael couldn't be as dangerous.

It would also be wrong. He was more dangerous without the ball, moving around screens, catching it in rhythm, ready to attack.

Because teams were used to guarding him with the ball, they had a game plan.

Guarding him without the ball can be more difficult, especially when the defensive player is rotating over as the help defender. Michael would hold on to the ball for five seconds, at most, before he took a jump shot, drove down the lane, or dished it to another player. He wasn't James Harden, holding the ball for an interminable ten or twelve seconds.

Sometimes, when I watched Harden play for the Houston Rockets, bouncing the ball up and down twenty feet from the basket, I felt as if my life were passing me by. I wanted to shout at the TV, "For God's sake, James, stop dribbling!"

At the outset of the 1989–90 season, we lost games we should have won. After wrapping up a seven-game road trip in November, our record was a mediocre 7-6.

Learning the triangle was similar to learning a foreign language. Just when we thought we had it down, we started to have trouble again. A few of us were hoping Phil might change his mind and scrap the whole thing. Now I could see why Doug had never been a convert.

Not a chance.

"This is what we are going to do," Phil told us, "and you guys are going to have to figure it out."

Through sheer repetition, we did just that.

Guys felt more confident in the holes they spotted in the defense and stopped second-guessing themselves. Maybe winning—we went 14-3 from late November through early January—made us believers. Or maybe believing in the system made us winners. Who knows? Who cares?

Either way, I fell in love with the triangle.

Every player on the court touched the ball on just about every possession, all feeling they were part of the offense whether they took the shot or not. Working together, we learned to value and trust one another. The players who believe in one another, and sacrifice for one another, are the players who win championships.

Phil was critical in a constructive way. He didn't embarrass us in front of our fans or teammates. He pulled guys off to the side or asked one of the assistant coaches to explain what we did wrong. I felt respected as a player and, more important, as a man.

I didn't go along with some of the Zen stuff he introduced to the team, such as the burning of sage and having us close our eyes and meditate.

Sorry, Phil. I know you meant well. That was just way too out there for a country boy like me.

Nor did I read the books he handed out every year as presents.

On the other hand, I totally bought into what he was saying about a basketball team being a pack, and not a collection of separate individuals. More than the X's and O's, that was Phil Jackson's most valuable contribution to the Chicago Bulls.

He got us to bond. To be one.

Instead of going directly from the hotel to the arena for practice, he mixed things up on occasion by taking the team on a tour of the DC landmarks or to visit the Statue of Liberty. There is a fine line between spending enough time with your teammates away from the court and spending too much time with them. Phil was a player for many years. He knew where the line was.

As for the X's and O's, while Tex ran the offense in practice, Johnny Bach ran the defense.

Johnny doesn't receive enough credit for our success. He had been close to Doug. Phil kept him around, regardless, and it was one of the smartest things he did. Johnny was highly respected by the players and knew defense as well as anyone else in the league. He was aware of what the other team was going to do before they were.

Phil trusted Tex and Johnny, and Jim Cleamons, the other assistant coach, to do their jobs. Not every coach in the NBA is that secure.

His back bothered Phil so much he couldn't stand in one place for more than a few minutes. He walked around the perimeter of the court, chiming in every so often with a suggestion that made me think about my role in a whole different way. I learned how to let the game come to me and not force the action if the opportunity didn't present itself. Instead of driving recklessly into the lane, I would pull up and take the midrange jumper.

Our practices were often more intense than the actual games. Being on the first unit, Michael and I played on the same team. We worked on our timing and execution. Every so often, Phil put me with the second unit to go against Michael, Horace, and the other starters.

I relished the challenge, and I wasn't alone.

So what if it was only practice? To beat a team that had Michael was a chance for the guys on the second unit to prove themselves. When they did win, they gained a ton of confidence. I believe that's why they came up big during that amazing fourth-quarter run in Game 6 of the 1992 Finals. The group that outplayed the Blazers for those vital three or four minutes was the same group that used to, on occasion, defeat Michael's team in practice. They knew they could do it.

My strategy in guarding him was no mystery:

Force him to drive away from the basket into what is known as *help*. That's where another defender switches from the player he is covering to help out. He was Michael Jordan. He wasn't passing the ball. He guarded me the same way. Both of us became better at that end of the court from defending the other.

Phil didn't push us too hard. Especially when guys reached their thirties. He saved our legs for when it counted.

The practices were structured, every movement, every drill having a purpose.

"Go hard, go short, make it productive," he told us.

That was another part of the man's genius. By the time the game got under way, we couldn't wait to unleash the energy that we had kept bottled up.

As much as he believed in the triangle, Phil believed in something else even more: winning.

If that meant dispensing with ball movement and player movement in the fourth quarter of a tight game, so be it. The offense would revert back to when Doug was in charge.

Translation: Give the ball to Michael. The rest of you, get the hell out of the way.

More often than not, that spelled trouble for opponents who had focused for three and a half quarters on the triangle. Now they had to abruptly change their entire strategy to focus on stopping one player. And not just any one player.

Good luck.

. . . .

In January of 1990, I was named to the All-Star team for the first time. Chosen as one of the Eastern Conference's seven reserves, I was on the same unit with such stars as Larry Bird, Patrick Ewing, and Dominique Wilkins. And, of course, Michael. I couldn't have been more excited.

And grateful.

When I underwent the back surgery in the summer of 1988, I wasn't thinking about playing in an All-Star Game someday. I was hoping to play in *any* game.

The All-Star Game was held in Miami. I scored 4 points and had 1 rebound, 1 steal, and 1 blocked shot. The highlight of the weekend was the slam dunk contest, where I finished fifth. I got the crowd going with my first attempt from the free throw line, receiving a score of 47.2 out of 50, then missed my second when I went for a more difficult, 360-degree turn. Oh well. Simply to be in the same competition with Dominique, one of the most spectacular dunkers of all time, was enough.

I was involved in another competition back then, which Michael and I came up with one day: for most steals in a season. We figured it would be a healthy battle, a way to get us to concentrate even more on our defense.

Phil didn't see it that way. In his opinion, just because a guy received credit for a steal didn't mean he was the player who caused it. More important, whenever you gamble by shooting the gap to steal the ball and don't succeed, the team might then be exposed to a wide-open shot or dribble penetration.

He had a point. In any case, as I later found out, it was never a fair fight.

Not because Michael was a better defender. Heavens, no. It was because Michael was better at getting people to do whatever he wanted. I saw it over and over, from the first training camp in 1987 to the last victory rally in 1998.

Here's how it worked:

Say I deflected the ball and tapped it over to him. I should get credit with the steal, right? Nope. More often than not, the steal went into his column on the stat sheet, and I could do nothing about it.

One night, a scorekeeper came into the locker room after the game to hand the stat sheets to Phil and the coaching staff. The sheet breaks down the points, rebounds, assists, steals, blocked shots, turnovers, and so on for everyone who played in the game.

I couldn't believe the look the guy gave Michael: "See, MJ, we take care of you."

No wonder, in the nine full seasons we played together, he averaged more steals than me in every year except two.

Even so, steals never tell the whole story of a player's impact at that end of the floor. There's no doubt in my mind I was superior to Michael in both individual and team defense. Of course, because the media believed Michael could do nothing wrong, he was in the running every season for the Defensive Player of the Year award. I was not.

I was considered the voice of the defense, the player who directed everyone where to go. My deep voice was perfect for the task, loud enough to be heard above the noise of the crowd and the other players on the court. Some voices get lost out there.

Being able to communicate well on the court is often the difference between winning and losing. You need to tell a teammate when his back is turned and the opponent is about to set a screen. Or when someone missed a rotation and you have to be the help defender.

Defense on our team was about trusting one another every bit as much as the triangle was. Perhaps more. Johnny Bach used to say our defense is on a string, meaning each man is connected to the other four. If, for example, the rotating man on the back end of defending a screen-and-roll doesn't move correctly, the whole defense will break down and the other team will likely score.

If it happens once or twice in a game, you can live with it. More often than that, you won't trust the man anymore, and that's a problem.

Not taking anything away from the triangle, but it was our defense, year after year, that gave us our identity. When we applied full-court pressure, it wasn't necessarily to force a turnover; it was to get our opponents to run some clock. By the time they got into their offense, they might have ten or twelve seconds to operate instead of sixteen or eighteen, often resulting in a low-percentage shot.

I enjoyed playing defense more than offense. I preferred to be the guy who stopped the last shot rather than the guy who made it. When you play defense the right way, you can break the other team's spirit. Players become lost, disoriented. It's a beautiful sight to see.

On defense, I could be "the man" in a way I could never be on offense. Not on a team that had Michael Jordan.

Another role I took on had to do with my buddy Horace Grant. He wasn't happy, and that's an understatement. Although he was playing well, Horace wasn't meeting Michael's high expectations—who could?—and Michael, as it was shown over and over with other players in the ESPN doc, wasn't shy about letting him know.

As for Horace, I never knew a player more sensitive to any slights, real or imagined. He despised the preferential treatment Michael received from Doug even more than I did. Michael and Horace had gotten into a pretty heated argument after a playoff loss to the Pistons in 1989.

Money was also an issue, and with good reason.

Horace was earning $320,000, lower than everyone else on the team with the exception of Ed Nealy and Charles Davis, who both played far fewer minutes.

In April of 1990, Horace couldn't take it anymore. He went public with a request to be traded. Horace had every right to feel disrespected. Just twenty-four years old, he was already one of the top power forwards in the league and was only going to get better.

The timing could not have been worse. The playoffs were about to get under way.

As usual, I was there for him. I told him his big payday would come, and no matter how critical Michael might be, everyone else in that locker room, Phil included, knew we wouldn't win a title without him. He soon stopped asking for a trade. Truth is, by this point Horace and I had begun to grow apart. While never enough to cause a serious rift, the difference was noticeable to both of us, and our teammates.

When we arrived at training camp in the fall of 1987, he and I were at a similar spot in our respective journeys, each hoping to make a mark in the game we loved. That was the case throughout our rookie season, and the season that followed it. The bond between us remained strong.

In the third season, everything changed.

I became an All-Star and, in the minds of the press and fans, rose to a level just below that of Michael. Horace felt left out. Being a twin— his brother, Harvey, played for the Washington Bullets—Horace believed everyone should be equal. Whenever I joined Michael for what I thought was an innocent game of cards, he saw it as a betrayal.

That I was trying to be like Mike.

I wasn't trying to be like Mike. I was trying to get along with every player on the team, from Michael to the last man on the bench. As Phil told us over and over, we would need everyone to contribute if we were going to do what we failed to do in 1988 and 1989.

To beat the fucking Pistons.

CHAPTER 8: ON A MISSION

What a difference a year makes.

Going into the 1990 playoffs, we were on a roll. Since the middle of February, our record was 26-7. That included two 9-game winning streaks.

The triangle was running more efficiently than ever, and in the fourth quarter, when the game was on the line, Michael took over as only he can. The 55 victories in the 1989–90 regular season were the most for the franchise since Richard Nixon was in the White House. Those victories meant nothing now. Anything less than a trip to the Finals and the season would be a failure.

We'd learned enough lessons my first two years in Chicago. The time had come to teach someone else a lesson.

In the best-of-five opening round, we beat the Milwaukee Bucks in four, scoring at least 109 points in each game. In Game 1, I recorded my first playoff triple-double: 17 points, 10 rebounds, and 13 assists. I also came up with 3 steals and 3 blocks.

So far, so good.

Next up were the Philadelphia 76ers, led by Charles Barkley, who would one day be my teammate in the 1992 and 1996 Summer Olympics and for one season with the Houston Rockets. We took the first two games at the Stadium and ended up beating the Sixers in five.

I don't remember much about that series. Basketball was the last thing on my mind.

Shortly before Game 2, one of my brothers called to say Dad had twenty-four hours to live. The news wasn't unexpected. His health had been declining for some time. When I arrived at the hospital in Arkansas, Dad was hooked to a feeding tube and didn't know I was there. He passed away the next day at the age of sixty-nine.

Losing him hit me hard. Ever since the stroke, he hadn't been active in my life. Yet he was still my dad, and it meant the world to me every time someone in the family told me he was watching one of my games on TV. I only wish I could, in those final hours, have told him one last time how much I loved him.

I didn't stay in Hamburg for long. My teammates needed me. We were trying to win a championship, and the Pistons would be next.

We were ready for them. No longer would Michael try to win the game on his own. This would be a better Bulls team than the one the Pistons were used to seeing in the playoffs.

More athletic. More physical. More disciplined. Better.

Or so we thought.

The Pistons captured the first two games in Detroit. In the opener, Michael scored 34 points, although only 3 of those points, on just one field goal, came in the fourth quarter. John Paxson, who had sprained his ankle in practice, played just sixteen minutes and was held scoreless. Our backup point guard, B. J. Armstrong, had only 4 points in twenty-nine minutes and finished with more turnovers (5) than assists (2). The final: 86–77.

I don't mean to come down too hard on B.J. It wasn't his fault we lost. That's a tough spot for a rookie.

In Game 2, trailing by 15 points at the half, we expected to hear an earful in the locker room. Which we got. From Michael. Not from Phil or the other coaches.

The press reported afterward that his tirade had been directed at his teammates, though Michael would claim he, too, had taken responsibility for our inept performance. Whomever he was angry with, the message came through loud and clear. We rallied in the third quarter and even seized the lead. Gaining a split on the road, always a goal in the playoffs, was still possible.

Not for long. The Pistons, determined to defend their crown—they had swept the Lakers the year before in the Finals—stormed back to win, 102–93. Their off guard, Joe Dumars, the unsung hero of that team, led the way with 31 points. Michael, still seething, bolted from the locker room without saying a word to the media. I didn't blame him.

Nevertheless, this was no time to panic. The Pistons did what they were supposed to do: hold serve.

Now it was our turn.

Two wins at the Stadium and the series would be even again. I felt so relaxed at practice I threw a rubber snake at Michael. He flinched, as usual. Michael was scared to death of snakes. I used to buy toy snakes and put them in his locker whenever I had the chance. The look on his face was priceless. I couldn't stop laughing.

There was nothing amusing about our play in the second quarter of Game 3. The Bad Boys outscored us, 32–19. In the third, they were leading by 14. Isiah was playing great. If we didn't get our act together, and fast, it *would* be time to panic. We clawed back, at last, Michael scoring 13 points in the quarter, while I added 12, and then held the Pistons off in the fourth to prevail, 107–102.

In the first two games, I had allowed Dennis Rodman, the Defensive Player of the Year, to get in my head.

That's not a good place for him to be. Rodman was an expert in using his feet and anticipating your next move. In Game 3, I was more aggressive. The result: 29 points, 11 rebounds, 5 assists. Game 4 went our way, as well: 108–101. Our defense in the first half was as suffocating as I had ever seen it. Detroit scored only 35 points. This was a brand-new series.

For about forty-eight hours.

In Game 5, their defense was suffocating, holding us to 33 percent from the field. Michael and I shot a combined 12 for 39, as we fell 97–83. Near the end of the game, I grabbed Laimbeer around the neck as he drove to the basket, probably in frustration more than anything else. After how hard we'd competed in Chicago, I expected a much better effort from my teammates. And from myself.

Here we were again, on the verge of losing to the Pistons for the third year in a row, and it didn't seem to make any difference who our coach was or what system we ran. Maybe they were too good.

Not so fast, Pip.

In Game 6, thanks to another gritty defensive effort, and a season-high 19 points from Craig Hodges, we evened the series once more with a convincing 109–91 triumph. Horace was also a factor with 14 boards. The victory didn't come without a price. Paxson aggravated the ankle he'd hurt before Game 1 and would miss Game 7. That was a huge blow.

Another key player wouldn't be on the court for Game 7. Yours truly.

Oh, I suited up, all right, and played forty-two minutes, third most behind Michael and Horace, who each logged forty-five. Except that wasn't Scottie Pippen wearing No. 33. That was an impostor.

About fifteen minutes before the opening tip, while I warmed up, my head started to throb and I couldn't see straight.

"Is there something wrong with the lights?" I asked my teammates. "Are they dimmer than usual?"

No, they said, the lights were just fine.

I asked our trainer for some aspirin. I'd had a slight headache the day before, which went away after a couple of hours. When I woke up on game day, I felt rested, ready to go.

Ready to book the first trip ever to the NBA Finals for the Chicago Bulls.

As I took the court for the jump ball, my head was killing me and I couldn't get my eyes to stop blinking. I was having a migraine.

I probably should have told Phil to put someone else in there, someone who could be an asset, not a liability. Why didn't I? Because I was a professional athlete and professional athletes play in pain, especially in a game as big as this. Don't forget, I had to leave the final game of the Detroit series the year before due to the elbow from Laimbeer, intentional or not. I would rather die than let my teammates down again.

We got off to a decent start, nonetheless, and were actually leading at the end of the first quarter, 19–17. Except it was the kind of low-scoring tussle the Pistons thrived on. The tempo was bound to catch up to us.

In the second quarter, they couldn't miss, shooting 82 percent from the field while we shot 21 percent. The lead was 15 points at halftime. We cut it to 10 after three quarters, though we never threatened down the stretch. The final: 93–74.

The game itself, to this day, remains a blur to me.

All I remember is my eyesight kept getting worse and worse. I could make out my teammates but couldn't tell how far away they were or read the numbers on the 24-second clock. During every time-out, I put a towel with ice around my head, hoping the pain would magically go away. It never did.

I was like a prizefighter between rounds who, when the bell rang, kept going back in the ring to take more punishment. If this had, indeed, been a boxing match, the ref would have stopped it in the first round. I finished 1 of 10 from the field for 2 points. How I ever made that one basket is beyond me.

The locker room afterward felt like a morgue. In 1989, when we lost to the Pistons, the guys were disappointed, not devastated. This time was different.

I'm not suggesting the Bulls would have won if Paxson hadn't hurt his ankle or if I hadn't come down with a migraine. Or if Hodges (3 for 13) and B.J. (1 for 8) hadn't shot the ball so poorly. Just that this was our first realistic chance to win a championship, and now it was gone.

The Pistons knew how to grind out playoff victories. We were still learning.

Jerry Krause went on a rant in the locker room. "This is never happening again," he told everyone. "We are better than this. We are going to beat this fucking team next year."

Jerry meant well, I suppose, although the guys were in no mood to listen. Michael also said a few words. He was especially tough on the younger players: "You need to be in the weight room and work on your games every single day. We can't do this without you."

He cried in the bus on the way to the airport. This was his sixth season without a trip to the Finals. That's not what he signed on for when he came aboard in 1984.

The press, meanwhile, let me have it. One writer even implied I faked the migraine, which was "unadvertised by any swelling or bandage, rather only by Pippen's word for it, a word that would be less suspicious if Pippen had not, in three previous trips to the Palace [of Auburn Hills], easily become road pooch of the playoffs."

Who cares what the press said? I didn't trust them anyway. Not since my rookie year when they sided with management after my back flared up. The reporters in Chicago were no different from Doug. Michael made covering the Bulls relevant for the first time ever, and, by extension, themselves relevant.

With Michael cast as the hero, someone had to play the villain. Care to guess whom they chose for the part?

Besides, I never felt I had to prove something to these "experts." The only people I had to prove something to were the men in the locker room. Who made the same sacrifices I did, year after year, and experienced the same setbacks.

Even so, I couldn't help wonder, *Why a migraine? And why now, of all possible days, on the afternoon of a Game 7?*

I went over every move I made in the previous twenty-four hours. There wasn't anything unusual that stuck out. I ate dinner, watched a movie, and went to bed. I thought for a short time it might have been food poisoning. It wasn't.

A few days later, my head still pounding, the doctors ordered a brain scan. Something wasn't right. I was scared it might be a tumor.

The scan showed nothing abnormal. Thank God.

So, I repeat, why a migraine?

One explanation was that perhaps the stress over the last few weeks, beginning with the death of my father, had been too much for me. I wouldn't rule out anything. Whatever the cause, I was sure the migraine would follow me for a long time, and I was right. People ask me today, more than thirty years later, if I still get headaches.

It wasn't just the migraine that gave me pause. It was also the concussion the year before.

Here were two straight elimination games, two moments of truth, one might say, when I wasn't there for my teammates, and it made no difference whether, in both cases, I had a legitimate excuse or not. To many fans, that couldn't be a coincidence.

Others were sympathetic. I ran into many folks that summer who told me they suffered migraines themselves and the fact that I was on the court for as long as I was (forty-two minutes) was remarkable. I appreciated their kind words. That wasn't the easiest time in my life.

■ ■ ■

We lost Game 7 to the Pistons on a Sunday.

On Tuesday, I was in the weight room.

My head was still hurting. My heart was hurting more. Call it revenge, redemption, whatever. I couldn't wait to get back to work. And I was far from alone.

Normally after a season ends, players will meet with the coaching staff to discuss the parts of the game they need to work on for the following year and then take off for the summer.

Not this summer.

One guy after another kept showing up in the weight room and would return the next day, and the day after that. This went on for weeks. There wasn't one coach, or player, who came up with the idea and the rest then followed along.

Everyone arrived at the same conclusion at the same time:

If we are to take down the Pistons, we have to work harder, and it doesn't start at training camp in October. It starts right here. Right now.

The next time, when Rodman, Laimbeer, and the other Bad Boys try to push us around, we will be too strong for them. Not that we will lower ourselves to their style of play. That's what they would want. We will focus instead on who we are: the more skilled, more athletic team.

While working out, we did something more important than lifting weights. We lifted each other. Becoming a team more than ever before.

Phil tried to create that feeling with the triangle and the meditation and his preaching about Oneness. He succeeded, to a point. We were more united than we were under Doug Collins. However, only when we, the players, made the commitment on our own after losing Game 7 to the Pistons did we truly begin to bond.

With any bond comes trust. Trust your teammate will be where he is supposed to be. That he will make the open shot. That he will help out when your man gets by you.

That he will sacrifice everything for the same goal you have: winning a championship.

. . . .

Before we knew it, the 1990–91 season was here.

The roster was the same, except for two key additions:

Cliff Levingston, a power forward from Atlanta, and Dennis Hopson, a shooting guard from New Jersey. Levingston wouldn't back down from Rodman and Laimbeer. He was exactly what we needed. In his most recent season with the Nets, Hopson averaged a little under 16 points a game. Both players were sure to fortify our bench.

In camp, we talked about the importance of securing home-court advantage throughout the playoffs. If Game 7 had been in Chicago, not Detroit, I believe we would have advanced to the Finals no matter how painful my migraine was or how many shots Hodges and B.J. missed. Our fans would have willed us to victory.

We were hoping to start strong. That's not what happened.

Three losses right out of the gate, to Philadelphia, Washington, and Boston. The Philly and Boston games were at the Stadium. The Celtics trailed by 11 points heading into the fourth quarter before rallying to win by 2. We missed 8 of our final 11 shots.

I wasn't quite over the migraine. Mentally, that is. I sat on the bench expecting my head to start pounding at any moment. The fear didn't go away for months.

That wasn't my only concern. So was the situation with my contract.

I was so frustrated I toyed with the idea of sitting out a few days of camp. My agent talked me out of it. I was severely underpaid, making $765,000. I know that sounds like a lot of money, and it was, but players at my level were earning a lot more. Reggie Miller was making $654,000 in the final year of his first contract when the Pacers upped the amount to $3.2 million. The late Reggie Lewis of the Celtics went from $400,000 to $3 million.

Not me. I worked for Jerry Reinsdorf. He didn't give me an extra dime.

Worse yet, I was being paid less than my teammate Stacey King, who came off the bench and was in only his second season. He was making $1 million. Stacey was a fine prospect. Still, $1 million? *Are you kidding me?* I've gotten a lot of criticism over the years for going public with my problems with ownership—I may hold the franchise record for most times asking for a trade—but a professional basketball player's window to make big money is narrow and can close before you know it.

In any case, as the weeks wore on, the 0-3 start felt like ancient history. By the end of December, we stood at 20-9, a game behind the Bucks in our division and just three and a half games behind the Celtics for the best record in the conference.

In early February, we got ready to take on the Pistons in Detroit for the second time that season.

Back in December, when they crushed us, 105–84, I was as atrocious (2 for 16 for 4 points) as I had been in Game 7. Only I didn't have an excuse this time. I could see how far away my teammates were and the numbers on the 24-second clock. I just couldn't make a basket.

For the second meeting at the Palace, I couldn't have been more motivated.

Another performance like the last two and people would have every right to wonder if I was, indeed, intimidated by the Detroit fans, and by Dennis Rodman. The Bulls also had a lot to prove as a group. Forget about the other teams we beat. Until we beat *this* team, in *this* building, many would doubt if we were for real.

With a little under three minutes to go, it looked as if those doubts would loom larger than ever.

The Pistons were up by 4 points, and they were without their best player, Isiah Thomas, out with a wrist injury. After Michael missed a jumper, Horace secured the biggest rebound of the game and passed it back to Michael, who converted a three-point play. He followed with two free throws on the next possession to give us a lead we wouldn't surrender. The final: 95–93.

I went to the hole with no hesitation, finishing with 20 points and 8 rebounds.

Dennis who?

Now if only my contract situation could be dealt with so easily. The Bulls promised in October they would take care of me before Christmas. Well, Christmas had come and gone, and nothing had been under the tree except more broken promises. I was the second-best player on the team but only the sixth-highest-paid player. If that wasn't a lack of respect, I don't know what is.

Just before the trade deadline, I made my position clear: treat me right or trade me now.

Meanwhile, Jerry Krause was pursuing Toni Kukoc, a six-foot-eleven forward from Yugoslavia, as if he were the Second Coming of Larry Bird. The money the Bulls could have paid me, they were saving for Toni, whom they had selected in the second round of the 1990 draft. Toni would decide a few months later to keep playing in Europe. For the time being.

Same old Jerry. Always more in love with what he didn't have. That went for players and coaches.

The press made what I said into a big deal, which I suppose it was. I could have chosen my words more carefully, that's for sure, and I probably didn't help my cause by going public. I was frustrated. I didn't know what else to do.

I didn't want the Bulls to trade me. Then or ever. I was just trying to get them to pay me what I was worth. People might roll their eyes when they read this but I'm serious.

I loved my teammates and I loved Chicago. No other city, in my opinion, came close. If I really wanted to get out of there, believe me, I could have created a lot more trouble for the organization than I ever did. Look how current stars such as Anthony Davis and James Harden put their teams in a position where they had no choice but to get rid of them.

Before long, the trading deadline passed and the story went away. For now.

On February 23, I scored a career-high 43 points (16 of 17 from the field) and added 6 steals and 6 assists in a 129–108 victory over the Charlotte Hornets at the Stadium. I was having a wonderful season, perhaps even better than the year before.

So why wasn't I on the All-Star team?

One explanation was that I hadn't been forgiven for the migraine. As if it were my fault that my head had been about to explode. Another was that I was being penalized for a slow start. Either way, I never felt the same about the All-Star Game after that. To me, it was a popularity contest, nothing more.

Anyway, the victory over the Hornets was our ninth in a row, a streak that stretched to 11 before the Pacers beat us by 21 points in early March. Without Horace, I might add.

Safe to say we didn't dwell on the loss for long.

Three days later, with a win against the Bucks, we launched another streak. This one didn't stop until 9, lifting us to a record of 50-15, a whopping 10 games ahead of the Pistons, still without Isiah, and a game and a half ahead of the Celtics for the coveted No. 1 seed. Which we soon secured, finishing 61-21, the best regular season in franchise history.

For the first time, the pressure in the playoffs would be on the Chicago Bulls.

Bring it on.

CHAPTER 9: THE FIRST DANCE

The magic number was 15.

With 15 victories, we would be the 1991 NBA champions. Phil scribbled the number on the whiteboard in our locker room. We couldn't miss it.

Every time we won a game, he erased it and jotted down the new number. That was his way of making certain we never got ahead of ourselves.

Our opponent in the first round was the New York Knicks, led by Patrick Ewing and my former teammate Charles Oakley. No one would be more determined to pull off the upset than Oak. I sometimes wonder how he feels about having left the Bulls when he did. Same with Doug Collins. Both are probably too proud to admit it, but deep down, it has to eat at them whenever they think of what they missed out on. Their total rings combined: zero.

The Knicks didn't have a prayer.

We took Game 1 by 41 points—Ewing had nearly as many fouls (5) as points (6)—and swept them in three.

Next were the Philadelphia 76ers. They did better than the Knicks. They won a game. We won the other four.

The number on the board was 8.

The more immediate number in our sights was 4, as in the 4 wins required to get past the Bad Boys in the Eastern Conference Finals.

We finished 11 games ahead of them during the regular season. So what? They were still the champions until someone knocked them off.

It wouldn't be easy.

For one thing, Isiah was back after being out for 32 games with the wrist injury. Next to Magic Johnson, he was the best point guard in the league.

I was a big fan of his when I was in college. Isiah was exciting to watch. Similar to Mo Cheeks, he was a small guy (only six foot one) who could penetrate into the lane almost at will. From a distance, he struck me as someone who played the game the way it should be played.

Boy, did I get that wrong.

Once I saw him up close, I discovered what a dirty player he was, with a knack for making the most inappropriate comments. Take the time after Game 7 of the 1987 Eastern Conference Finals against the Celtics when he acknowledged Larry Bird was a "very, very good basketball player," but if he were black, he would be "just another good guy." That "just another good guy" is in the Hall of Fame.

Nonetheless, Isiah, still in his prime, was sure to cause us problems. Throw in Dumars, Rodman, Laimbeer, and another talented big man, James Edwards, along with their excellent bench (shooting guard Vinnie "the Microwave" Johnson, forwards Mark Aguirre and John Salley), and it was bound to be a long series.

At least Games 1 and 2 would be in Chicago. That was a first.

In Game 1, the Pistons focused on stopping MJ, and it paid off. He was only 6 for 15 from the field and committed 6 turnovers. A game like that from Michael would have meant certain defeat in the old days.

These were not the old days.

Our bench bailed us out, scoring 30 points in a comfortable 94–83 victory. B.J., no longer a rookie, scored 9, while Levingston finished with 8 and Perdue 6. Hodges added 7 (3 of 6), as well, a stark contrast with his performance in Game 7 the year before. To show how much the game has evolved, a three-pointer from Hodges was our only three, in just five attempts.

Some teams nowadays put up that many threes before the national anthem.

I enjoy watching today's players light it up from long range—Steph Curry, in particular—and there is certainly no going back to those primitive times before the three was in vogue. That would be like getting rid of the 24-second clock.

On the other hand, the three has become routine, and that's unfortunate. The three in my era was a dagger.

The guys came up with another strong effort in Game 2, prevailing, 105–97.

Prior to the opening tip, Michael accepted the season's MVP trophy, his second. He proceeded to show why he was so deserving, scoring 35 points and dishing out 7 assists. Our bench was a factor once more, making critical shots and playing good defense. Over the first two games, the Pistons had led for a total of three minutes and twenty seconds. Folks, that is called being in total control.

Even so, the series was far from over. The Pistons were warriors. They would fight until the very end and would now be playing in front of their fans at the Palace, the scene of our previous disasters.

It didn't make any difference.

In Game 3, Michael was superb with 33 points, 7 assists, and 5 blocks. I wasn't too shabby myself: 26 points and 10 rebounds. Horace chipped in with 17 points and 8 boards. Good thing the Bulls didn't grant him his wish to be traded. In the summer of 1990, they gave Horace a three-year extension for $6 million. Safe to say the investment was paying off.

Now the series *was* over. No team had ever come back from a 3–0 deficit.

Two days later, it became official: Bulls 115, Pistons 94. We had dethroned the Bad Boys, at last, and in the most satisfying manner, a sweep.

Of course, it's not the game itself people remember most about that Monday afternoon in Auburn Hills.

With 7.9 seconds to go, a number of Pistons left their bench and walked right by us on the way to the locker room. No waiting until the buzzer sounded. No shaking hands. No congratulating us on a job well done or wishing us good luck in the Finals.

No respect. Nothing.

In other words, precisely the type of juvenile behavior we had come to expect from a group led by Isiah Thomas and Bill Laimbeer. They couldn't deal with our being the better team and their reign in the East being over. They were lucky their reign didn't end in 1990.

In *The Last Dance*, Isiah claimed that what the Pistons did wasn't unusual. He said the Celtics did the same thing when the Pistons were about to beat them in the 1988 Eastern Conference Finals.

"During that period of time," Isiah suggested, "that's just not how it was passed. . . . When you lost, you left the floor."

I beg to differ. That, most definitely, was not how "it was passed."

The Celtics left in the final seconds because the fans in Detroit were starting to storm the court. The Celtics were on enemy ground. The Pistons were not. No one was storming the court. After we lost to the Pistons in 1988, 1989, and 1990, we shook everyone's hands and wished them well in their next series.

"That's sportsmanship," Michael pointed out in the doc, "no matter how much it hurts, and believe me, it fuckin' hurt."

Amen to that.

Since our playing days ended, I have had nothing to do with Isiah, and it will remain that way. When I ran into him at an event in Florida some years back, I didn't say a word.

In the spring of 2020, while the doc was being aired, Isiah was interested in the two of us declaring a truce. He reached out to B. J. Armstrong, who called me.

"Would you be willing to talk to him?" B.J. asked.

"Dude, are you kidding me? When I came into the league, he was never nice to me. Why would I want to meet with him now?"

Isiah is no fool. He knows better than anyone else how poorly he came across in *The Last Dance*, and with good reason. I wasn't about to make it easier for him.

As for Game 4 itself, we were up by 8 points in the second quarter when Rodman shoved me out of bounds with both hands after I drove to the basket. A dirty play, without question, even by his standards. In today's NBA, Rodman, who was fined $5,000, would have been ejected and suspended for a couple of games, maybe more.

My teammates rushed to my side to make sure I was okay. I was. The shove resulted in nothing more than a cut on my chin that would require a half dozen stitches.

All hell might have broken loose if I had gotten up right away and gone after Rodman.

Instead, I sat on the floor, got my bearings, and calmly returned to the court. Taking my lead, my teammates didn't start anything, either, and we were better off for it. Say we had retaliated, which was what the Pistons were hoping for. The game would have become more physical, and that kind of game always suited those guys.

When we didn't retaliate, they didn't know how to respond. They were done.

The day was important for me on a personal level, as well.

On this same floor, eleven months earlier, I scored two points. *Two points.* Migraine or not, that's a black mark on my résumé I can't remove. Nor can I do anything about the concussion that knocked me out the year before. I have to live with those two disappointments till the day I die.

At least now I had something else to live with. In Game 4, I scored 23 points and had 10 assists, 6 rebounds, and 3 steals.

The celebration on the bus afterward was something I will always remember. Except for the image of Jerry Krause dancing down the aisle. That, I wish I could forget.

All kidding aside, beating Detroit felt like winning a championship. The whole regular season, that was the team we targeted, not any team in the West.

Our fans couldn't have been more excited. When we landed at O'Hare on Monday evening, people were lined up by the fence to cheer us on.

The guys were touched, although our work was far from done.

Which was why we couldn't have had a better coach in that situation than Phil Jackson. Phil always reminded us we were on a journey, and the journey didn't end till we won a championship. Every so often he showed us the ring he earned with the Knicks in 1973.

You want one of these, guys? Then go out and earn it.

We were confident, no doubt, but we weren't cocky, and there's a big difference. Given the success the franchise would enjoy the rest of the decade, it's easy to forget that, in June of 1991, we weren't yet the Bulls whom people would long remember. We were just another hungry team hoping to make a dream come true.

The number on the board was four.

. . . .

When Ronnie Martin and I went one-on-one at the Pine Street courts in Hamburg, I didn't always pretend I was Dr. J or Mo Cheeks or Larry Bird or Kareem Abdul-Jabbar.

Sometimes I pretended I was Earvin "Magic" Johnson, the six-foot-nine point guard for the Lakers, who, along with Bird, was taking the NBA to a whole new level in the early 1980s. Magic was unlike any other point guard the sport had ever seen. He could see the play before it happened. I studied his game for years. Be like Mike? I wanted to be like Magic.

Now I would be able to study him up close.

The Lakers were—sorry, Boston fans—the most glorious franchise in the league. They won five titles in the 1980s. They were in the eighties what we aspired to be in the nineties.

They were known as the "Showtime" Lakers, with Magic racing downcourt at breakneck speed, finding James Worthy, Michael Cooper, and Byron Scott for easy baskets. When they didn't score on a fast break, they threw it to Kareem in the low post. His patented skyhook was impossible to defend.

Except we were in the nineties now. Showtime was over.

The current version could easily have been called the Slowtime Lakers. Magic was thirty-one years old and didn't barrel down the lane the way he did in his twenties. Kareem had retired while Cooper had gone off to play in Italy.

Nonetheless, their half-court offense featuring Worthy, Scott, Sam Perkins, A. C. Green, and Vlade Divac was more than effective. The Lakers won 58 games in the '90–91 season, only three fewer than us, and beat the top-seeded Blazers in six games to capture the West. Magic was tremendous in that series, averaging 20.7 points, 12.7 assists, and 8 rebounds.

We would have to be at our very best.

However, as far as NBC, who would carry the Finals, was concerned, this was not about the Chicago Bulls versus the Los Angeles Lakers. This was about Michael Jordan versus Magic Johnson. Every promo put them front and center. The rest of the Bulls and the Lakers didn't exist. The papers presented the same narrative. One headline in the *Chicago Tribune* read, "Manifest Destiny: Michael vs. Magic."

They were missing the whole point. Basketball, I will keep saying until my last breath, is a team game, not an individual game, and should be promoted in that fashion.

Besides, Michael and Magic didn't play the same position. Magic wasn't going to cover Michael. Not in a million years.

Game 1 at the Stadium was set for Sunday, June 2, 1991.

Jogging onto the court for warm-ups was reminiscent of the day I played in my first NBA game. Everything felt new and exciting. The players who have been fortunate enough to make it to this stage know exactly what I mean. Those who haven't never will.

In Game 1, Michael scored 15 points in the first quarter. He seemed intent on showing Magic, and the entire western hemisphere, who was the superior player. Except, we were barely ahead, 30–29. Michael could score 50 and he wasn't going to win the game on his own.

Magic, meanwhile, was . . . Magic.

Anytime a teammate got in the clear, even for a split second, Magic found him in perfect rhythm. I swear the man had eyes in the back of his head. He made his share of key baskets, as well. His two three-pointers to close the third quarter gave his team a 75–68 advantage.

Magic was too much for Michael to handle. I should have been on him. Only Michael didn't want to give him up. His pride was on the line. When Magic took a breather in the beginning of the fourth quarter, we went on a 10–0 run to seize a 3-point lead. The Lakers were in trouble whenever Magic went to the bench. Once he came back, the game remained tight the rest of the way.

With 23.5 seconds left, the Lakers had the ball, down by 2 points. Magic, guarded by Michael, dribbled near the top of the key and threw it to Perkins, who was wide open behind the arc.

Bingo!

The Lakers, suddenly, were on top, 92–91. Fourteen seconds to go. We called time. Everyone knew who was going to take the last shot.

After scoring just 8 points in the second and third quarters combined, Michael had 13 in the fourth.

I threw it in. Michael drove to the hoop. With guys converging on him, he dished it underneath to Horace. It was knocked out of bounds. Still Chicago ball.

Another time-out. Nine seconds left.

Back to Michael, who could not have gotten a better look from about 17 feet, similar to the shot he nailed against Georgetown to win the NCAA title.

It looked good the moment the ball left his hands.

It wasn't. Around the rim and out.

Byron Scott made 1 of 2 free throws to increase the lead to 2. With no time-outs left, we were forced to go the length of the court. Bill Cartwright threw the ball to me a couple of strides before the half-court line. I took one dribble and let it fly.

No good. Ball game.

Gone, just like that, was our precious home-court advantage. We would now have to win at least one game in Los Angeles.

There was no reason to panic. As poorly as we played, the final margin was only 2 points. If this was the best the Lakers had to offer, everything would be fine. Furthermore, we weren't going to sweep those guys. The Lakers had been here before. We had not. None of us, with the exception of Phil, had ever played in the Finals.

Michael scored 36 points and I chipped in with 19. The problem was no one else finished with more than 6. That wasn't going to happen again. At the same time, the coaching staff needed to make adjustments, typical for the team that loses a playoff game. The biggest adjustment would be putting me on Magic.

In Game 1, he had a triple-double: 19 points, 11 assists, 10 rebounds. He was the Magic of old.

I was excited. This was the challenge I was hoping for.

Nothing against Michael as a defender. Only I was convinced I could do a better job. While he would start the game on Magic, I was told to be ready.

Another adjustment we made was to double-team Worthy and Perkins from the baseline instead of from the first player at the top of the key. Both were scoring easily in the low post.

Early on in Game 2, we couldn't miss. Even so, the Lakers hung in there.

Then it happened.

With about four minutes to go in the first quarter, and the Bulls leading by 2, Michael picked up his second foul. We couldn't afford for him to pick up a third with so much time left in the game.

Magic was now mine.

I knew exactly what I wanted to do: force the ball out of his right hand.

Magic was a maestro with his right hand. He could make passes from anywhere. From half-court, full court, from Pasadena, if need be. I stayed on his right side, and when he dribbled with his right hand, I made him turn and shift the ball to his left, the way Coach Ireland taught me all those years ago. Magic didn't pass with his left hand. He also loved to throw it off the bounce, so any time I could get him to stop his dribble, he wasn't as effective.

On just about every possession, I picked up Magic as soon as he came over the half-court line. No one ever did that. I wanted him to use more clock—and more energy. If he was forced to waste valuable seconds before he got everyone into the offense, it would reduce the chances of the Lakers getting off a high-percentage shot.

I didn't want Magic coming toward me with any thrust, the way LeBron comes at opponents today. Like a linebacker running the 40. Impossible to stop.

Instead I would come to him.

Magic managed to dish out 10 assists. However, he shot only 4 of 13 from the field. We won going away, 107–86. Michael was at the top of his game. He got others involved early on and then took over in the second half, making 13 shots in a row. He finished with 33 points and 13 assists.

In that game, Michael made a shot everyone remembers, perhaps as much as *The Shot*. In the fourth quarter, he drove toward the hoop, the ball stretched out in his right hand. He was going to slam it home. Except, on this occasion, with Perkins near him in the lane, Michael, in midair, switched the ball to his left hand and laid it in off the glass.

Having been his teammate for four years, I figured I had seen everything the man could do. Apparently not. Dr. J doesn't make that play. Nor does Pete Maravich or Earl Monroe.

Only Michael Jordan, basketball's Baryshnikov. The Stadium went wild.

Horace and Pax also came up big in Game 2. Horace scored 20 points while Pax went 8 for 8 from the field.

As for myself, while quite proud of the job I did on Magic, I didn't get carried away. Magic was not the same player who had won three MVPs and led his team to five championships in nine years.

Thank God I didn't have to cover that Magic.

Meanwhile, after Game 2, I signed the contract extension the organization had promised since the dawn of time: five years for $18 million. The deal would take me through the 1997–98 season, when I would be thirty-two.

I was set. At last.

Only why the rush to sign me now? The Bulls waited for months. What difference would a few more days make?

Plenty.

The two Jerrys, if they hoped to use the salary cap money they had originally put aside for Toni Kukoc, needed to sign me first, according to league rules, prior to midnight on the last day of the Finals. That day would arrive before we returned to Chicago, if either us or the Lakers won all three games in Los Angeles. Since Toni, only twenty-two, had hooked up with a team in Italy, the Bulls could sign me now and still have enough cap room to pay him down the road.

. . . .

I was excited to be back in the City of Angels and playing again at the Forum.

Excuse me . . . the *Great Western Forum*.

I remembered hearing about the Forum all the time as a kid when I watched Lakers games on TV, and the building certainly lived up to its reputation. With its circular façade of gorgeous white columns, the place had an unmistakable grandeur, like something you would have come across in ancient Rome.

All that was missing were the chariots.

The Forum was filled with the rich and famous, with celebrities such as Jack Nicholson, Dyan Cannon, and Denzel Washington, to name a few, who were as much a part of Lakers Nation as Magic Johnson and James Worthy.

One evening, I appeared as a guest on *The Arsenio Hall Show*. Arsenio was a tremendous talent, although far eclipsed by the king of late-night TV, Johnny Carson.

Remind you of anyone?

Anyway, back to the stars on the court.

In Game 3, the Lakers went on an 18–2 tear in the third quarter to seize a 13-point advantage. Showtime was back. Magic was making passes only he makes, while Vlade Divac, in just his second season, was playing extremely well. The crowd came alive.

The question was, Would the Bulls?

The answer: an emphatic yes.

Scoring the last 6 points of the quarter, we sliced the lead to 6 heading to the fourth.

We were just getting started.

After an 8–2 run to begin the quarter, the score was tied at 74 with a little under nine minutes to go. From then on, it was anyone's game. That we were still in it proved for about the one trillionth time the Bulls were far from a one-man team. After scoring 11 points in the first quarter, Michael had managed only 10 the next three quarters combined.

With 10.9 seconds left, Vlade scored in the lane while being fouled by yours truly, my sixth. I was done for the night. Vlade hit the free throw to put the Lakers ahead, 92–90.

Time-out, Bulls.

Phil opted to go the full length of the court instead of taking it out on the side. He felt it would be easier that way to get the ball to number 23. So what if Michael was 8 for 24? It would not have mattered if he was 8 for 54. No one came through like he did with the game on the line.

Pax threw it in to Michael, who raced up the court, guarded by Byron Scott. When he got to about 14 feet away, he let it go over Vlade.

The shot looked good the moment the ball left his hands. Like the jumper in the closing seconds of Game 1.

This time, it was good: 92–92, with 3.4 seconds left.

After a time-out, the Lakers got off a last shot, though not a very good one, an off-balance jumper by Scott. The teams were headed to OT.

I was devastated I couldn't be out there. The next five minutes would prove to be the most important five minutes of the whole series.

Thank goodness, with Michael scoring 6 of our 12 points, we survived, 104–96. I wouldn't have forgiven myself if we had lost that game. The victory guaranteed the worst that could happen now was going back to Chicago down 3 games to 2.

Forget about going back to Chicago with the outcome still in doubt. Why not wrap it up right here? In front of Jack, Dyan, and Denzel.

In Game 4, we set out to do just that. The final: 97–82. All five starters, led by Michael with 28 points, scored in double figures. The Lakers were hurting, especially Worthy, with a sprained left ankle.

There was a new number on the board: 1.

It is often said a closeout game is the toughest game to win. That's because it's true.

In Game 5, the Lakers, playing without Worthy, a future Hall of Famer, hung in there, the game knotted at 80 entering the fourth quarter. Two rookies, Elden Campbell and Tony Smith, were coming up big. During the first six minutes of the quarter, Michael tried to win it on his own. He made a couple. They weren't enough. With about five minutes to go, the score was tied at 93.

Phil wasn't pleased. During a time-out, he asked Michael who was open whenever the Lakers ganged up on him. Paxson was, Michael said.

"Then get him the ball!" Phil said.

Michael did exactly what Phil told him and, in doing so, showed a level of trust in a teammate he had never shown before, and it was about time. From then on, through the nineties, Michael, to a large degree, bought into what Phil and Tex had been preaching from day one.

Take what the defense is giving you. Find the open man.

Paxson was automatic down the stretch. The biggest basket was his 18-footer that put us ahead by 4 points with less than a minute to go. After Perkins missed a long jumper, I secured the rebound and soon followed with two free throws. That pretty much was it.

Final score: Bulls, 108; Lakers, 101.

The ball was in my hands when the buzzer sounded, and I wasn't about to let go. A few fans tried to pry it away, as did a couple of teammates. They didn't have a prayer. I took that precious cargo with me on the plane back to Chicago.

Michael might have the MVP trophy, but I have the basketball. It's tucked away in a safe place. Along with my memories, of the evening itself (my stat line: 32 points, 13 rebounds, 7 assists, and 5 steals) and everything I had to go through to get there.

Of watching my brother and father turn into invalids.

Of Coach Wayne kicking me off the team in high school and later forcing me to run the bleachers.

Of being overlooked by one college after another until Coach Dyer gave me a chance.

Of the shooting pains in my back and being terrified my career might be over.

Of the concussion and the migraine and fans wondering if I would ever show up when it counted most.

The journey to that point had been difficult, sometimes almost unbearable, but each of those experiences made me stronger. They made me a champion.

I think about the 1991 title a lot, it being the first. We were so young then, so innocent.

The season wasn't as smooth as it appeared, someone always complaining about one slight or another, me included. Every team goes through periods like that over the course of 82 games. What matters is how you cope with those periods, and no one coped better than Phil Jackson.

He kept us believing in ourselves. He kept us as One.

CHAPTER 10: **TOGETHER AGAIN**

I was still on cloud nine from winning that first championship when the call came in late July from C. M. Newton, the athletic director at the University of Kentucky.

I was about to climb even higher.

Newton, who would soon be the president of USA Basketball, asked if I was interested in being one of the twelve players to participate in the 1992 Summer Olympics in Barcelona, Spain.

Was I interested?

This wasn't just any basketball team, mind you. These twelve players would become known forever as the Dream Team, the first time NBA stars were allowed to compete in the Olympics.

Other countries had been relying on professionals for years. Why shouldn't we?

The final straw came at the 1988 Games in Seoul, South Korea, when the US squad, coached by Georgetown's John Thompson and featuring outstanding college players such as David Robinson, Danny Manning, and Stacey Augmon, was forced to settle for a bronze medal after losing to the Soviet Union. People were furious. The US basketball team doesn't lose in the Olympics. And certainly not to the Russians . . . unless, as in 1972, something funny is going on.

I said yes to Newton in record time. I didn't want to give the man an opportunity to change his mind.

I was surprised he called. I'm not suggesting I wasn't worthy. Quite the opposite. I was one of the top players in the game. Except I had been in the league for just four years and made only one All-Star team. There were others with more impressive credentials.

I only wish my father were still around. Having served his country in World War II, he would have been proud of me.

Once I returned to Earth, Newton and I chatted for a while about some of the logistics. If the Bulls made it to the Finals again, a strong possibility, I would have practically no time off before having to show up at training camp in La Jolla, California. The Games would begin on July 25.

So be it. This wasn't some exhibition in Peoria. This was the Olympics! If necessary, I would go from Grant Park directly to O'Hare.

I asked Newton, for vastly different reasons, if either Michael Jordan or Isiah Thomas would be on the team.

"Michael has a spot," he said. "He just hasn't committed yet."

Newton asked me to keep our chat a secret until the committee could issue a formal announcement.

"No problem," I said. "I won't say a word."

Unless I'm mistaken, the only person I told right away was my brother Billy, who shared the news with the rest of the family. I trusted them 100 percent.

Shortly afterward, however, while the committee was still putting the team together, I approached Michael. I couldn't keep quiet a moment longer. I told him about the call from Newton.

"Are you going to be on the Dream Team?" I asked.

"I don't know yet," Michael said. "I'm thinking about it."

I had once asked Michael the same question after we learned the United States would use professionals in Barcelona.

"Are you kidding me?" he said then. "I already have a gold medal. I want to enjoy my summer." He played for Bobby Knight at the 1984 Games in Los Angeles.

In the end, Michael decided to join the team.

Not because he felt a sudden sense of duty to Uncle Sam. He played to help grow the game and, let's be frank, his brand. Two of his biggest corporate sponsors, McDonald's and Gatorade, would also be sponsoring the Games. The optics would have been awful if he had stayed home.

As for Isiah, I asked Newton because here was someone I hoped would be staying home.

"No, he won't be on the team," Newton told me, and that was all he had to say on the matter. That was enough.

In late September, the Dream Team was finally announced.

It would include me, Michael, Patrick Ewing, David Robinson, Larry Bird, Charles Barkley, Magic Johnson, John Stockton, Karl Malone, and Chris Mullin. Two additional players were to be chosen at a later date, one from the NBA, one from college. They'd end up being Clyde Drexler and the kid from Duke, Christian Laettner.

I agreed with each pick except Laettner. I didn't think he would fit in, and I was right. The committee should have chosen another NBA player, and plenty were worthy. My preference was Dominique Wilkins, otherwise known as the Human Highlight Reel. Dominique was only thirty-one and still at the top of his game.

Much has been written over the years about why Isiah didn't make the team. What is true, without a doubt, is that a number of guys wouldn't have participated if he had been selected, Michael and me included. Newton and other members of the committee knew how we felt.

Not even Chuck Daly, the team's head coach—and Isiah's coach since 1983—lobbied for him. What does that tell you?

Looking at his numbers, it would be difficult to argue Isiah wasn't deserving.

He was a ten-time All-Star, a two-time champion, and a sure Hall of Famer. Except putting a basketball team together is about more than numbers. It is about chemistry, and with Isiah on the Dream Team, the chemistry would have been horrible.

I couldn't wait for the Games to begin.

■ ■ ■ ■

First, there was another season to get through. And another shock to absorb.

The news came from Los Angeles on Thursday, November 7.

Magic Johnson had been diagnosed with HIV. He said he would immediately retire.

Just five months earlier, we faced him and the Lakers in the NBA Finals. He couldn't have looked any healthier.

Now he was dying. At least, that's what we feared.

I was devastated. I wished I could have spoken to him. To believe he would get through this. To believe we would get through this. Magic and I didn't enjoy that kind of relationship. He came into the league eight years before I did. Eight years is a generation in the National Basketball Association.

To me, him contracting the virus was another reminder of how quickly everything can be taken away. Not that I needed any more. I just had to think of my own family.

No one displayed a pure love for the game as enthusiastically, and as genuinely, as Magic Johnson did. Then or ever since.

As incredible as he was on the court, I admire him more for how he has conducted himself off the court. A death sentence? Hardly. There is no one I've ever met who is more alive.

We knew so little about AIDS in those days. Ironically, just a week before, Phil had stressed the importance of being careful with members of the opposite sex. A few guys made jokes, as young men tend to do in these kinds of conversations.

There were no jokes this time.

Everyone was concerned. Like many people, they assumed only homosexuals contracted the virus. Now that it had claimed Magic Johnson, the epitome of heterosexuality, it dawned on them AIDS could claim anyone.

About a week later, there was more news from off the court. A new book, *The Jordan Rules*, chronicling our championship season, hit the shelves. To this day, I haven't read one word of Sam Smith's book, and I won't. I don't need to read it. I lived it.

Besides, I've heard so often what's in there, I feel as if I *have* read it.

That Michael had a fight with Will Perdue. That Michael didn't want any of us to pass the ball to Bill Cartwright in crunch time. That Michael met with a psychic when he went through a shooting slump. Etc., etc., etc.

(I made the last one up.)

The book blew things way out of proportion. The tensions that were spelled out—between players, and between players and management—are there on every team . . . in every season.

The only reason this particular account was newsworthy can be summed up in two words: Michael Jordan.

As for who the sources might have been, a topic of much specu- lation over the years, I don't buy for a second that it was primarily Horace, as Michael suggested in *The Last Dance.* Sam Smith, who covered the team for the *Chicago Tribune*, picked up his juicy tidbits from a number of players and coaches, and from people affiliated with the organization, and, yes, that included Jerry Krause.

Doesn't make sense, does it?

Jerry was known for keeping information from reporters, not the other way around. And what about the reports he was so out- raged by what came out in the book that he marked up dozens of sections he felt were blatant lies?

None of that changes my opinion one bit.

Think about it: Jerry spent years trying to assemble a championship roster, and now that his dream had come to fruition, he wasn't getting the credit. Michael was. Jerry was the most insecure man I ever met. It made him work hard and become an excellent general manager. It also made him petty and vindictive.

So he decided to take Michael down. Just a notch.

Jerry assumed he could control what Sam wrote. That was his mistake. He had been around the media long enough to know better.

In any case, the book didn't take Michael down. Not even close. Okay, so he wasn't a saint. Who is? He was the most beloved athlete in the world, except for maybe Muhammad Ali. Nothing in a reporter's tell-all book was going to change that.

Nor, for that matter, did it take the team down. Quite the opposite, and that was because of Phil.

Phil was always able to make us believe it was us against the world, especially after we won our first championship. That's what happens when you become the best. People want to destroy you. We often felt as if we were fighting members of our own organization—and the media—as much as we were fighting the other teams.

The book turned out to be a blessing. From then on, we were more guarded with what we said to one another, and to the press, sparing us, no doubt, further controversy.

Not that Michael was thrilled with everything reported in the book. He didn't speak to Sam for the longest time. I didn't blame Michael one bit. If I had been in his position, I might not have spoken to Sam ever again. Sam, to be fair, was no different from the other members of the fourth estate, always on the prowl for the next victim.

Michael had been through a lot that fall already.

In early October, the team visited the White House to be honored by President George Bush. It was pretty cool, I have to admit. Meeting the leader of the free world was something I never imagined myself doing.

There was one notable no-show: Michael.

Which wasn't a problem until Horace made it a problem. Larry Bird skipped a similar visit in 1984, and I don't remember it leading to the end of Western civilization.

"I'm very disappointed because it was a great honor for the whole city of Chicago as well as the Bulls' organization," Horace said. "Not to have your best player and your team leader there is just like sending somebody else besides George Bush to Saudi Arabia."

Now I think the world of Horace, always have, and I understood how much the double standard that Doug—and to some extent, Phil—allowed to exist between Michael and the rest of the team bothered him. Only here was an occasion, and there were certainly others, where he should have kept his opinion to himself. The season had yet to begin. Michael had earned the right to do whatever he wanted with his own time. That included not going to 1600 Pennsylvania Avenue.

Before long, Michael and Horace made up and the whole episode was forgotten. Except to serve as another reminder that, now that we were the champions, every minor incident had the potential to become a major story.

The challenges we faced in the 1991–92 season were formidable. That's always the case when you're trying to defend a title. Will guys work as hard? Will they keep putting the team above themselves? Will they complain about their contracts?

Most important, Will they remain healthy?

During the '90–91 season, ten players on our roster appeared in at least 73 games, four (Michael, me, Paxson, and B.J.) in all 82 games. That was incredibly good fortune and would never happen today.

Load management? The term didn't exist in the early nineties.

There was more to it than pure luck. We spaced the floor and didn't find ourselves in too many collisions, at least of our own doing, and when someone did get injured, he was taped up and back on the court in no time.

Phil came up with a slogan for every season. The year before it was Commitment. This time, it was Together Again.

Together, indeed.

In addition to signing me to the five-year extension, the Bulls inked deals with Cartwright and Pax, both in their thirties, which showed the organization's faith in keeping our core group intact. Phil didn't like to make a ton of changes in personnel. Getting new players to pick up the nuances of the triangle would take time.

The only change of any real significance occurred in early November when we shipped Dennis Hopson, who had never fit in, to the Sacramento Kings for eight-year veteran Bobby Hansen. Hansen was known primarily for his defense, not scoring. We had enough scorers.

Or so we thought.

On the very same day, Craig Hodges injured his left knee when he collided with Stacey King in practice. Hodges would miss 19 games. Shortly afterward, Bill fractured his left hand, and he, too, would be out for a while. I suppose we were due for our share of bad breaks.

■ ■ ■ ■

Early that season, I ran into my buddy Isiah Thomas.

Same old Isiah. He shoved me from behind for no reason during our 110–93 victory at the Stadium. The teams had gotten into a near-brawl. Both of us had to be restrained. I wonder if it had anything to do with his not being on the Dream Team. I didn't bother to ask.

Anyway, the win was our fourth in a row, and we went on to make it 14 straight before losing on the road to the Sixers by 3 points in early December. Shortly after the first of the year, we launched another winning streak, this one coming to an end at 13 when the Spurs defeated us, 109–104. David Robinson was a monster: 21 points, 13 rebounds, and 8 blocked shots.

Our record was 37-6, and being the first team to win 70 games was within reach.

Except what would that prove? They don't give out trophies for breaking the record for most wins. Better to pace ourselves, let guys get a breather every now and then, and be ready for May and June. When they do give out a trophy.

Meanwhile, I was playing the best basketball of my life.

In early March, I was the only player in the league in the top 15 in scoring, assists, and steals, and the only one to average more than 20 points, 7 assists, and 7 rebounds. There was talk I might win the MVP. I didn't believe it. I could have a triple-double every night and the writers would never vote for me over Michael.

Lo and behold, Michael won the award for the third time in five years. I came in ninth.

After we finished 67-15, our opponent in the first round of the play-offs was the Miami Heat. We swept them in three games.

Next were the New York Knicks. These weren't the same Knicks we swept the year before. Their new coach was Pat Riley, formerly of the Showtime Lakers, the owner of four rings. Riley, similar to Phil, was a tremendous motivator. In his first season in New York, the Knicks won 51 games, a dozen more than the year before.

Their center, Patrick Ewing, was one of the toughest players we ever had to guard. He could hit the midrange jumper and do a ton of damage in the paint. Double-teams didn't seem to bother him. Oakley was another problem. Playing against Oak was like going to war. You knew he would come at you for every rebound. Their other big man, Anthony Mason, in his third year, was also a bruiser.

The Knicks were, essentially, the new Pistons. Just our luck. We had only recently figured out how to beat the old Pistons.

Even so, we were extremely confident heading into Game 1 at the Stadium.

Perhaps too confident.

The Knicks beat us, 94–89. Ewing scored 34 points (16 in the fourth quarter), pulled down 16 rebounds, and blocked 6 shots.

If losing at home wasn't upsetting enough, I also sprained my ankle. The injury would hinder me for the rest of the series. I couldn't get the normal lift on my shots, and lift is everything in basketball. In Game 2, I finished 2 for 12, scoring only 6 points. I hadn't played this poorly in a playoff game since the migraine. Fortunately, we prevailed, 86–78, to square the series.

In Game 3, I bounced back, sprained ankle or not, with 26 points, including 12 in the fourth quarter, as we won in the Garden, 94–86, to regain home-court advantage. New York took Game 4, 93–86, and the series was even again. Phil was thrown out late in the third quarter after getting on the officials for allowing the Knicks to push Horace and me around.

The new Pistons, indeed.

Between Games 4 and 5, another battle raged. This one was in the press, between the two coaches.

Phil started it.

In his postgame interview at the Garden, still fuming, he went after the NBA.

"I think they're probably licking their chops on Fifth Avenue," Phil said, referring to the league's headquarters in New York. "I don't like orchestration; it sounds fishy, but they do control who sends the referees. If it goes seven games, everybody will be really happy. Everybody will get the TV revenue and ratings they want."

The next day, Riley responded. He was no wallflower: "The fact that he's whining and whimpering about the officiating is an insult to how hard our guys are playing and how much our guys want to win."

Those were the days, weren't they?

The teams split the next two games to set up a deciding Game 7 at the Stadium.

The pressure was on us entirely. After losing just 15 times the entire regular season, we were now suddenly one loss from being eliminated. The Knicks, on the other hand, had already exceeded expectations by forcing a Game 7.

The pressure was on me, as well.

In the series so far, I was averaging less than 16 points and was shooting only 37 percent from the field. During the regular season, I averaged 21 points and shot 51 percent.

Robin to Michael's Batman? I was acting more like the Riddler. From game to game, no one knew what to expect from number 33. Me included.

Speaking of villains, the Knicks had a real one, the bald-headed small forward Xavier McDaniel. The X-Man, as he was called, had been pushing me around the whole series, and we let him get away with it.

Not anymore.

With about three minutes to go in the first quarter of Game 7, McDaniel was called for an offensive foul. As the teams headed down the court, he and I exchanged a few words. I don't recall the nature of our *conversation*. Let's just say I wasn't asking him about his plans for the summer.

That's when Michael came over and got right in McDaniel's face, and I mean literally. If their foreheads weren't touching, they were awfully close. Both received a technical.

What Michael did was as important as the 42 points he would put up that day. He was our leading scorer. He wasn't our enforcer. We hadn't had an enforcer since Oak left. For Michael to take on that role sent a powerful message to the Knicks: this is our court and our game and we are not going to back down to you thugs for one second.

The Knicks didn't back down, either. Early in the third quarter, when they cut an 11-point deficit to 3, Phil called time. Phil didn't like to call time when the team got out of sync. He preferred the guys figure things out on their own.

Except this was a Game 7. We could figure things out another time.

I don't remember what he told us in the huddle. Whatever it was, it worked.

We went on a run of our own and led by 15 after three quarters. Our defense was as stingy as ever, and we were unwilling to settle for jump shots. That the NBA appointed a veteran crew to officiate the game also helped. The final: 110–81.

The Knicks gave us a much tougher challenge than we anticipated. What a relief to get them out of the way.

For me, it was vindication. If that appears to be something I harp on, it's because I received constant criticism from my close friends in the press. I finished with a triple-double: 17 points, 11 rebounds, 11 assists.

That shut them up. For the time being.

On to the conference finals, to face another familiar foe, the Cleveland Cavaliers. After winning only 33 games the year before, the Cavs (57-25) were back to being one of the best teams in the league. They still had Brad Daugherty in the post and Mark Price at the point and had just eliminated the Celtics.

Game 1 was a breeze, 103–89, as I nearly posted another triple-double: 29 points, 12 boards, 9 assists. Perhaps most encouraging was our performance from the free-throw line: 19 of 19. In the Knicks series, we made only 70 percent of our free throws.

Two routs in a row. We were back on track for another ring.

Back, all right. To the drawing board.

I don't have an explanation for what happened in Game 2. Except this: we stank. We missed our first 13 shots and shot only 14 percent in the first quarter. The Cavs were up by 26 at the half. In our building!

Phil put it best: "This team deserved to be booed off the floor."

Fortunately, momentum can change in a hurry in the playoffs. In Game 3, it was our turn.

At one point in the first quarter, the score was 26–4 in favor of the Bulls. In addition to Michael and me, Horace (15 points, 11 rebounds, 4 blocks), Pax (5 of 6 from the field), and Scott Williams (10 points, 6 boards) came up big in a 105–96 victory.

Having regained the home-court advantage, we set out in Game 4 to dash any lingering hopes the Cavs might still harbor.

Forget it. They were in control from the start, winning 99–85. Worse yet, I felt we had gone back in time. Michael took 33 shots. The other four starters took a total of 29. In the entire second half, I had 3 attempts. That's not a typo. I finished with 13 points.

Tex must have wanted to shoot himself. Or us.

As usual when we lost an important game, I took the heat. For how I played, and for having the nerve to tell the reporters, when asked why I didn't score more, that I hadn't received "any opportunities."

They thought I was criticizing the coaches. I was not.

The following day, I skipped a session with the media. Why bother? They were going to find something negative to write about me whether I showed up or not.

Once again, the pressure was on us, and on me.

Once again, I came through.

In Game 5, I scored 14 points and pulled down a team-high 15 rebounds, as we prevailed, 112–89. In Game 6, we closed out the Cavs in Cleveland, 99–94. My line: 29 points, 12 rebounds, 5 assists, 4 steals, 4 blocks.

The 1991–92 season felt as if it had been going on forever:

Magic diagnosed with HIV and having to retire. The controversy generated by the release of *The Jordan Rules*. The games with the Knicks that were more like brawls.

Yet here we were, still standing in the month of June. We couldn't ask for anything more.

CHAPTER 11: FROM ONE DREAM TO ANOTHER

Instead of the Lakers in the NBA Finals, it was the Portland Trail Blazers.

No, the Blazers didn't possess a legendary player such as a Magic Johnson or a legendary past. The franchise could boast of only one championship (1976–77) since entering the league as an expansion team in 1970. They would probably have had more but their star center, Bill Walton, injured his foot in 1978 and would never be the same. It wasn't long before the team, which had gotten to 50-10 at one point in the 1977–78 season, went back to what it was before Walton arrived: irrelevant.

Which was precisely the fate we hoped to avoid. The list of NBA champions includes one-hit wonders who disappeared as rapidly as they surfaced.

The Blazers, who defeated the Utah Jazz in the Western Conference Finals, were more athletic than the Lakers and they were deep, with center Kevin Duckworth, guards Terry Porter and Danny Ainge, and forwards Jerome Kersey, Cliff Robinson, and Buck Williams.

Oh, and, of course, there was Clyde.

Clyde Drexler, at six foot seven, would be my man. As usual, I looked forward to the challenge.

I'd studied his game for years, like I studied Magic's. Clyde was a right-handed penetrator who seldom dribbled to his left. Our mission in every playoff series, as Phil put it, was to cut off the head of the opponent's snake. On the Blazers, the snake was Clyde. He averaged 25 points that season, finishing second to MJ in the MVP race. Some put the two in the same category.

As you might expect, Michael didn't like to be compared to Clyde. Michael didn't like to be compared to anyone.

Ironically, the only reason he ended up with the Bulls in the first place was because the Blazers, who owned the pick ahead of them in 1984, already had Clyde (drafted the year before) and thought they didn't need a player with a similar skill set.

Guess again.

Anyway, in Game 1 at the Stadium, Michael wasted no time in proving his point. Watching him knock down one three-pointer after another against Clyde, I was mesmerized. He was always coming up with something we hadn't seen before.

He finished with 39 points, including 6 threes, in our 122–89 triumph. Lost in his performance, which included the famous shrug after he hit his last three, was a near triple-double (24 points, 10 assists, 9 rebounds) from yours truly, though I was just as pleased with holding Clyde to 16 points on 5 of 14 from the field. So much for the head of the snake.

Were the Blazers overwhelmed by the moment?

Perhaps. There was certainly no excuse for losing Game 1 of the NBA Finals by 33 points. I don't care if Michael had made *16* threes.

Two nights later, in Game 2, we outscored Portland 32–16 in the third quarter to go up by 7. With four and a half minutes left, the lead was 10. Clyde had fouled out. Ball game.

Not so fast.

A layup by Kersey. A jumper by Porter. Two free throws from Porter. A scoop shot by Ainge. Another layup by Kersey.

Suddenly, incredibly, it was 95–95.

The game still tied with a couple of seconds to go, Michael fired from a few feet right of the foul line. No good. We were headed to OT.

And to more frustration. Portland outscored us 18–7 in the extra five minutes to even the series. The hero was Ainge, who had half of those 18 points. The Blazers were overwhelmed by the moment, all right. All they did was score on 16 of their final 17 possessions. I couldn't, for the life of me, recall us ever blowing a lead like that in a game this big.

We couldn't afford to dwell on the loss for long. Game 3 in Portland was only two days away. The year before, we needed to win at least one game in Los Angeles to keep our season alive. We won three. There was no reason we couldn't win three in Portland. As long as we made the proper adjustments.

Instead of pressuring their guards as they moved the ball up the court, we switched to an interior zone, forcing the Blazers to settle for long jump shots. Which, to our good fortune, they didn't knock down. In Game 3, they shot 36 percent from the floor and scored just 84 points, while we put up 94. In their previous 17 playoff games, the Blazers averaged more than 113 points.

Two down, two to go, and now we had the momentum.

Naturally, with how these up-and-down playoffs were going, the momentum didn't last.

The Blazers took Game 4, 93–88.

There were many to blame for the defeat, and I was definitely on the list. With a little over four minutes to go, I was on the line with a chance to extend our lead to 4 points. I missed both free throws. From then on, the Blazers outscored us, 13–6, to tie the series 2–2.

Enter Michael and me to the rescue. In Game 5, which we won, 119–106, Michael scored 46 points, while I chipped in with 24, along with 11 rebounds and 9 assists. We were one angry group for letting the Blazers hang around this long. Playing angry is often when you play your best.

Now it was time to put them away for good.

Like everyone else, I was excited about the opportunity to close the deal on our own court. That was the only thing missing from the 1991 title. Not that we took anything for granted. The Lakers, without James Worthy, fought from start to finish in last year's elimination game. We expected the same effort from the Blazers.

We got it.

From the opening tip, the Blazers were the looser, more poised team. They looked as if they were trying to close *us* out.

At halftime, we were fortunate their lead was only 6. The third quarter wasn't any better. Before we knew it, the lead was in double digits. Going into the fourth, we were down by 15. The fans were antsy. So were we.

Phil sent me out with the second unit to start the quarter. The first unit didn't have it. That included Michael.

Not for one moment, however, did I believe the game was over.

Having played with the guys (B. J. Armstrong, Bobby Hansen, Stacey King, Scott Williams) on the second unit countless times in practice, I knew what they were made of. Each player was aware of the little—I should say big—things required to win a basketball game, especially a game such as this: taking charges, setting screens, making the extra pass.

Most of all, believing in themselves and one another.

The plan was to get the Blazers rattled. If we could do that, the crowd would rattle them some more. We needed to treat every possession as if it were the last, at both ends. Whenever we trailed by double digits, our mindset was, if we could get five stops in a row, and score on at least four of our own trips, we would be right back in it.

I was never one to give pep talks. That was Phil's job or Michael's. This time, I did have a suggestion.

"You get a shot," I told the guys in the huddle, "shoot it!"

Bobby Hansen did just that. He nailed a three from the corner the first time we had the ball and followed with a steal at the other end. Which led to a pivotal moment in the game involving Stacey King.

Stacey, who was a star at Oklahoma, hadn't turned out to be the player we hoped he would be. Perhaps we didn't give him enough minutes. Or perhaps he didn't do enough with the minutes we gave him. He had the misfortune of joining us at the precise time Horace was developing into one of the top power forwards in the NBA. I don't know what else Stacey could have done to break through.

Whatever the reason, we needed him now, and he delivered. He went strong to the hoop and got hacked by Kersey. The refs signaled for a flagrant. Stacey went to the line for two free throws and we would maintain possession. The crowd was loving it. After Stacey converted one of the two, I scored in the lane to get us within 9. Two possessions later, I scored inside again, and Clyde then turned it over.

There were less than ten minutes to go. Normally, around this point, Phil would have put Michael back in. Not this time. The second unit was on a roll, and he didn't want to mess with it. Not yet.

I wasn't shocked. Phil was never afraid to make the decision no one expected.

B.J. hit a jumper. After Buck Williams committed an offensive foul, Stacey followed with a jumper of his own. The Blazers were rattled, indeed. The lead was only 3.

With about eight and a half minutes left, Michael finally went back in. The second unit had done its job, and then some. Michael, the best closer in the game, and I could take it from there. The final score: 97–93. Michael finished with 33 points, 12 in the final quarter. I added 26, going 5 for 5 in the fourth.

Once it was over, I made my way to the locker room to get the party started. Without the basketball this time. One souvenir was enough.

As for what this championship meant to me, it meant a lot. They all did, though I will never put one over another. Each stood out in a different way. This one stood out for what the second unit did during those crucial three and a half minutes in the fourth quarter. Without cutting into the Portland lead the way those guys did, the game might well have been over.

Who knows what would have happened in a Game 7. I'm just grateful we didn't have to find out.

In the locker room, as we were soaking it, in more ways than one, the word quickly got around: "They aren't going home."

The "they" were the fans. Few had taken off for the exits.

There was only one thing to do: go out there and join them. I jumped on the scorer's table, along with Horace and Michael. Our arms linked together, we did a little dance. We stayed out there for a half hour, maybe longer. I didn't want the night to ever end.

Two days later, on a beautiful, sunny afternoon, a more formal celebration took place at Grant Park in downtown Chicago. It felt as if the whole state of Illinois was there.

Several of us went to the podium to say a few words. When it was my turn, I said what I believed was on everyone's mind:

"Let's go for a three-peat."

.....

After the usual exit meetings with the coaching staff, everyone took off for the summer, except for Michael and me. We had one week before reporting to camp in La Jolla.

There was a gold medal to win.

I remember the first day of camp very well. As I looked around at the faces of my new teammates—and former (and future) adversaries—I couldn't quite believe my good fortune. It's one thing to hang out with these amazing players, some of them true legends, during the weekend of the All-Star Game. Quite another to realize we would be together for six weeks. On the court. Off the court. Everywhere.

I didn't know these guys. I knew their games, yes, as well as anyone. Where they liked to catch the ball. How they defended their man. What their favorite shot was. Etc., etc., etc. What I didn't know was who they were, what made them tick. What made them great. What made them human.

I wondered, for instance, Would they be able to check their egos at the door?

Think about it: You are asking the most talented basketball players in the universe (everyone, with the exception of Laettner, would wind up in the Hall of Fame for their individual accomplishments) not to be selfish. Not to do what propelled them to become stars in the first place.

Midway through the first practice, I stopped wondering. If anything, the guys were too *unselfish*, passing up one easy scoring opportunity after another to look for their teammates. One doesn't see that often, not even in practice. Tex would have been in heaven.

A couple of days later, Coach Daly put us through our first scrimmage. The opponent was a group of college players, such as Bobby Hurley, Grant Hill, Chris Webber, Penny Hardaway, Allan Houston, and Jamal Mashburn. The coach was Roy Williams from the University of Kansas.

These kids were extremely gifted, with bright futures in the league. Of course they would be no match for . . . the Dream Team.

Lo and behold, the kids beat us by about 10 points. Houston hit from everywhere, and I don't remember anybody else on their team missing many shots, either. Boy, were they proud of themselves afterward. You would have thought they had just won the gold medal.

Some people, including our assistant coach, Duke's Mike Krzyzewski, have long believed that Coach Daly lost the game on purpose. Which would explain why he didn't put the best five players, including

Michael, on the court when the outcome was still in doubt. Coach Daly, as this theory goes, saw it as a chance to get across an important message:

On any given day, if you guys don't play hard enough, anyone can beat you.

The message got through loud and clear. The next day, in another scrimmage, we killed the same team by like 50 points.

Let's face it: there was no way we were leaving Barcelona without the gold.

We knew it, and the teams we were playing knew it, and what's more, they didn't seem to mind one bit. Their players behaved more like fans than foes. Many asked for our autographs or to have their pictures taken with us after the game. Sometimes before the game. That didn't keep every man on the Dream Team from taking his job seriously. Lots of times in the NBA, when a coach goes over a scouting report, guys, to put it kindly, don't give it their full, undivided attention.

That didn't happen with us, no matter the quality of the opposition. We treated every game as if it were Game 7 of the NBA Finals.

As for me, I didn't care how many minutes I got. I told Coach Daly and his assistants, If you need me in crunch time, wonderful. If you need me in garbage time, that's wonderful, too. At twenty-six, the youngest player besides Laettner, I felt blessed merely to be a member of this incredibly special group. I was in paradise.

When Coach Daly put Larry Bird in the starting lineup for our first game, I was on board 100 percent.

This was Larry Bird, one of the best players of all time. In the end, I logged about twenty-one minutes a game, trailing only Michael and Chris Mullin. Coach Daly relied on me for defense. We had plenty of guys who could put the ball in the hole.

Everyone found it refreshing to not have to be *the man* night after night. All they had to do was go out there and execute, and we would be up by 30 points before the first time-out. I'm exaggerating, obviously. Not by much.

Occasionally, certain individuals tried to do too much. The person who comes to mind is Clyde Drexler.

Clyde, still hurting from losing to the Bulls in the Finals, was out to prove he belonged on the same level as Michael. As if the six games the teams had just played hadn't proven the exact opposite.

Here is what someone should have told him:

Clyde, you should feel fortunate. You are one of the best basketball players in the world. You're just not Michael Jordan and that's no crime. No one is.

His energy was terrible. He always had his head down and acted as if Michael and I were his adversaries, not his teammates. Clyde didn't fit in with the whole team, and it was a shame.

The Dream Team had a definite hierarchy, as there is on any team. It went like this: Magic and Larry at the top, Michael one rung just below.

Give Michael credit. He deferred to Magic and Larry, letting them share the honor of being cocaptains. Michael was the best player in the game, but Magic and Larry had paved the way for Michael. The NBA wasn't very popular before those two arrived in the fall of 1979. The Finals—*the Finals*—were often shown on tape delay after the eleven o'clock news. That didn't change for good until the Lakers played the Sixers in 1982.

Seeing Magic on the court again, where he belonged, gave everyone a lift. There was a time we didn't think that would ever be possible.

He was the same Magic from before the HIV diagnosis. Firing up his teammates. Talking trash. Making those behind-the-back passes no one else could make.

Having more fun playing the game of basketball than a person has any right to have.

Larry, on the other hand, was in pain every day. Some days, he could barely move. Having experienced my share of back problems, I thought it was a miracle he was out there at all. He would retire later that summer at the age of thirty-five.

Like Magic, Larry was a master at talking trash. His digs often revolved around which of us had championship rings and which did not. Thank God I had a couple by then so I didn't have to be one of his victims.

Seven of the eleven veterans on the Dream Team didn't have rings, one of them being Patrick Ewing.

Yet Larry and Patrick became good friends. A white guy from Indiana bonding with a black guy from Jamaica. Go figure. They sat together every morning in the breakfast room at the hotel, cracking each other up over the silliest things. The rest of us referred to the two as "the Harry and Larry Show." How Patrick got the name Harry is beyond me.

I also made a new friend: Karl Malone.

The two of us had much in common. Karl, too, was from a small town in the South (Summerfield, Louisiana), was the youngest child in a large family—he had eight brothers and sisters—and went to a school, Louisiana Tech, that didn't exactly have NBA scouts lining up.

He was the best power forward in the league, and it was no accident. I never saw another human being with a body like his, as if he were carved out of a rock. Karl didn't take a day off. Spending time in the gym with him, I didn't realize anyone could work that hard. I couldn't have gotten more prepared.

Having played so recently in the Finals also worked to my advantage. I was in excellent shape coming in.

I would have to be. As C. M. Newton explained to me one day, "Larry and Magic are getting up there a bit. So we are going to be relying on guys like you, Michael, Charles—guys who are younger—to carry this ball club."

No problem, Mr. Newton. We'll be ready.

However, no matter how serious we were, we made sure to have a good time.

Many days after practice, Charles, Michael, Magic, and I ordered some food and met in Magic's room to play tonk. We played for hours, sometimes until five in the morning, for $500 per game. I didn't make a fortune. I didn't lose a fortune, either. As exclusive as this group was, not once did I feel the urge to pinch myself. I deserved to be there as much as they did.

After a few days in Southern California, we headed to Portland to play six games in something called the Tournament of the Americas. Teams needed to do well there to qualify for the Games themselves.

Our first opponent was Cuba. We won by 79 points.

I would be lying if I said I was surprised. We were that much better than anyone else. The next day, we took on Canada. The game was closer. We won by 44. After leading by only 9 late in the first half—what was wrong with us?—the team went on a 13–5 run to go up by 17. We put the Canadians away in the first few minutes of the second half. Over our next four games, against Panama, Argentina, Puerto Rico, and Venezuela, the average margin of victory was 46 points. Finishing 6-0, we booked our ticket to Barcelona.

Here's the amazing thing: the guys were still learning how to play with one another. Just think how dominant we would have been with another week or two of practice.

In La Jolla and Portland, I felt I was as much of an Olympic athlete as Carl Lewis and Oscar De La Hoya. Though not until I left the country did it hit home how big of a deal this whole Dream Team thing was. That I wasn't playing for the Chicago Bulls. I was playing for the United States of America.

Wherever we went, people waited for hours to catch a glimpse of the famous Americans. I didn't feel like a basketball player. I felt like a rock star.

One night in Monte Carlo, the team went to a dinner hosted by Prince Rainier. That's the man who had been married to the late American actress Grace Kelly. Safe to say, meeting a real prince wasn't something that happened every day to a kid from Hamburg, Arkansas.

Guys spent a fair amount of time playing blackjack at the casino or hanging out on the beach. I had never been to the beach before. I couldn't believe how beautiful the women were and that many of them were topless.

However, when I think of Monte Carlo, I don't think of the prince or the casino. Or even the women.

I think of the game one day in practice between the Blue Team led by Magic (which included Barkley, Mullin, Robinson, and Laettner) and the White Team led by Michael. Of all the basketball that was played from La Jolla through Barcelona, the game in Monte Carlo was at a level beyond anything else.

The Last Dance captured it well: the trash talking between Magic and Michael and how Michael's team, which I was on (the other three players were Larry, Karl, and Patrick), came back to win. What the doc could not capture—no footage possibly could—was what it felt like to watch the best players in the world put their heart and soul into a game that meant nothing. And everything.

It was as if we had gone back in time, to when we were boys on courts such as Pine Street, playing for the pure love of the game. The game that gave us a life even more amazing than the one in our dreams.

From Monte Carlo, we went to Barcelona, and what we saw when we got there I will never forget.

The plan was to enter the city from a remote location to avoid any crowds. The security from day one, as you might imagine, was always a top priority, and this was nearly a full decade before 9/11. None of us could go anywhere without an officer tagging along.

The plan didn't work.

When we arrived at the airport, roughly an hour outside town, people were everywhere. The official estimate was four thousand. It seemed like four *hundred* thousand.

We took a bus into the athletes' village, escorted by about a half dozen police cars and a police helicopter. After getting off the bus, we went to the building where we picked up our credentials. Dream Team or not, we needed to go through the same process as every other Olympic athlete. I wouldn't have wanted it any other way.

Barcelona was a blast. Some nights, Charles and I went for long walks along Las Ramblas, a well-known tree-lined, pedestrian street in the central part of town that was packed with locals and tourists. I never went for walks like that in Chicago.

On July 26, we played our first game. The opponent was Angola, a country on the west coast of southern Africa. I crack up every time I think of the famous quote from Charles.

"I don't know anything about Angola," he said at a press conference, "but Angola's in trouble."

Big trouble.

Dream Team, 116; Angola, 48. That included a run of 46–1. Which was a combination of us being awesome and Angola being, well, Angola.

That was also the game in which Charles slammed his elbow into the chest of a 174-pound player, Herlander Coimbra. Charles caught a lot of heat for that. I thought the whole incident was blown way out of proportion. Charles didn't hit him very hard.

Next up was Croatia.

I had been looking forward to this matchup since the schedule came out in early July. Croatia was the team Toni Kukoc played for— you know, the guy Jerry Krause was in love with.

As with Isiah Thomas, this is another subplot of the Dream Team that has received a ton of coverage. Almost as much as the games themselves.

What has been reported for years is absolutely true. That Michael and I set out to make things difficult for Toni by hounding him every time he touched the ball. He finished with just 4 points, on 2 of 11 from the floor, and committed 7 turnovers, resulting in another blowout for Uncle Sam: 103–70.

However, there was nothing personal between Toni and me. How could there be? I didn't know the guy. Toni and I would get along quite well once we became teammates in 1993. People don't realize how good he was. We wouldn't have won our last three championships without him.

It *was* personal between Jerry and me. Extremely personal.

I was still angry with him for flying to Europe in pursuit of Toni while leaving my contract situation up in the air. There seemed no end to the amount of ways Jerry would insult me, and Michael, for that matter. We were the ones busting our butts night after night, year after year, for the Chicago Bulls. Not Toni Kukoc.

The next five games—against Germany, Brazil, Spain, Puerto Rico, and Lithuania—were as lopsided as the others. Only Puerto Rico came within 40 points.

Finally, the big day was here. All that stood between us and the gold was another meeting with Croatia.

Again, no contest: 117–85.

Give Toni credit. He put the 2-for-11 embarrassment behind him and came up with a solid performance: 16 points and 9 assists. For us, Michael led the way with 22 points, while Patrick added 15 along with 6 rebounds. I finished with 12 points, 4 assists, and 2 steals.

Before long, I was standing on the podium with my teammates, listening to "The Star-Spangled Banner," a gold medal wrapped around my neck. I was overcome with emotion. For years I watched athletes, male and female, in moments like this, in the Summer and Winter Olympics, wondering what they were feeling.

Now I knew. There is no feeling like it. That includes winning an NBA championship.

I'm proud of my role on the Dream Team. I led us in assists, with nearly 6 a game, and played tough defense. I wanted to shut down everyone, not just Toni.

More important, I'm proud of the role we, as a team, played in helping to make the game popular throughout the globe. That is our legacy more than the medals we took home. Many of the international players who came into the NBA in the late 1990s, and ever since, fell in love with basketball by watching us in the '92 Olympics.

Today, nearly thirty years later, when I run into other members of the Dream Team, we reminisce about those days.

The Harry and Larry Show. Playing tonk in Magic's room. The scrimmage in Monte Carlo.

The night we won the gold.

These guys feel like teammates, even if we were together for only a short time.

What a time it was.

CHAPTER 12

THIRD TIME'S A CHARM

Something else happened on the way toward the United States capturing the gold medal in Barcelona. I gained respect from a place where it had been absent for the longest time.

From Michael Jordan.

He came to the conclusion that I was the best all-around player on the team—and on occasion even outplayed him. He never told me that himself. That wouldn't be like him. He told Phil at training camp in the fall of 1992, and I didn't hear about it until many years later. Either way, that is high praise from someone with three MVPs, and to this day, it means a lot to me.

At the same time, and I can't express this emphatically enough, it doesn't mean everything.

When I joined the Bulls in 1987, I set out to be the best basketball player I could be. I didn't set out to gain Michael's seal of approval—or anyone else's, for that matter. That was still the case when I played on the Dream Team.

I was a two-time All-Star with two rings. That was enough validation to last a lifetime.

Whether Michael was accurate in his assessment, one thing's for certain: I gained a ton of confidence from my play in Barcelona, on both ends of the court, and looked forward to carrying that confidence into the 1992–93 season.

Only I was in no rush.

The last regular season, like every regular season, had been a grind. Tack on the four rounds in the playoffs, an additional 22 games, and the six weeks on the Dream Team, with a week of rest in between, and you can understand why I might be burned out. That's the only downside of playing into mid-June.

Come October, however, I wouldn't have a choice. The NBA waits for no one.

At least, thanks to Phil, Michael and I didn't have to work as hard as usual at training camp. We took part only in the morning sessions of the two-a-day drills.

Phil had been around the game long enough to know how much the minutes and the travel catch up to you, no matter how fit you may be. He realized that if the Bulls stood any chance of a three-peat, which no team had pulled off since Bill Russell's Celtics won eight straight titles in the late 1950s and 1960s, Michael and I would need to pace ourselves from October until June.

Otherwise, both of us would hit a wall and break down.

Nor did Phil make securing home-court advantage a big priority this time, another shrewd move on his part. We'd proven we could win playoff games on the road. In the Finals, the team was 5-1 the last two years away from Chicago, as opposed to 3-2 at the Stadium. Guys were sometimes more focused on the road.

No family obligations. No hustling to scrounge up tickets for friends and relatives you haven't heard from in years. Nothing except dealing with the task in front of you: winning a championship.

The other players, I could tell, weren't thrilled with Michael and me having it easier in camp. I didn't blame them. I would have felt the same way.

All of them kept their opinions to themselves.

All, except Horace.

The preferential treatment he always complained Michael received, well, now that apparently applied to me, as well. I wasn't surprised that he felt that way. The two of us had drifted further apart than ever. This wasn't 1987 anymore. This was 1992.

He couldn't have been more mistaken. Not for a moment did he consider how much Michael and I had given to our team—and our country—over the past twelve months. He was able to enjoy a normal summer vacation. We were not. Mind you, I'm not complaining. I would have given up ten summer vacations for a chance to play on the Dream Team.

I didn't argue with Horace. I knew how stubborn he could get.

Many nights, since his rookie year, I had listened to him go on and on about one slight or another. I couldn't listen any longer. That fall, I believe, is when he concluded he wouldn't re-sign with the Bulls when his contract expired after the 1993–94 season no matter how much money they might offer him. He'd been insulted long enough.

Horace walked out of practice one day after participating in what was known as the "Hiawatha drill." That's where every player ran in a single file, and when the whistle blew, whoever was the last in line had to move up to the front and lead the pack for the next stretch. Michael and I were sitting this one out, which was, I suspect, what put Horace over the top.

In no time, ready or not, the 1992–93 season was under way.

After escaping with a victory on opening night in Cleveland, we flew to Chicago to receive our championship rings prior to a game against the Atlanta Hawks.

I looked forward to ring night more than any other night of the regular season. The night meant even more than the celebrations in Grant Park. Nothing against Grant Park. I loved looking at the mass of people extending out for what seemed like miles and miles. There was just something about receiving a ring, an object I could touch and look at whenever I wanted, that made what we accomplished more real than ever, a reminder of the sacrifices each of us made, large and small.

Too bad the evening ended on a sour note with a 100–99 defeat.

The Hawks were ahead by 22 before we rallied in the fourth quarter to take a 1-point lead when I hit a jumper with about a minute and a half to go. Those were the last points we scored. The 20 turnovers (6 for Michael, 5 for myself) we committed were a killer. There would be no ring ceremony next year if we kept playing like that.

About a week later, I received some sad news from home. Grandma was gone.

It was hard to believe. The woman was invincible, afraid of nothing, including death.

At the cemetery in Hamburg, I almost expected her to rise up from her coffin with a stern warning to everybody who was paying their respects:

"Get off my grave!"

. . . .

Six straight wins in November. Seven straight in December and early January. We were used to streaks like this.

Even so, at the end of January, our record was 28-15. Which would have been acceptable for any other team in the NBA.

The Chicago Bulls weren't any other team. We were the two-time defending champions who had lost 15 games the whole previous *season*. Injuries definitely played a part. In the 1992–93 season, eleven players missed a total of 119 games. The season before, eight players were out for 45 games, the second-lowest total in the league.

Paxson and Cartwright, both getting up there in age, were dealing with knee issues that had required surgery during the summer. That year, they would miss 23 and 19 games, respectively. B.J. was inserted into the starting lineup for Pax, while Will and Stacey filled in for Bill.

I wasn't in ideal shape, either.

The ankle I hurt against the Knicks in the 1992 playoffs had turned into chronic tendonitis. I didn't possess my usual explosiveness when going to the basket, and that was an integral part of my game.

Fortunately, as the playoffs approached, guys started to recover, as we captured 15 of 18. With two games remaining, against the Hornets and Knicks, our record was 57-23. Win both and we would be the No. 1 seed in the East for the third year in a row. Not this time. The Hornets defeated us, 104–103, coming from 4 down with over a minute left. Two nights later, we fell to the Knicks, 89–84.

The New York game didn't mean anything in the seedings. Nonetheless, Phil was concerned enough afterward that Michael felt the need to reassure him:

"Don't worry. We'll get it together for the playoffs."

Would we really? It was hard to tell.

In the first round, we took on the Atlanta Hawks. Game 1 was on a Friday. The series was over on Tuesday. Maybe Michael knew something I didn't.

Next were the Cleveland Cavaliers. Those guys had to be thinking to themselves, *Can't we play someone else for a change?* The Cavs had lost to the Bulls in 1988, 1989, and 1992.

This series, too, lacked any drama, with the exception of Game 4, when we were going for the sweep.

With 18.5 seconds to go, the score was tied at 101. Time-out, Bulls. I'll give you one guess who was assigned to take the last shot.

Michael was guarded tightly by Gerald Wilkins, Dominique's younger brother. Gerald covered Michael about as well as anyone. He was able to slap the ball away for an instant, but MJ regained control and let it go from 18 feet before the buzzer sounded.

Goodbye, Cleveland.

Four years later, from almost the same spot on the court, and in the same arena against the same opponent, The Shot now had its encore and we were headed to the Eastern Conference Finals.

Where our opponent would be another adversary we knew quite well.

This time, the Knicks, with 60 wins in the regular season, would have the home court, definitely a cause for concern. The Knicks were practically unbeatable at the Garden, the mecca of basketball (37-4 during the regular season, 5-0 in the playoffs). Riley, in his second season as the head coach, was no doubt anxious to avenge the playoff loss of the year before.

I was looking for payback, too. Ewing, Oakley, Mason, and McDaniel had pushed me around in the '92 playoffs, and while we won the series, I was tentative at times, although some of that was due to my injured ankle. I needed to be tougher. The way Michael was when he got in McDaniel's face in Game 7.

We wouldn't have to worry about the X-Man any longer. He signed with the Celtics during the off-season. Charles Smith replaced him at small forward. Smith was not as intimidating. Nonetheless, the Knicks had plenty of big bodies to throw at us, the series promising to be another rugby match. The Pistons felt being aggressive—and dirty, whenever possible—was the formula to beat Michael Jordan and the Bulls, and for a while, it was. The Knicks felt the same.

Except, by the spring of '93, I was a different man. Whenever anyone shoved me, I shoved him right back. I was determined to rid the Knicks—and the media—once and for all of the notion I was a finesse player who would look for the nearest exit whenever there was too much physical contact. If anything, I was too physical.

In Game 1, Doc Rivers, New York's veteran guard, was going in for a breakaway layup midway through the third quarter when I knocked him to the ground. A foul, no doubt, but a totally legitimate, hard-nosed basketball play. The Knicks didn't think so and neither did the fans. They wanted a flagrant. The refs wouldn't call it, and from then on, the intensity in the building rose to a whole other level.

So, it seemed, did the Knicks, who prevailed, 98–90, thanks to Ewing and their pesky guard, John Starks, who each scored 25 points. Starks hit 5 of 7 three-pointers. The Knicks killed us on the boards, 48–28, and over the final six and a half minutes, Michael didn't make a single field goal.

I wasn't too concerned. Phil and the other coaches would make the necessary adjustments.

It didn't make a difference. The Knicks took Game 2, 96–91. We hadn't dropped the first two games of a playoff series since 1990 against the Pistons.

Losing the game was disturbing enough. I also lost my composure. That didn't happen often.

About five minutes through the fourth quarter, with the Knicks up by 12, I was called for a double dribble by referee Bill Oakes. The call was outrageous and I let him know it. No problem. Except when I tossed the ball to him, I apparently tossed it a bit too hard.

Big problem.

He caught it just under his chin. That was the end of the night for me.

My getting booted did the team some good. We went on a 12–3 run to cut the deficit to 3. The outcome was still up in the air when, with about fifty seconds remaining, Starks got a little opening and slammed it home with authority over Horace and Michael. The Garden exploded. These fans were dying for a championship. Twenty years was a long time to wait.

Still, there was no reason to be discouraged. The series was far from over. Barring a total collapse in Chicago, we would get one more crack at these guys in New York. Probably two.

First, we had to deal with Atlantic City, and I don't mean the movie. Although this wouldn't be lacking in drama, either.

The *New York Times* reported, according to anonymous sources, that before Game 2, Michael was spotted gambling at Bally's Grand Casino until as late as two-thirty in the morning. Michael said the timing was off, that he left Atlantic City around 11:00 p.m. and was in bed by 1:00 a.m.

The timing didn't make a difference to me. I wouldn't have cared if Michael was at the tables the whole night. He was a grown man, for God's sake. If taking a limo to Atlantic City to gamble for a few hours was what he felt he needed to blow off some steam, who was I or anyone, the press especially, to find fault with him? No one could begin to understand the pressure he was under, night after night, year after year.

Besides, Michael was on time for our shootaround the next morning, as fired up as ever. Nothing else mattered.

Sure, he wasn't at his best (12 of 32 from the field) in Game 2. So what? This wasn't his first poor shooting game in the playoffs, and it wouldn't be the last. And by no means was that the only reason we lost. Horace had 2 points and 2 rebounds and 4 fouls. I missed 4 of my 7 free throws. I could go on.

Anyway, once the *Times* ran the story, it seemed that every other media outlet in the country got on Michael's case. Nobody was talking about anything else.

The "controversy" was similar to when *The Jordan Rules* came out two years earlier. We were on top and someone was trying to take us down. They failed then and they would fail this time. If anything, as in '91, it brought the team closer together. When Michael boycotted the media, the rest of us did the same—for a while. Not that I would consider avoiding the reporters to be a sacrifice. More like a blessing.

In Game 3, we looked like a different team. Our full-court defense and trapping in the half-court forced them into 20 turnovers. The final: 103–83.

Michael came up big, if not in the manner you would expect. His shooting was still off (3 for 18), but he got guys involved with a team-high 11 assists. Meanwhile, I was on fire, hitting 10 of 12 to finish with 29 points. Two nights later, our 105–95 victory evened the series at two games apiece. Michael regained his touch, and that's an understatement. He hit 6 of 9 from three-point range (18 of 30 overall), ending up with 54 points.

The win was huge. So was the comment by Ewing afterward.

"We don't have to win in Chicago," he told the press.

Think about it: You are pretty much conceding you are not going to win any games in your opponent's building. Talk about putting pressure on your team to win in your building.

When Ewing said that, we thought, *We've got 'em now.*

Game 5 at the Garden was intense from start to finish. And what a finish.

With the Knicks down by 1 with thirteen seconds to go, Charles Smith caught a pass from Ewing a few feet from the basket. When he tried to lay it in, Horace came up with a tremendous block. Smith got it back and tried again. This time, Michael stripped it. Smith got the ball back a third time. Now it was my turn to block the shot. A fourth time, I blocked it again.

Finally, Michael emerged from the pack with the ball and we hung on, 97–94, to take a 3–2 lead.

That one play, more than any other, epitomized who the Chicago Bulls were. Not just in that series and not just in that season. That's who we were throughout our reign in the nineties.

When we desperately needed a stop, we got it. The key to playing great defense is to never give up on a play. Never. We didn't have a true shot blocker in the mold of an Hakeem Olajuwon or a Dikembe Mutombo. We had something just as vital. Guys who battled in the paint as if their lives were on the line. Johnny Bach called Horace, Michael, and me Dobermans, and that's exactly what we were.

As the team made its way toward the locker room, I heard some-thing I'd never heard in Madison Square Garden. Silence. The sound was music to my ears.

We closed the Knicks out two days later in Chicago, 96–88. Good riddance. I ended up with 24 points, on 9 of 18 from the field, along with 7 assists and 6 rebounds. The '92–93 regular season wasn't my best. For the first time, my scoring average went down, from 21.0 to 18.6 points per game. Maybe it was the ankle. Maybe post-Olympic fatigue. Maybe something else.

Whatever it was, when my teammates needed me the most, I was there for them. And we weren't done yet.

■ ■ ■ ■

I felt blessed to be back in the NBA Finals.

There was never a guarantee, not even on a team with Michael Jor-dan, I would ever make it to one Finals, let alone three in three years. Chris Paul, a certain Hall of Famer, didn't make the Finals until his sixteenth season.

Our opponent would be the Phoenix Suns, who got there by beat-ing the Lakers, Spurs, and SuperSonics.

The Suns, the winners of 62 games, the most in the league, were led by my teammate from the Olympics Charles Barkley. Charles was the MVP that season, averaging 25.6 points and 12.2 rebounds. When I came into the league, Charles was almost an impossible cover. He was so quick he could go around you or he could shoot over you. Our strategy would be to force him out on the perimeter, to around 17 feet, where a defender could deal with him one-on-one.

Then, in the last few minutes of the game, the pressure on, we'd come with a double-team. Just to give him a different look.

We also needed to contain their speedy point guard, Kevin Johnson, who had a scorer's mentality, and their dangerous forwards, Dan Majerle and Richard Dumas. Boy, did we want to contain Majerle. He was (like Toni Kukoc) a player Jerry Krause was in love with, and anyone Jerry was in love with, we wanted to embarrass as much as possible.

The Suns scored a ton of points, 113.4 per game, best in the NBA.

No problem. We were relieved to be playing a team that favored an up-and-down, less physical brand of basketball. The battle with the Knicks had taken its toll. Against the Suns, we knew we could make a hard cut without taking a shoulder to the chest.

I couldn't wait for the Finals to start.

For the games themselves, and for everyone to stop talking about Michael Jordan and his gambling. Which was again a big story.

According to a new book by Richard Esquinas, a San Diego businessman, Michael owed him more than $1 million from bets they'd made on the golf course. Michael didn't deny losing money to this guy, only that the amount reported was, in his words, "preposterous."

To me, this was no different from MJ going to the casino in Atlantic City. I didn't care about the details. He could have lost $10 million and it would have been no big deal. There was nothing illegal about gambling on the golf course, and let's not forget, whatever amount he lost was his money.

Charles couldn't have put it any better: "It isn't gambling if you can afford to lose."

The story went away, eventually, and it was time to focus on basketball. Our goal again was to leave town with at least a split.

Mission accomplished. In Game 1, we beat the Suns 100–92.

In the second quarter, we went ahead by 20 points. The Suns rallied to cut the deficit to 3 but that was it. The game can be boiled down to the difference between the two stars: Charles finished 9 of 25, while Michael went 14 of 28 for 31 points, along with 7 rebounds, 5 assists, and 5 steals.

Now that we had secured the split, we went for more.

In Game 2, the Suns were still hanging around midway through the fourth quarter. Until Michael decided enough was enough. He scored 10 points to put us up by 8 with about a minute and a half to go. The final margin was 3. MJ finished with 42 points, 12 rebounds, and 9 assists, while I posted a triple-double: 15 points, 12 boards, and 12 assists.

On to Chicago we went for what everyone assumed would be a coronation.

Everyone except the Suns.

In Game 3, they outlasted us in triple overtime, 129–121. Majerle played out of his mind with 6 three-pointers. Charles and Kevin Johnson also stepped up. To put forth a sizzling performance like that after losing the first two in your own building showed a lot of character.

We bounced back ourselves, taking Game 4, 111–105, thanks to 55 points from Michael, as well as 17 points, 16 rebounds, and 3 blocks from Horace.

The champagne was on ice. The commissioner was in attendance. The crowd was ready to celebrate.

Everything was in its proper place.

Well, not everything.

Our minds weren't where they needed to be. We were thinking about where we would rank in history and where we would party afterward. We weren't thinking about the game itself.

And it showed.

The Suns captured Game 5, 108–98. Dumas went 12 of 14 from the field for 25 points, while Johnson (25 points, 8 assists) and Charles (24 points, 6 assists, 6 rebounds) had big nights as well. That meant flying back to Phoenix for one game or possibly two, a journey we didn't think we'd have to make.

Leave it to Michael to look at the bright side. When he boarded the plane at O'Hare, he had one cigar in his mouth and a whole box under his arm. He referred to them as victory cigars and said he packed only one suit for the trip.

Translation: there will be no Game 7.

I wasn't as convinced.

I was even less convinced as Game 6 neared its conclusion. With about fifty seconds to go, the Suns had the ball, ahead by 4. We had scored a grand total of 7 points (all by Michael) in the entire fourth quarter.

Hey, MJ, what was that you were saying about packing only one suit?

After backup guard Frank Johnson missed a jumper, Michael grabbed the rebound and went coast to coast to lay it in. The lead was down to 2. We weren't dead yet.

On its next possession, Phoenix moved it nicely from one man to the next, the ball ending up in the hands of Majerle, who was open on the baseline, about 15 feet from the basket.

Majerle makes that shot 60 percent of the time.

He missed.

He didn't even hit the rim, resulting in a 24-second violation. Time-out, Bulls: 14.1 seconds left.

The Suns assumed Michael would take the last shot. When didn't he take the last shot?

The official handed the ball to Michael, who threw it in bounds to B.J., who promptly threw it back to him.

MJ dribbled toward half-court, and with Kevin Johnson on him, he tossed it to me a few steps behind the top of the key. I drove past Charles, then dished the ball to Horace, who had a clear path for a layup on the left baseline. He didn't take it. Instead he threw it to a wide-open Paxson, just behind the three-point line.

Everything happened in slow motion.

Then, and in how I have remembered it ever since.

Pax catches the ball. Rises in perfect rhythm. Lets it go.

Bang! We go from down 2 to up 1 with 3.9 seconds remaining.

That shot, of the thousands of shots we took in our magical run, might be the biggest shot of them all.

Precisely because it did *not* come from Michael, who averaged an NBA-record 41 points in the 1993 Finals. Because it came from a guy who scored 35 points the whole series. In that possession, which lasted just over ten seconds, every player touched the ball. Ball movement. Player movement. Open shot.

The way Tex explained it in the fall of 1989 and kept explaining it until it finally sank in.

The Suns still had a chance.

After a time-out, Kevin Johnson threw it in to their center, Oliver Miller, who gave it right back. Johnson dribbled to the top of the key and let it fly.

The ball was knocked away by Horace. The buzzer sounded. Bulls, 99; Suns, 98. We'd done it again. We'd won it all for the third year in a row.

What a sequence for Horace Grant. The two plays (the pass to Paxson and the blocked shot) were probably the difference between us winning and losing, and now not having to play a Game 7. This was after a Game 5 in which he scored only 1 point in thirty-eight minutes. Talk about redeeming yourself. Horace doesn't receive enough credit for our first three titles. We wouldn't have won any of them without him. I know it. The guys know it. And so does Michael.

What took place during those final fifty seconds or so of Game 6 was remarkable. Everything had to go right for us to win, and it did.

After popping champagne in the locker room, we went back to the hotel. The plan was to spend the night in Phoenix—we were staying at the Ritz—and fly to Chicago in the morning.

The plan changed. Why stay one minute longer than we needed

to? Our work was done. We packed our bags and headed to the airport. We could still smell the champagne.

Before long, everybody was up in the clouds, celebrating in a manner like never before. We weren't surrounded, for a change, by people we didn't know who were trying to be part of *the scene.* On the plane were only the players and coaches, and there was something so fitting and wonderful about that.

We were the ones who realized what it took to win a championship. No one else.

Lots of times, on a plane, on a bus, at the hotel, guys used to break into smaller groups. Not everyone is close with everyone else. That's the case with every team, and there is nothing wrong with that. We come from different backgrounds with different priorities. Unlike college, where everyone is pretty much the same age, the players in the NBA range from their early twenties to late thirties. The difference in how you see yourselves, one another, and the world is vast.

No one broke into smaller groups this time. We celebrated the same way we won. Together. As a team.

The third time felt different from the first two. We didn't just earn another ring. We earned a place in history.

CHAPTER 13: 1.8 SECONDS

The summer of 1993 couldn't have gotten off to a better start. I hung out for a few weeks with my family and friends in Hamburg.

Joking with my brother Ronnie.

Shooting the breeze with Ronnie Martin.

Making sure Mom didn't need anything.

No matter how much I enjoyed living in the big city, there was nothing like going home. I was grateful to get away from the feeling I was always being judged—too harshly, if you ask me, and by people who didn't know what they were talking about.

I was able to reflect on what I had accomplished over the last twelve months.

The victory over the Blazers. The gold medal. The victory over the Suns. There was never a moment to step back and take it all in.

Come August, however, I was reminded once again of how fragile life really is.

The body of Michael's father, James Jordan, was found in a swamp in South Carolina. Everyone had feared the worst when he went missing a few weeks earlier in North Carolina. Still, there was hope he would turn up, and now the hope was gone. He was shot while sleeping in his car off the interstate. He was fifty-six years old.

James Jordan was the kindest soul one could ever meet. He spent a lot of time with the team, at home and on the road, even when

Michael wasn't around. I don't believe he missed a single playoff game. It's no exaggeration to say I had more communication with him than I did with his son.

He wasn't always in a hurry. He didn't need to be the center of attention.

Michael was blessed to have him for a father, someone he could trust in a world where everyone wanted something from him. His time. His money. His approval. There was no end to the demands on Michael Jordan. After many games, I saw the two of them at the hotel, kidding around, grabbing a bite. Michael was happy to have his dad with him. His dad was his best friend.

As soon as I heard the news, I contacted Tim Hallam, the PR guy for the Bulls. I was hoping Tim could let Michael know how badly I felt for him and his family. I couldn't call Michael myself. I didn't have his number. Besides, he had a strong support group around him. He didn't need to hear from me. What could I possibly say others couldn't?

Tim told me no one from the organization had been in contact with Michael. When I heard that, I should immediately have tried another way. I knew plenty of people who could have easily gotten a message to him.

Instead I told myself I was off the hook because I had made my "attempt." I would express my condolences the next time we saw each other, at training camp in October.

Looking back, I wish I could blame my youth for being so incredibly insensitive. I can't. There is no excuse. A friend of mine lost his father and I didn't say a word to him. I will have to live with that for the rest of my life.

Why didn't I make a stronger effort?

Perhaps I didn't want to deal with Michael's grief. Just as I didn't deal with my own grief when my dad passed away three years earlier. I've always been good at running away from that kind of pain. Too good.

For as long as I can remember, I have been surrounded by a loving and supportive family.

My older brother, Ronnie, who was severely injured when he was thirteen, has shown more courage than anyone I have ever known.

As one of the managers for the Hamburg Lions football team, I got to spend time with friends and be around a game I enjoyed.

After my growth spurt, I learned how to take advantage of my size and swiftness and wound up with my share of dunks at Central Arkansas.

I arrived at college without a scholarship, but I was in the starting lineup by my sophomore year and became a two-time All-American.

From the day he took over as the Bulls coach in 1989, Phil Jackson knew what we needed to become champions.

Our 1991 championship, the first of six, was so special. These were our starters, but the entire team contributed.

It was an incredible honor to play with the greatest players in the world on the Dream Team and help the United States win a gold medal in Barcelona.

We couldn't have won any of the first three titles without Horace Grant, who came up with two key plays down the stretch during Game 6 in the 1993 Finals against the Phoenix Suns.

I dearly miss my mother, Ethel Pippen, who did a remarkable job raising twelve children under very trying circumstances.

Winning the MVP in the 1994 NBA All-Star Game, where I scored 29 points and had 11 rebounds, is one of my proudest achievements.

Of all the times I dunked the ball, nothing tops the emphatic one I had over Patrick Ewing during the 1994 playoffs. It was our final game at Chicago Stadium.

We took a lot of pride in defending like Dobermans. I loved the challenge of stopping opponents whom we considered to be the head of the snake.

Michael Jordan and I, savoring the moment after our last championship in 1998, when we defeated the Jazz for the second year in a row.

Winning the title in 1998, which we celebrated with another rally at Grant Park, capped our dominant run of six championships in eight years.

I considered the possibility of coaching after my playing days were over but was happy to be surrounded by another team—my family.

When it came to deciding who would present me at my Hall of Fame enshrinement, there was only one real choice.

I was grateful to have my family at my side when the Bulls unveiled a bronze statue of me at the United Center in 2011.

My oldest son, Scotty Jr., plays for Vanderbilt and has a real chance to make it in the NBA.

My college coach, Don Dyer, and high school coach, Donald Wayne, could be very strict, but both helped me become a better player—and a better man.

Nothing has given me greater satisfaction than what my children have accomplished. Like the day we celebrated when my son Preston (second from right) graduated from high school.

As I look back, it was quite a journey from Hamburg, Arkansas, to the NBA, and I couldn't be more blessed.

. . . .

When October finally arrived, I waited for the right moment to approach Michael.

The moment never came. That was because another one did.

It was Tuesday evening, October 5, 1993. I was on my way to a private box at Comiskey Park to watch the Chicago White Sox take on the Toronto Blue Jays in Game 1 of the American League Championship Series. The South Side was buzzing. The White Sox hadn't been in the playoffs in ten years.

The reporters asked if I had heard a rumor that Michael was going to retire.

"Yeah, right," I told them. And I'll be starting at third base for the Sox tonight.

No, really, they said, that's the word going around the ballpark. I still didn't believe it, but I decided to reach out to Michael regardless. He was in another private box, having thrown out the game's ceremonial first pitch. It would be worth a good laugh, if nothing else. He and I were always getting a kick out of the wild rumors people put out there.

This was no wild rumor.

"It's true," Michael told me. "I'm making the announcement tomorrow."

I was in shock. I didn't stick around for the whole game. My mind was a million miles away.

Like others on the team, I saw the toll the past season had taken on him—the games themselves, as well as the gambling stories that popped up. And that was *before* his dad was killed. Some reporters had the nerve to suggest Michael's gambling debts may have had something to do with the murder. Just when I thought the media couldn't go any lower, I was proven wrong.

Yet during the regular season, and in the playoffs, I never got the slightest indication he was thinking of hanging it up. The competition meant too much to him, and both of us believed there were more championships to come.

The next morning, we met as a team shortly before Michael was to address the media. Phil felt it was important everyone got a chance to tell Michael what he had meant to them. I thanked him for showing me the way with his dedication and refusal to ever give in.

The press conference was held at the Berto Center in Deerfield, our practice facility for the last year.

The building was packed. The retirement was such a huge story it was carried live on national television. NBC sent its nightly news anchor, Tom Brokaw. No other athlete would have generated that kind of coverage.

Michael sat at the front table with his wife, Juanita, along with Phil, Jerry Krause, Jerry Reinsdorf, and Commissioner Stern. I stood in the back with several of my teammates, wearing shades. I had a feeling I might shed a few tears before the day was over.

So what if Michael and I weren't as close off the court as people assumed? The two of us would forever be linked together on a franchise that won three straight championships. I was overcome with a deep sense of loss as I listened to him explain why he was leaving. That a part of me was leaving, too.

I noticed something different about Michael that day. He was happy. I'd seen him happy before, of course. Just not like this. As if he had been freed from something. Which he was.

No more practices. No more press conferences. No more plane rides from one end of the country to the other. He could now enjoy his wealth and time any way he pleased.

I could relate to what Michael had been going through. Not to the demands he faced every day, obviously, or the expectations that he be awesome every night. That he be Michael Jordan.

Rather, to the fatigue he experienced, physically and mentally. I compare it to what a running back in the NFL has to endure over the years. The hits add up. Till you get to the point where your body tells you enough is enough. Your body doesn't lie.

Fortunately, I'd gotten a bit of a rest that off season by delaying surgery on my right ankle and left wrist. This was the same ankle that had been bothering me since the Knicks series in 1992. I waited until the end of August, as I felt it was time I made a decision for myself, and not for the Chicago Bulls. I'd given enough to them already. Surgery would have meant another lost summer and being on crutches for weeks.

That ain't resting. That's struggling.

Furthermore, I was certain I'd be ready for the first game of the season on November 5. The team (with Michael on board, I assumed) could get along just fine in the meantime without me.

That wasn't the only reason for the delay. I had an obligation with Nike to go around the world promoting shoes that would be hitting the stores the following season. I couldn't very well do that wearing a boot on my foot. The money I received in my Nike deal was a game changer given how severely underpaid I was in my day job.

Once it sank in that Michael wouldn't be coming back, I began to ponder what it would mean for myself, and the team.

I won't lie. As much as I would miss Michael, a part of me was looking forward to seeing what life would be like without him. Even before he retired, I had come to the conclusion that I was our best all-around player.

Before you jump down my throat, let me explain.

I mean player, not scorer, and there is a big difference. I was the facilitator for the offense and the anchor for the defense—the guy who made everyone else better. The way Magic was on the Lakers. The chemistry, the caring, the sharing—that was the culture I created and nurtured, not Michael. And that's the culture that made us champions. Granted, we wouldn't have been in that position if not for his heroics.

I wasn't the only person who saw the advantages to him being gone. So did Jerry Krause.

Jerry would never have admitted it. They would have run him out of town. Consider this: without Michael, who was already on the team when Jerry became the general manager in 1985, he'd now be able to claim he had put the entire roster together. So if we were to succeed with this revised cast, maybe make it back to the Finals, he would receive the credit for once, not Michael.

Phil, meanwhile, said the right things, explaining what he expected from me as the team's new leader. I was appointed cocaptain with Bill Cartwright and took over Michael's locker stall.

At the same time, I never got the sense Phil believed in me. Not the way he believed in Michael.

He ran plays for other guys. He hardly ever ran a play for me. His explanation: "You have the ball in your hands the whole time. You're running the offense. You can run any route you want." Maybe. Yet it would still have been nice for him to draw up a specific play for me more often than once every two or three games. As a sign of respect, if nothing else.

I let it slide. I let a lot of things slide. Until, and I know I'm getting ahead of myself, the fateful possession against the Knicks. That, I would never let slide.

As for the team itself, I was optimistic.

Besides Horace, Paxson, and myself, we now had Toni Kukoc, who finally decided to leave Europe; Steve Kerr, a shooting guard; Bill Wennington, a center; and my friend from Arkansas Pete Myers, who would succeed—no one could replace—MJ in the starting lineup.

They were all excellent additions, who were great to have in the locker room. Steve was one of the best shooters in the league. Bill could contribute on both ends. Pete, meanwhile, continued to amaze. He had been out of the NBA for three years and most recently was a member of Scavolini Pesaro, a team in Italy. If that isn't perseverance, I don't know what is.

Were we a championship contender?

Probably not. You can't lose a player of Michael's caliber and expect to sustain the same level of play. On the other hand, the guys remaining knew what it took to be a champion, and that surely had to count for something.

Toni and I talked early on about what happened in Barcelona. It was good to get that out in the open. There was no animosity between us, and I was relieved. We were on the same side now.

I probably pushed Toni harder in practice than I ever pushed anyone else. I learned that from Michael, who busted my butt every day. To his credit, Toni never held it against me. He was under a lot of pressure. Jerry had been trying forever to get him in a Bulls uniform, and now that day had finally come.

Would he live up to the hype?

We were about to find out.

* * * *

Ring night on November 6, 1993, felt much different from the two ring nights before.

How could it not? The man who had been the MVP in the Finals each time was wearing a suit instead of a uniform. I had thought a lot about the reasons Michael gave for retiring, and they seemed to make sense.

Only I couldn't help but wonder then, and still wonder today, Was there more to it?

I've never summoned the courage to ask Michael, and, no, I don't believe the rumors that the league was planning to suspend him because of his gambling. Seriously, why would the NBA shut down its No. 1 attraction, who was still at the height of his powers?

Anyway, picking up our rings, as always, was a special moment. Winning this championship was as tough, maybe tougher, than the other two.

From then on, the evening went downhill—and fast.

The Miami Heat crushed us, 95–71. In the second quarter, we scored 6 points, a new franchise low, and only 25 in the half, another low. A number of fans left in the third quarter. I wished I could have joined them. If the game wasn't humiliating enough, several of the Heat players kept mocking us . . . *The Chicago Bulls. The three-time NBA champions.*

"You're a bum, Pippen," said Grant Long, who wasn't even in uniform. Added John Salley, the former Piston, "No more MJ, boys."

Even without MJ, there was no excuse.

Losing to the Heat was the least of our troubles. Two days later, I was placed on the injured list and would end up being out for 10 games. The consensus was that I came back too early from the surgery. My ankle still wasn't right. I also hurt my foot when Scott Williams accidentally stepped on it on opening night in Charlotte. The team lost 6 of the 10 games I missed.

I returned to the lineup on November 30 at the Stadium against the Suns, who were surely looking for a little payback for their loss in the Finals.

They'd have to look for it another time.

The Bulls coasted to a 132–113 victory. The building was rockin' for perhaps the first time in the post–Michael Jordan era. I scored 29 points, pulled down 11 rebounds, and recorded 6 assists.

We were just getting started.

Over the next month, we dropped only 1 of 13 games, in overtime at Philadelphia. The win over the New Jersey Nets in late December was our tenth in a row. Our longest winning streak in the 1992–93 season was seven.

Michael who?

To me, it was no mystery why we were playing so well. Guys were passing the ball as never before, not content until they spotted the open man.

From game to game—possession to possession—our opponents didn't know whom they needed to worry about, quite a contrast from the old days. The players we added in the off-season were veterans with a high basketball IQ who picked up the nuances of the triangle faster than those who were on the team in 1989. Having four or five guys learn a new system instead of twelve also helped.

I'd never had so much fun. Without Michael judging every move, no one was afraid to make a mistake. The change in Horace was most noticeable. He was playing with more confidence. I can't recall him complaining once, about anything, though he was still almost certain to leave when he became a free agent at the end of the season. The damage caused by the organization was too severe, and Jerry Krause wasn't going anywhere.

My goal was never to replace Michael as a scorer. I attempted less than 2 shots (17.8 to 16.4) more per game than the season before. My goal, as always, was to be the facilitator, to push the ball up the court to get easy baskets in transition.

Teams couldn't stop us. Tex couldn't say a word.

The guys were there for one another on the other end of the floor, as well. Take Steve Kerr, who was plagued with a bad left knee. He couldn't cover speedy guards such as Kevin Johnson or Gary Payton. So it was up to the other four players on the court to communicate with Steve: *Send him right. I got your help.*

Our fans played a role in our success. They had always been incredibly supportive. Except now, in our final season at Chicago Stadium—we would move into a new building, the United Center, in the fall—they realized that without Michael around to be his usual spectacular self, they would have to generate the energy themselves. Did they ever.

Come January, I was beginning to believe we could make a serious run at another championship. All we needed was to add a piece or two, and it didn't have to be a star. Like what the Knicks had just done, picking up Derek Harper, a veteran point guard, from the Dallas Mavericks.

Well, day after day went by, and Jerry Krause failed to make a move. I was becoming frustrated. I kept those feelings to myself. Until I couldn't.

"If people expect the Bulls to contend," I told the press, "we have to have something to go to war with."

I also made a comment about Jerry traveling with the team on road trips, a familiar complaint among the guys.

"We need him on the phone, not in the locker room," I said.

Nothing I said would do any good. (In late February, while other teams in contention helped themselves, the Bulls pretty much stood pat. I was sure it would come back to haunt us. The only move of any consequence was sending Stacey King to Minnesota for seven-foot-two center Luc Longley.)

I made other headlines that winter—this time, not intentionally.

One evening, after we beat the Washington Bullets at the Stadium, I went to P. J. Clarke's, a restaurant on the city's North Side, to hang out with a few friends. Around midnight, someone said I needed to go outside.

A police officer had already searched my car, a black four-door 1994 Range Rover. The officer said the car was illegally parked and would have to be towed. However, since it was in locked position and couldn't be moved, he asked for the key. I gave it to him. He claimed to have found a .380-caliber semiautomatic handgun in plain view between the front seat and the console.

I was arrested and taken to the district police station, where I was charged with a misdemeanor: unlawful use of a weapon. Because I was registered to own a gun didn't mean I wasn't licensed to carry one. The maximum penalty was one year in jail and a $1,000 fine. After I posted a $100 cash bond, they let me go.

The arrest was a big story in Chicago for a few days. Even the mayor, Richard Daley, weighed in. Everyone got way too carried away.

First of all, I purchased the gun for my protection. As a public figure, I was an obvious target. Keep in mind it had been less than six months since Michael's father was murdered, and I was living in a city where people were gunned down every day.

Second, the weapon wasn't where the officer said it was. I kept it hidden inside the console, for obvious reasons.

The charge was dropped about a month later when a judge ruled the police had no legal jurisdiction to search my car. The judge restored my faith in the system.

To a point.

More than anything else, the episode served as another reminder of the racism that was rampant in Chicago and still is.

I would never have been treated that way—they put me in hand-cuffs, for God's sake—if I were white. The officer uttered a racial slur after I walked out of the restaurant. I didn't say anything. What good would that have done? It's not as if I hadn't heard the same slur before. I came from the South. I heard it all the time.

Another reminder came in late February when the Cavs beat us at the Stadium, 89–81.

The fans began to boo. I got so upset that, during a time-out in the third quarter, the Cavs leading by 18, I gave the finger to a person behind the bench. How dare these folks turn on us? Had they not noticed the effort we were putting forth, night after night? Our record was 37-18, the second best in the Eastern Conference. Not too shabby, if you ask me, after losing a three-time MVP.

Yes, we had an off night. So what? Every team is entitled to have an off night. Besides, one would assume that winning three championships in a row would keep the natives satisfied for a while.

Apparently not.

Afterward, when the press asked if I was depressed about the boos, I didn't hold back:

"Personally, the only thing that's depressing is that in my seven years here, I've never seen a white guy get booed in the Stadium. . . . Toni was oh for whatever tonight, and I never heard one fan get on him." (Toni was 0 for 9, with 4 turnovers.)

I didn't regret saying what I did for one second. If anything, I should have spoken up sooner.

The Bulls, as you would expect, went ballistic. Whether what I said was true didn't concern them in the least. All they cared about was defusing the situation as rapidly as possible.

Jerry Krause drafted a statement of apology, which read, in part:

"In my comments after the game I in no way meant to imply that there was racism involved. That small minority booed all the Bulls players. In past years, they have booed players of both races."

There was plenty in the statement I didn't agree with. I signed off anyway. I was as anxious to get the matter over with as Jerry was. My job wasn't to speak out against racism. My job was to help the Chicago Bulls win basketball games.

Which, by the way, we were suddenly having trouble doing.

From the All-Star break through the second week of March, the team dropped 9 of 13 games. I was right. Not getting any significant help before the trade deadline was coming back to haunt us. We could have picked up the Clippers' Ron Harper or Philadelphia's Jeff Hornacek, both extremely capable, and still kept our core group pretty much intact. Nice job, Jerry.

Our offense was struggling, to put it mildly. In that 13-game stretch, we scored fewer than 90 points on six occasions, including an 86–68 loss to the Knicks. We fell by 19 to the Blazers, 25 to the Nuggets, and 31 to the Hawks.

I was part of the problem. Here are some of my *highlights*:

Seven of 24 against the Heat.

Five of 19 against the Nuggets.

Three of 10 against the Cavs.

I couldn't figure out where this was coming from. Prior to our slump, I was playing as well as ever. At the All-Star Game in mid-February, I was the MVP with 29 points and 11 rebounds, hitting 5 of 9 three-pointers as the East beat the West in Minneapolis, 127–118.

For once, it was nice to win something of my own instead of watching Michael walk off with another trophy.

That was a crazy day. Before the game, I hung out in my hotel room with a buddy, Michael Clarke, a former teammate of Pete Myers's at U of A in Little Rock. Michael and I played tonk, the loser drinking a shot of beer. This went on for hours. I probably drank the equivalent of three beers.

Suddenly, it was time to leave for the arena.

So I was a little tipsy. So what? I wasn't planning on putting much energy into what is nothing more than an exhibition. And, you may recall, ever since I was snubbed in 1991, I didn't think much of the All-Star Game to begin with.

The strangest thing then happened. When I got on the court to warm up, my level of concentration was off the charts. I hit every shot, including three-pointers. I can think of a similar experience one other time in my career. Michael and I drank a couple of beers prior to a preseason game. Both of us were sick of these games, also meaningless. I couldn't miss then, either.

Fortunately, the team got back in sync in mid-March, going 17-5 the rest of the way, which included a 10-game winning streak, to finish the regular season 55-27. No one thought we would win that many games. Not even Phil.

If only we could have won the final two.

Instead, losing at home to the Celtics, a team headed for the lottery, in double OT in the second-to-last game severely hurt our chances of securing the top seed in the East. In the first overtime, I missed 2 free throws with less than thirty seconds left and a jumper at the buzzer. For the night, I was 11 of 31.

That defeat, and the one two days later against the Knicks, left us as the No. 3 seed.

. . . .

In the playoffs, we would sorely miss No. 23.

Not so much in the first round, against the Cleveland Cavaliers, whom we swept in three games. The team Magic said was destined to rule the nineties wouldn't make it to an NBA Finals until 2007.

Definitely in the next round, when we took on Patrick Ewing and the Knicks.

The Knicks couldn't have been more motivated, having lost to us in 1991, 1992, and in 1993 after being ahead in the series, 2–0. We were the one team that kept getting in their way, as the Pistons got in our way for what seemed like . . . forever.

After taking the first two games at the Garden, the Knicks again found themselves in great position.

The date: May 13, 1994. The place: Chicago Stadium.

Sounds as if I'm setting the scene for some kind of major crime. Which, in the opinion of many, was exactly what transpired.

Fast-forward to the late stages of Game 3. We had the ball, up 102–100, with less than eighteen seconds remaining. Our lead had been as high as 22 points late in the third quarter. Time-out, Bulls.

I was thrilled that the play, for a change, was designed for me. Everyone else would clear the right side of the floor, where I could take a jumper or drive to the basket. Except Toni stayed on the same side, near the corner. I waved him off. He didn't move. I was forced to throw up a desperate heave, which failed to touch the rim, resulting in a shot-clock violation.

The Knicks called time: 5.5 seconds to go.

Toni messed up big-time. To make matters worse, Ewing hit a hook shot in the lane to tie the game. Another time-out: 1.8 seconds left.

1.8. 1.8. 1.8 . . . I have been reminded of 1.8 so many times in the last twenty-seven years that I am almost convinced it will follow me, literally, to my grave:

SCOTTIE MAURICE PIPPEN
BELOVED HUSBAND AND FATHER
1965–
Seven-time NBA All-Star.

Six-time NBA champion.

**Sat out the final 1.8 seconds of a playoff game
between the Chicago Bulls and the New York Knicks.**

Well, allow me, once and for all, to set the record straight.

For one thing, I do not consider it the lowest moment of my career. I consider it one of the highest. Believe me or not, I don't care.

During the time-out, in case you don't know, Phil called for Toni to take the last shot. The same Toni who botched the previous play. I was told to throw the ball in bounds.

I was furious and let Phil know it.

"Just do what I said," he barked.

"Fuck you!" I told him.

After I chose not to go back on the floor for those final 1.8 seconds, Bill Cartwright and Johnny Bach urged me to change my mind. No chance. Phil put Pete Myers in to make the entry pass.

The rest, as they say, is history. Toni hit an 18-footer over Anthony Mason. Bulls, 104; Knicks, 102.

The locker room felt like a morgue. One would never have imagined that this group had just won a game it desperately needed to get back in the series. According to my teammates, coaches—and, I suspect, basketball fans everywhere—I committed one of the worst sins a professional athlete can ever commit.

I quit on my team.

Cartwright, the cocaptain, had tears in his eyes when he addressed everyone in the locker room:

"This is our chance to do it on our own, without Michael, and you blow it with your selfishness. I've never been so disappointed in my whole life."

I felt horrible. Not for sitting out the final play. I will never feel horrible for that. For how the guys reacted. I worked hard for years to earn their trust, and now that trust was gone.

There was only one thing for me to do. Apologize.

I felt we, as a team, needed to move on from this incident as fast as possible. Game 4 was less than forty-eight hours away, and we couldn't afford to go down 3–1 with the series headed back to the Garden. I wasn't angry with Bill or any of the other players. If I had been in their position, I would have felt the same way.

There was one person I was angry with: Phil Jackson.

Michael was gone. This was my team now, my chance to be the hero, and Phil was giving that chance to . . . Toni Kukoc? Are you serious? Toni was a rookie with no rings. I was in my seventh year with three rings. And, by the way, in the MVP race that season, I finished third behind Hakeem Olajuwon and David Robinson.

The most humiliating part was Phil telling me I would throw the ball in bounds. At least when you're on the floor, you can be a decoy. The Knicks would have put two defenders on me. Someone would have gotten a good look.

By not going back in the game, I did the right thing not just for myself and my pride. Also for the players who would come after me. Who, one day, might very well find themselves in the same position.

Phil and I spoke about the matter the next day. He said something about my being the best passer on the team and referred to the three game-winning shots Toni hit during the regular season.

Nothing he said changed my mind.

"Are you telling me that, if Michael was playing, you would have had him take the ball out because Toni hit those shots?" I asked.

I don't recall how he responded. All I recall is that I was done with Phil Jackson.

Not totally done, of course.

For the rest of my days in Chicago, I would play hard for him and do what he asked. I still felt an obligation to my teammates and to the fans. Except our relationship would never be the same no matter what triumphs would lie ahead. The moment of truth had come, and he had abandoned me. What would stop him from abandoning me again the next time?

By the way, it's not as if we would have lost the game if I had missed the shot. The game was tied. The worst thing was that we would have gone to overtime.

I wonder, What if Toni had missed the shot? Would Phil have wanted me to play in the overtime? Would *I* have wanted to play in the overtime? And what if we had lost Game 3 and the Knicks had gone on to sweep us? What would have happened then?

I know exactly what.

The fans in Chicago would have demanded the Bulls get rid of my ass as soon as possible, and Jerry Krause would happily have obliged. He was always looking to get rid of me.

Sometimes I think a trade that summer might have been the best thing in the long run. To get away from the two Jerrys. To get away from Phil. To get away from the members of the media who didn't like me for one reason and only reason alone: I wasn't Michael Jordan.

Speaking of Michael, he reached out to Phil the day after the game.

"I don't know if Scottie is ever going to live this down," Michael said.

I had no problem with Michael calling Phil. Though it would have been nice if he had also called me. I was the one being vilified on television and in the newspapers. Not Phil. I needed all the support I could get.

Not that I expected Michael to call. That would have been out of character for him. Then again, I didn't call him, either.

People who watched *The Last Dance* were surprised when, referring to the 1.8-seconds incident, I said, "If I had a chance to do it over again, I probably wouldn't change it."

Let me amend that statement:

I definitely wouldn't change it. I stood up for myself. I would never have forgiven myself if I didn't.

Many were also surprised in June, when, during a couple of interviews, I suggested Phil was a racist and that was why he designated Toni to take the last shot.

Nothing could be farther from the truth.

I was so hurt when he picked Toni over me that I needed to come up with an explanation for why I was rejected. For why, after everything I had given to the Chicago Bulls, I wasn't allowed to have my moment. So I told myself at the time that Phil's decision must have been racially motivated, and I allowed myself to believe that lie for nearly thirty years. Only when I saw my words in print did it dawn on me how wrong I was.

In any case, there was still a Game 4 to play. That's what is so wonderful about the NBA. There is always another game. Until there isn't.

We caught a break when Derek Harper, the Knicks guard, was suspended for two games by the league for getting into a brawl in Game 3 with one of our subs, Jo Jo English. You take the breaks anywhere you can get them.

To prove how much Game 3 was behind me, I scored the team's first 8 points, finishing with 25, along with 8 rebounds and 6 assists. We prevailed, 95–83, despite spotting the Knicks a 12–0 lead. The fans were on my side from the opening tip. That meant the world to me. I wasn't sure how they would react.

Back to the Garden for another Game 5. Another Game 5 to remember. All too well, I'm afraid.

With about ten seconds to go, the Bulls up, 86–85, B.J. missed a jumper from the top of the key. The Knicks called time. One more stop, that's all we needed. One more lousy stop.

Mason threw the ball to Starks, who drew a few defenders before kicking it out to his backcourt mate, Hubert Davis, who was wide open by the top of the key. I hurried over to contest the shot. Davis let it go.

No good!

What happened next was hard to believe. Then, and it still is.

The official Hue Hollins called a foul. He claimed I hit Davis on the right forearm. Davis was awarded two free throws.

I can't think of a worse call at a worse time. Against me or anyone else.

Yes, there was contact, except it came after Davis released the ball. Bottom line: it didn't affect the shot. Technically, a player is still in the act of shooting until his feet touch the ground, though, in those days, a foul was hardly ever called once the ball was out of his hands.

Certainly not in a game this big.

Davis made the free throws with 2.1 seconds left, putting the Knicks on top, 87–86, and that's how it would end. Everyone on our team felt robbed. Even Darell Garretson, another official working that night, would admit a couple of months later that Hollins screwed up.

"All I can say is that it was a terrible call," Garretson said.

We could complain about Hollins for only so long. Game 6 in Chicago was two days away. The season would be on the line.

The season was saved: Bulls, 93; Knicks, 79. B.J. led the way with 20 points, while Horace scored 16 and pulled down 12 rebounds.

The game is remembered for my thunderous, one-handed dunk over Ewing midway through the third quarter and the technical I received after I appeared to be taunting him by standing over his prone body on the floor. I didn't deserve a T. I wasn't taunting him. I was fired up. If you are not fired up in a game like this, you're never fired up.

I then got into it with the Knicks' No. 1 fan, the filmmaker Spike Lee, who was sitting in the front row wearing a John Starks jersey. I did nothing wrong there, either. Spike started it.

"Sit your ass down," I told him.

Okay, so maybe I'm leaving a word or two out.

Back to the Garden for one last time.

The pressure was on the Knicks. Their fans would never forgive them for losing to the Bulls for the fourth year in a row. Especially with No. 23 off playing baseball.

In Game 7, we certainly had our chances. With two and a half minutes left in the third quarter, we were leading, 63–59. The Knicks, however, went on an 8–0 run to go up by 4 heading into the final twelve minutes.

Those are twelve minutes I would like to forget.

We scored only 14 points. Credit the Knicks, who won going away, 87–77. Ewing, held scoreless in the first half, finished with 18 points and 17 rebounds, while Oakley had 17 points and 20 rebounds.

I had almost forgotten what it felt like to lose.

The pain went away, eventually, replaced by pride.

No one thought we would go as far as we did. If Hollins hadn't made that call, and we'd won that series, I believe we would have beaten the Pacers in the conference finals. We were 4-1 against them that season.

The Rockets would have been our opponent in the Finals. I believe we would have beaten them, as well.

Now wouldn't that have been something, winning a championship without Michael Jordan? I wonder how that would have affected his legacy. And mine.

CHAPTER 14: **HE'S BACK**

How did the Bulls reward me for my MVP-type 1993–94 season? The only way they knew how. With the same disrespect they had shown from the day I arrived in Chicago.

They tried to get rid of my ass.

The worst part was they didn't have the courage to tell me themselves. I had to find out what was going on from my "friends" in the media.

When I confronted Jerry Krause, he denied the Bulls were actively seeking a trade. That wasn't the point. Even the Bulls just listening to offers was upsetting enough. Organizations don't part with their best player. Most organizations, that is. And if they do decide, for whatever reason, to shop the player around, at least they have the decency to let him know something might be in the works.

The Bulls, according to various press accounts, were hoping to send me to the Seattle SuperSonics for forward Shawn Kemp and guard Ricky Pierce. The teams would also exchange draft picks. Everything appeared to be set—until the Seattle owner, Barry Ackerley, vetoed the deal.

The word was the fans in the Pacific Northwest weren't too keen on giving up Kemp, who was only twenty-four. I would turn twenty nine in September.

To me, it made no difference that, in the end, the trade didn't go through. The damage had been done.

For months afterward, I was the one hoping for a trade. To go somewhere in the league—anywhere—where I was wanted. Which was clearly not the case in Chicago.

A different rumor seemed to crop up every day. I started one myself, that I was headed to the Suns for Dan Majerle, rookie Wesley Person, and possible draft picks. It got around in no time.

No doubt there was life after the Chicago Bulls.

Just ask Horace, who signed a six-year deal with the Orlando Magic in July of 1994 for $22.3 million. I was happy for him. He was finally gaining the respect he deserved. People asked if I tried to persuade him to stay in Chicago. Absolutely not. I would never stand in the way of a player and the payday he had coming.

John Paxson, Bill Cartwright, and Scott Williams also left the team that summer. Pax retired, while Bill signed as a free agent with the Sonics, Scott with the Sixers.

That old gang of mine was breaking up. The only players left from the three championship teams were me, B. J. Armstrong, and Will Perdue.

Even Johnny Bach wouldn't be sticking around. Though that wasn't his choice. Phil fired him. I never found out the whole story. Johnny and Jerry hadn't been getting along for years, everyone knew that. I'm pretty sure Sam Smith's book had something to do with it. Jerry believed Johnny was one of Sam's sources. What a hypocrite.

Losing that many players meant we needed to bring in a bunch of new ones.

They included forwards Larry Krystkowiak, Jud Buechler, and Dickey Simpkins, a rookie from Providence, and, most important, the man I wanted us to acquire the year before, Ron Harper. Harp, a guard, signed as a free agent for five years at $19.2 million. He wasn't the same athlete since he tore his ACL in 1990. That didn't make him any less valuable.

I wasn't thrilled, however, with another move the Bulls made.

Which was signing Toni to a new deal for $26 million over six years, the largest in the history of the franchise. It figured. They leave me underpaid, year after year, then hand Toni a fortune. First the last shot, and now this.

The press—and Jerry Krause, no doubt—waited for me to lash out. I had been known to lash out before.

Not this time. I knew it would do no good to say a word. And, by this point, I was sure my payday would come, eventually. If not with the Bulls, with someone else. As it had come for Horace.

One more piece of business had to be attended to before the summer break came to an end. Saying goodbye to the Stadium, which was set to be demolished in 1995. I loved that building. The way it sounded, the way it smelled. More of a gym than an arena. And so much history had taken place there, and not just in sports. That's where the Democratic Party first nominated Franklin Delano Roosevelt way back in 1932. Safe to say that turned out all right.

On September 9, we staged the final game ever to be played at the Stadium, the Scottie Pippen All-Star Classic. B.J., Horace, Toni, and a few other NBA players joined me in raising more than $150,000 for charity. There wasn't an empty seat.

Oops, I almost forgot to mention one other name on that list.

Michael Jordan.

I was happy he showed up. He did more than show up. He scored 52 points in his team's 187–150 victory. Dunks. Fallaways. Reverse layups. The whole works. The fans loved the trip down memory lane. So did I.

After the game was over, the two of us hugged. Michael then kissed the Bulls logo at midcourt.

Soon he would be gone again, to the new dream he was chasing as the right fielder for the Birmingham Barons, a White Sox Class AA affiliate in the minor leagues.

While the group he left behind faced a future more uncertain than ever.

. . . .

The opening weekend of the 1994–95 regular season was most revealing.

In back-to-back nights at the United Center, our new home across the street from the Stadium, we struggled against two teams, the Charlotte Hornets and Washington Bullets, who hadn't made the playoffs the year before.

In the Charlotte game, we committed 27 turnovers. I was responsible for 6 of them. Good thing the Hornets threw the ball away 23 times themselves, allowing us to hang on, 89–83. The Bullets, meanwhile, beat us, 100–99, in OT. That one hurt. I missed a game-winning shot at the buzzer. I was hacked on the arm, but there was no call. I wasn't surprised. The refs don't call a foul like that at the end of a game. Unless it's Hue Hollins.

The story was pretty much the same the whole month of November. Our longest winning streak was a whopping 2 games.

Even so, I showed up at work every day with a positive attitude. That didn't mean I'd changed my mind about Phil Jackson. And what took place on November 19, when we squared off against the Mavericks in Dallas, certainly didn't narrow the gap between us.

A little background to set the scene:

A week earlier, Jamal Mashburn, a starting forward for the Mavs, had torched us for 50 points in their overtime victory in Chicago. I took it personally, as I did whenever my man got the better of me. Which wasn't often.

So, as we got ready to play them again, I let the guys know I would be going for 50.

I said it on the plane to Dallas. I said it in the locker room before the opening tip. I practically taped it to my forehead. Phil couldn't have missed it.

Everything went according to plan.

Well, almost everything. I had scored 17 points by the half, 36 (along with 14 rebounds) after three quarters. I was on my way. . . .

To the bench.

Where Phil would leave me the whole fourth quarter. I get it. We were killing the Mavs. He saw no reason for me to be out there.

I saw a very good reason. I needed to answer Mashburn, point for point. Believe me, if it had been Michael in the same scenario, I guarantee Phil would have kept him in the game until he scored 50, maybe 60. This felt no different from when he chose Toni to take the last shot. Phil didn't allow me to have my moment.

The month of December wasn't any better. Two games stand out, both at the United Center, and it's difficult to choose which was more humiliating.

On December 19, the Cavs knocked us off, 77–63, a franchise low in points. I was the high scorer with 14. At least the Cavs were a good team, in the middle of what would, ultimately, be an 11-game winning streak.

One week later, the Los Angeles Clippers beat us, 95–92.

The Clippers.

The Clippers (4-23) hadn't won in Chicago since 1979, when they were based in San Diego. In the second quarter, I received my second T (technical) of the game for arguing with an official after he had signaled me for an offensive foul. The first T was for taunting. I was done for the night.

There was no mystery over why we were stinking up the joint. We missed Horace. Almost as much as we missed Michael. Horace controlled the boards and held his own against the top power forwards in the league.

The defeat put our record at 13-13—and me in a foul mood. I

wasn't used to such mediocrity at any level of the game: high school, college, or the pros. Which might explain why I unloaded on Jerry Krause the next day.

"He lies about everything," I told the reporters. "You don't even bother yourself in dealing with him."

I was referring to when Jerry lied about the near trade to Seattle. I was also frustrated he didn't make a more concerted effort to re-sign Horace. I'm not suggesting it would have made a difference, although you never know.

It wasn't just the lying, and the losing, that bothered me so deeply. I was still angry about being underpaid. Toni, B.J., and Harp were each making more than I was.

As usual, I didn't allow how I felt to hinder my effort on the court. I was leading the team in each of the five major statistical cat-egories: points, rebounds, assists, blocks, and steals. No player had accomplished that feat since Dave Cowens, a center for the Celtics, in the late 1970s.

But what I was going through was having on effect on me, and it was bound to show up.

On January 24, we took on the San Antonio Spurs at the United Center.

Late in the first half, Dennis Rodman, now on the Spurs, mixed it up with Luc Longley. I couldn't believe Rodman wasn't called for a foul. I shared my opinion with Joey Crawford, the official, who didn't appreciate what I had to say. He gave me a T. Now I was really ticked off, resulting in another T.

Before I left for the locker room, I made sure to leave one last impression.

As I walked past our bench, I picked up a folding chair and tossed it onto the court, similar to what Indiana coach Bobby Knight fa-mously did in 1985. I never liked Joey Crawford. He was one of those refs, and there were several, who used the whistle to show how much power they had.

Looking back, I wish I hadn't thrown the chair. Someone could have gotten hurt.

Even so, I didn't apologize then and I won't apologize now. Fine, I overreacted. So did Crawford, and I don't recall him ever saying he was sorry.

Soon, another trade deadline came and went, and I stayed exactly where I was. The latest reports had me headed to the Clippers. Maybe. Maybe not. I never knew what to believe.

Speaking of going nowhere, the Bulls' record in February was 5-8, the worst since April of 1989 when Doug Collins was the coach. The script was the same night after night. We would grab the lead and then fall apart in the second half.

In early March, the team was 28-30, eight and one-half games be-hind the Hornets in our division and light-years behind the Orlando Magic (44-13), who owned the best record in the Eastern Conference.

The Magic featured two of the game's most exciting young tal-ents: Shaquille O'Neal, a seven-foot-one, 325-pound center, and Penny Hardaway, a six-foot-seven guard/forward. Shaq will be for-ever linked with Kobe Bryant, and rightfully so, but Penny was his first true costar. Penny could shoot from the outside and on the block and was a tremendous passer.

The odds were Horace would pick up another ring before I did, and if that happened, I would never hear the end of it.

. . . .

When he showed up for practice at the Berto Center on March 7, it seemed like no big deal. Michael had worked out with the team on a number of occasions since his retirement. He still loved the game, and that was never going to change. Except something was different this time. He worked with the second unit and participated in a film session. He even ran sprints after practice.

Guys began to ask themselves, Is the man actually thinking about coming back?

The speculation went on for several days, and no one knew the answer. The local TV and print reporters were on top of the story from the beginning. There hadn't been that many members of the media in the Berto Center since Michael's farewell press conference in 1993. Which felt like a hundred years ago.

As usual, Michael didn't confide in me. Nor did I dare to ask him what his plans might be. I knew how far our relationship went, and I didn't take it a step further. I wasn't alone. Everyone on the team, with the possible exception of his pal B. J. Armstrong, was kept in the dark.

With each passing day, Michael's return appeared more likely, especially with baseball not being an option anytime soon. The players had gone on strike the previous August, which resulted in the cancellation of the rest of the 1994 season. By the following March, there was still no end in sight to the labor troubles. Some guys were willing to cross the picket lines to join replacement players in the minor leagues. Not Michael.

On March 18, he made it official with his famous fax: *I'm back*.

I was overjoyed, which I think surprised some people. They figured I wouldn't want to be demoted to No. 2 again. That I preferred to be Batman to Robin. I won't lie. I enjoyed being the man, proving to the critics I could take my game to a whole other level if I didn't have to defer to Michael.

Jerry Krause, meanwhile, had more to prove. Winning 55 games in the 1993–94 season wasn't enough. No wonder he wasn't excited about having Michael back.

"Scottie, Horace, those are your kids," Michael used to tell Jerry. "You didn't draft me."

That would irritate Jerry to no end. Which only encouraged Michael to keep saying it. He always knew which of Jerry's buttons to push, and there were many.

Not that Michael would be able to cure everything that was wrong with the Chicago Bulls. He wasn't Horace Grant. He couldn't battle with the big men in the post, and we still needed a lot of help on the boards.

Furthermore, he wasn't in what I like to refer to as *midseason condition*.

I don't care who you are. You can't show up for a few practices and expect to be the player you were before. Your body won't let you. It's not just the games themselves. It's the practices, the travel, the mental focus that is required day after day. Michael hadn't been through that kind of regimen since we defeated the Suns in the 1993 Finals, nearly two full years earlier.

The rest of us had to make an adjustment, too. Mostly, the guys who had never played with him.

Not just where to get him the ball or where to position themselves when he drove to the basket. To play with Michael meant adjusting to the attention he generated from fans, reporters, photographers, celebrities, you name it, which was, incredibly enough, more overwhelming than ever.

Guys were starstruck, as if he were a matinee idol, which, I suppose, he was. I'm talking about grown men who had been in the league for years. They didn't know how to approach him. In many cases, they didn't bother. Better to keep their distance than say the wrong thing and get on his bad side.

I can't tell you how many times a teammate would come up to me and ask, "Hey, do you think I can get MJ to sign this?"

Every time, whether it was a jersey for their kid brother or a program from a game where Michael scored 50 points, I gave them the same look: *Good luck*.

No one was more intimidated than Toni.

Toni always wanted to play with Michael. When Michael retired, he was devastated.

Be careful what you wish for. Toni was already having to deal with Phil, who constantly got on his case about not playing defense the right way. Now here comes Michael, who, to put it kindly, wasn't shy about expressing himself.

Michael's first game back was on March 19 against the Pacers in Indianapolis. It felt more like June 19. That's how amped-up the fans were in Market Square Arena and how many members of the media were in attendance.

Wearing the number 45 jersey, the first number he used in high school, instead of his familiar 23, Michael was rusty, as one would expect. He hit only 7 of his 28 shots, as we lost in overtime, 103–96. After beating the Celtics in the next game, we took on the Orlando Magic at the United Center. This was a big test for us, the Magic the clear favorites to come out of the East.

We failed. Michael was out of sync once more (7 for 23), Orlando winning, 106–99.

There was no reason to be concerned. He was Michael Jordan. He would find his rhythm before long.

Try the very next game.

With 5.9 seconds to go and trailing the Hawks by 1, MJ caught the inbounds pass and went the full length of the court to hit a 14-foot game winner at the buzzer. He finished with 32 points. Not bad for someone who had spent all those months trying to hit curveballs.

Then came the night at the Garden. The night no one saw coming.

Michael hit 6 of his first 7 shots on his way to 20 points in the quarter. He added 15 in the second and 14 in the third. He ended up with 55, the most anyone had scored the entire season, and fed Bill Wennington for the game-winning dunk, as we defeated the Knicks, 113–111. It would become known as the double nickel game.

The fax told the world, *I'm back*.

The performance at the Garden made it official.

Michael played in 17 games before the playoffs got under way in late April. We won 13 of them to finish the season at 47–35 to secure the No. 5 seed in the East.

We were the Bulls again. Anything was possible.

. . . .

Our opponent in the first round, a best-of-five series, would be the Hornets, with Game 1 in Charlotte. The last time we started the playoffs on the road was 1989.

The Hornets won 50 games in the '94–95 season, with a future Hall of Fame center, Alonzo Mourning, forward Larry Johnson, and a lightning-quick point guard who brought back wonderful memories from my life-changing week at the predraft tournament in Portsmouth, Virginia: Muggsy Bogues. I will never be able to thank Muggsy enough.

This being a short series, Game 1 took on greater significance than normal. The final in overtime was Bulls, 108, Hornets, 100.

The credit goes to Michael, who poured in 48, including 10 of our 16 points in the OT. The Hornets came back to take Game 2, 106–89, Mourning leading the way with 23 points and 20 rebounds. In Game 3, we held him in check (13 points, 7 rebounds) in a convincing 103–80 triumph.

One more victory at the Stadium and it would be on to the next round.

Easier said than done. Especially with Michael having an off night.

During a sixteen-minute stretch in the third and fourth quarters of Game 4, he didn't score a single point. I wouldn't have thought that was possible. Picking up the slack were me and Toni, who finished with 21 points and 11 rebounds. Even so, the Hornets were in position to steal it at the end. Down by a point with a few seconds to go, Johnson took a jump shot from behind the free throw line. Air ball.

An over-the-back follow attempt by Hersey Hawkins was also off the mark. We survived. Barely.

The top-seeded Magic were next. No one doubted their talent. The question was, Were they ready to climb the next hurdle? It takes time to knock off the champs, as we found out against the Pistons, and with MJ back, we felt that's who we still were: the champs.

As if the 1993–94 season had never happened.

Our toughest challenge would be containing Shaq. He was a beast. That season, only his third in the league, he averaged 29.3 points and 10.8 rebounds. We didn't have anyone who could guard him straight up. By the way, no one else did, either. His weakness was free throws. He made only 53 percent. I never understood why Shaq didn't work harder on that part of his game. As dominant as he was, he could have been even better.

Fortunately, with three capable big men—Bill Wennington, Luc Longley and Will Perdue—we could be aggressive with Shaq, having 18 fouls (6 fouls apiece) to play with. They were known as the "three-headed monster."

Anyway, so much for Shaq's weakness.

In Game 1, he hit 12 of 16 from the line, scoring 26 points and pulling down 12 rebounds. Nonetheless, we were in it the whole way, thanks to another stellar effort by Toni (17 points, 9 rebounds, 7 assists) and 34 points from our bench.

With eighteen seconds to go, we were ahead, 91–90. Michael dribbled up the court, trailed closely by guard Nick Anderson. The Magic would likely have to commit a foul.

Or would they?

Anderson stripped it away from Michael, Penny gaining control of the loose ball. He raced downcourt and fed Horace, who slammed it home. The Magic were now up, 92–91.

To suggest Michael was in shock—that the entire basketball world was in shock—would be an understatement. No one steals the ball from Michael Jordan in crunch time.

Except this wasn't the same Michael. This was the Michael who had been away from the game for nearly two years.

Time-out, Chicago; 6.2 seconds to go.

It wasn't over yet. Michael would have a chance to redeem himself.

He caught the ball near half-court and dribbled toward the free throw line. He jumped and, in midair, instead of taking the shot, threw the ball to me. I wasn't expecting him to pass. No one was. The ball floated behind me out of bounds, as I had already edged toward the basket for a possible rebound. The Magic won, 94–91.

A quarter of a century later, people recall the Anderson steal as proof Michael wasn't infallible. Gee, I could have told them that. What they probably don't recall is that Michael scored 38 points (17 of 30) in Game 2 as we evened the series, 104–94. If not infallible, he was still Michael Jordan. In that game, he switched back to wearing number 23. Number 45 hadn't felt right.

Off to Chicago we went, with the split we were looking for. And all the momentum in the world.

Too bad it didn't last.

In Game 3, the Magic beat us, 110–101. Shaq scored 28 points, including 8 of 10 from the line. *Who is this big dude impersonating Shaquille O'Neal?*

We rebounded in Game 4, 106–95, to square the series again. The Magic then captured Game 5, 103–95, as Shaq dominated with 23 points, 22 rebounds, and 5 blocked shots. A beast, I'm telling you. Horace was also great: 24 points and 11 rebounds. Still, if we could just take care of business in Chicago, the pressure would be on the Magic. They would be in a place they had never been before.

A Game 7.

No problem. With over three minutes remaining in Game 6, B.J.

nailed a three-pointer from the corner to give us an 8-point advantage. The atmosphere in the United Center was electric. Like the Stadium used to be.

Time-out, Orlando.

Two possessions later, Shaq scored in the paint to narrow the lead to 6. Following a Bulls turnover, Anderson hit a three. We failed to score the next time downcourt, our third unsuccessful trip in a row. Not a good time to go cold. The Magic took advantage, Brian Shaw converting two free throws. The 8-point lead had all but evaporated.

After Michael threw up an air ball, Anderson hit another jumper. Now it *was* gone, the Magic up by 1.

Phil called time with 42.8 seconds to go.

This simply could not be happening.

Not to the Chicago Bulls, the franchise with three rings in the past four years. Not in our own building. And not with Michael Jordan back in the fold.

Down the stretch, we had two chances to tie or take the lead.

First, Luc missed an easy one a couple feet from the basket after a perfect dish from Michael. After small forward Dennis Scott hit a free throw to give the Magic a 2-point advantage, Michael turned it over again. That was it. The final: 108–102. Over the last three minutes, Orlando outscored us, 14–0.

The celebration got under way. The Magic players carried Horace, the returning conquering hero, on their shoulders as he waved a white towel. I hated to lose, obviously, although a small part of me didn't mind seeing Horace rub the loss in Jerry Krause's face.

Who knows? Maybe I would get the same opportunity one day.

If the Bulls had their way, I would have been gone sooner than later. They reached out to several teams shortly after we were eliminated to see if there was any interest in a trade. Just because Michael was back didn't mean they wanted me back.

Believe it or not, I wanted to come back. I know, wasn't I the guy who, earlier that same season, had been hoping to leave? Indeed. A lot had changed since then, Michael's return at the top of the list.

Our reign, if interrupted, was far from over.

Guys such as Steve Kerr, Bill Wennington, Ron Harper, Toni Kukoc, and Luc Longley now knew how to play with Michael and how to deal with the spectacle always surrounding him. The final two months of the 1994–95 season were a perfect dress rehearsal.

All we needed was a rebounder and defender to replace Horace.

I could never have imagined who that player would be.

CHAPTER 15: **TWO MORE RINGS**

The first time I heard his name was during my junior year at Central Arkansas.

He gave me hope. I realized I didn't have to be at a big-time school to get drafted by the NBA. As long as one possessed the talent and dedication, the dream was still possible. Dennis Rodman, whose unlikely journey took him from a poor neighborhood in Dallas, Texas, to Southeastern Oklahoma State to, eventually, the Basketball Hall of Fame, had an abundance of both.

I came into the league a year after Dennis did. The two of us were rivals, then enemies. We hated the Bad Boys and they hated us. They hated everyone. Yet even while the Pistons kept beating the Bulls in the playoffs, I admired his ability to play defense and rebound. He knew where the ball was headed the moment it left the shooter's hands and was able to wrestle rebounds away from players five inches taller and fifty pounds heavier.

That didn't happen by accident.

He studied the tendencies of his opponents and teammates, planting himself in perfect rebounding position even before guys got into a shooting mode. Dennis possessed an unbelievable basketball IQ. He could have a tremendous impact on a game without scoring a single point. How many players can you say that about?

As vital as Isiah Thomas, Bill Laimbeer, and Joe Dumars were to their success, the Pistons wouldn't have won their two championships without Dennis.

How he even made it to the NBA in the first place is quite a story.

His father took off when Dennis was only three years old. Dennis didn't see him again for forty-two years. His mother worked a series of jobs to keep the family afloat. After graduating from high school, Dennis was a janitor at the airport in Dallas when he was caught on camera stealing watches from a gift shop. He was fortunate the charges were dropped. Or the story might have ended right there.

A miracle then took place. Dennis grew, and grew . . . and grew.

He went from five foot nine to six foot eight in one year—and I thought I went through a fast growth spurt. He tried basketball for the second time. The first time, in high school, it didn't work out. This time, he hooked up with a small community college in Gainesville, Texas. From there, he went to Southeastern Oklahoma State. He was on his way.

So, in the summer of 1995, when Phil asked how I felt about the possibility of the Bulls acquiring Dennis, who was then thirty-four, I didn't object. Nor did Michael. Not that there weren't some concerns. Of course there were. Michael's reaction was something to the effect of "Dennis Rodman? . . . Really?"

Yes, really, and it made a lot of sense.

The year before, Phil had experimented at power forward with Toni, Larry Krystkowiak, Dickey Simpkins, and Greg Foster, on his fourth team in five years. In the playoffs against the Magic, I assumed the role. No one came close to replacing Horace.

The power forward is a key position in basketball. It is where a lot of games are won or lost. We needed someone to get around 10 rebounds, block his share of shots, and handle bruisers such as Karl Malone, Charles Barkley, Charles Oakley, etc.

No one was better suited for the assignment than Dennis Rodman.

Believe me, I had no illusions of what this man was capable of. On or off the court.

I was the guy he shoved out of bounds in Game 4 of the 1991 Eastern Conference Finals, causing six stitches on my chin. That's not something one tends to forget.

Phil assured Michael and me that the team would be able to get rid of Dennis if he became too much of a distraction. That would be stated explicitly in the contract. *Good to know.* I didn't see it ever getting that far. Not with Phil's ability to handle a wide range of personalities, yours truly included. And not with veterans such as Michael and me, who would insist Dennis put in the work and be prepared to play night after night.

On the other hand, I was realistic. We're talking about Dennis freakin' Rodman. The one, you know, with the strange hair colors and tattoos from practically head to toe. The one who took his shirt off after games and tossed it into the crowd. The one who dated Madonna.

Anything was possible.

Ask the San Antonio Spurs. They were dying to unload Dennis. He had been nothing but trouble from the moment they acquired him from the Pistons in the fall of 1993. I don't know what the record was for fines and suspensions in a season. I got to believe he made a run at it.

In early October, the deal became official: Rodman to the Bulls for Will Perdue. I'm sure more than a few fans in Chicago were asking themselves, *What the hell are we getting ourselves into?*

One thing was for sure: there wouldn't be a dull moment.

Take the first preseason game against the Cavs at Carver Arena in Peoria.

When Dennis walked onto the court for the opening tip, his hair red, the crowd cheered as if he were Elvis. The reaction would be the same the whole season. Which, I believe, caught Dennis off guard, given how despised he was by the Chicago fans when he played for the Bad Boys. He finished with 7 points and 10 rebounds that night and got into a brief scuffle with one of the Cleveland players. Of course he did.

Over the eight preseason games, Dennis received 5 technical fouls. I repeat: *preseason*. What was going to happen when the games started counting for real?

As the days wore on, I was surprised at how reserved he was. There is Dennis Rodman the spectacle, and Dennis Rodman the man, and the two are very different. Dennis kept to himself most of the time in training camp, working on his conditioning and his craft. He was often the first player to arrive at the gym and the last to leave. I never saw anyone else learn the triangle as fast as he did. Learn it? He mastered it.

Everyone was watching him, waiting for the slightest sign of trouble. And he knew it.

Another takeaway from camp was how sharp Michael looked. This was the Michael of old, not the Michael who allowed Nick Anderson to steal the ball.

The loss to the Magic made him angry. It's not generally a good idea to make Michael Jordan angry.

Perhaps he also realized, after being away from the game for twenty-one months, how fortunate he truly was, and that this blessed career of his wouldn't last forever. Whatever time he might have left, he would make the most of it. He was thirty-two years old. That's getting up there for a basketball player.

While in Los Angeles the summer before to shoot *Space Jam*, Michael worked out with other NBA players in a gym the studio built specifically for him.

Then, back in Chicago, every morning around seven o'clock, Ron Harper and I met at Michael's house in the suburbs to lift weights in his basement. After an hour or so, we enjoyed a breakfast cooked by his chef that included pancakes, oatmeal, grits, eggs over easy, fresh-squeezed orange juice, etc. Hence, the nickname for the group: the Breakfast Club.

The idea was Harp's. He saw it as a way for guys to bond. He couldn't believe it when I told him Michael and I basically had no relationship away from the court. Like everyone else who came to the Bulls, he assumed we were tight.

I loved lifting weights. I still lift almost every day. How ironic, indeed, given how I felt about lifting weights in high school and how it nearly ended my basketball career.

After leaving Michael's house, we headed to the Berto Center for practice, where we worked on our defense and the triangle. The new guys had a lot to learn. A second weight session wasn't necessary. I took part, regardless. I didn't want Al Vermeil, the strength coach, to think he wasn't doing his job.

With Dennis, MJ, and me in top form, there seemed no limit to what we could accomplish.

B.J. was gone, taken by the Toronto Raptors in the expansion draft. I was sorry to see him go. Same for Will Perdue and for Pete Myers, who signed with the Hornets and was traded a month later to the Heat. On the flip side, we made some nice additions to our bench: guard Randy Brown, former Detroit center James Edwards, and power forward Jason Caffey, a promising rookie from Alabama. Edwards was still capable at the age of thirty-nine.

When I leafed through the schedule early that season, I told the guys: "I don't think we're going to lose a game for three months."

. . . .

I wasn't far off.

By the first week of December, our record was 13-2, the best start in franchise history. That included winning 6 of 7 on the first long road trip, the lone setback to the Sonics, 97–92. Our defense was more stingy than ever. During that trip, only Portland and Dallas scored more than 100 points. The other early loss was to the Magic in Orlando.

Amazingly enough, we weren't playing our best and were without Dennis, who missed 12 games with a calf injury. He returned on December 6 against the Knicks at the United Center. In thirty-eight minutes, he had 20 rebounds. The Knicks had a total of 39.

From then on, and for the rest of the season, we *did* play our best. The best any team has ever played.

In December, we went 13-1. The loss was on the road to the Pacers the day after Christmas, 103–97. The guys were, in one sense, relieved. Trying to keep a winning streak intact—it had reached 13—adds a significant amount of pressure, and there was enough pressure already.

Three days later, we launched another streak, defeating the Pacers in Chicago, 120–93.

This one lasted 18 games, not coming to a halt until the Denver Nuggets defeated us, 105–99, on February 4, 1996. That's forty days between losses. During the modern, post-1950 NBA, only the 1971–72 Lakers (33 games, with Wilt) and the 1970–71 Bucks (20, with Kareem) had put together longer winning streaks.

Our record after the Denver loss was 41-4. People were asking the obvious question:

Can the Bulls become the first team to win 70 games?

Why not? Michael and Dennis weren't the only ones playing at a high level. So were Harp and Toni. On many nights, Harp shut down the opponent's top scorer, while Toni gave us a tremendous boost off the bench. He would be named the league's Sixth Man of the Year.

I was also at the top of my game.

In December, I was the NBA's Player of the Month for the second time. The first was in April of the 1993–94 season. Over the 14 games,

I averaged 25.5 points, 7 rebounds, 6 assists, and 2.36 steals. I shot 54 percent from the floor and 48 percent (39 of 80) from behind the arc. Those are MVP-type numbers.

Everything was going well. Too well. The season is long. Something was bound to go wrong, especially when you have Dennis Rodman on your team. Sooner or later, he is going to lose it. The question is when. And how bad it will be.

Pretty bad.

It happened on March 16, 1996. We were playing the Nets in New Jersey. With about a minute and a half to go in the first quarter, Dennis was called for a foul on Rick Mahorn. To express his disgust, Dennis put his hands in his pants. To suggest it showed a lack of respect, to the official and to the game itself, goes without saying.

The official, Ted Bernhardt, gave him a T, his second of the game. Dennis was done for the night.

Well, not completely done. Being Dennis, that is.

He had a tantrum. No problem. Players have tantrums all the time. I certainly had my share. (Please see my relationship with my favorite folding chair.) Only Dennis did something that was anything but fine. He headbutted Bernhardt and would be suspended by the league for six games.

Missing him didn't kill us—we went 5-1—although it was definitely a cause for concern.

Phil and Michael felt he let the team down, and I had to agree with them. Up until his meltdown in New Jersey, while Dennis was picking up a lot of technicals (he would finish the season with a league-leading 28), he was, for the most part, a model citizen and needed to remain one for us to compete for another championship.

When Dennis returned to the lineup in early April, the guys were 62-8. Take 8 of our final 12 and we would reach the magic 70.

With our record at 69-9, the opportunity came on April 16 against the Bucks in Milwaukee.

The team took a bus, with Chicago only about ninety miles away. The trip was unlike any other we ever made. TV helicopters followed us for miles while fans held signs of support along the highway. We were treated more like soldiers going off to the battlefield than athletes going to a basketball game.

During our march to history, the Chicago Bulls were the hottest ticket in sports. People didn't root for us, or against us, as much as they were simply eager to be *around* us.

We took care of business, 86–80, Michael leading the way with 22 points and 9 rebounds. A work of art? Hardly. So what? The record was ours. We finished the season at 72-10. The previous record had belonged to the '71–72 Lakers at 69–13.

I'm proud of what we achieved. Though winning 70 games was not something we constantly dwelled on.

Look what happened to the Golden State Warriors during the 2015–16 season. They went 73-9 and then lost in the Finals to LeBron and the Cavaliers. The Warriors spent too much energy on breaking our record.

Harp put it best before the playoffs got under way:

"Seventy-two and ten don't mean a thing without the ring."

. . . .

The opening series against the Miami Heat, coached by Pat Riley, was a mismatch. We swept them in three games, no margin of victory less than 17 points.

Next was Riley's former team, the Knicks, now coached by Jeff Van Gundy. The Knicks still had Ewing, Mason, Starks, Oakley, and Harper.

This series promised to be much more competitive. And it was.

After dropping the first two games in Chicago, the Knicks survived, 102–99, in OT at the Garden to give themselves a chance.

Then, in Game 4, with roughly thirty seconds to go, the Knicks had the ball, down by only 1.

Ewing took a turnaround jumper from the baseline. No good. The rebound was secured by—who else?—Dennis Rodman, his nineteenth of the night. We went on to win, 94–91, and take the series in five, to send us to the Eastern Conference Finals for the first time since 1993. Our opponent: the Orlando Magic.

The Magic won 60 games themselves that season. The only reason they didn't generate more attention was because we won 72.

Getting swept by the Rockets in the NBA Finals the year before had been tough for them to swallow, no question. However, the loss was bound to help the Magic grow, as our losses to the Pistons helped us grow.

From the first day of training camp, this was the team the guys wanted to face. The Magic players celebrating in our building, carrying Horace on their shoulders, was an image we couldn't get out of our heads. Getting revenge was the only way.

We got off to a great start, capturing Game 1, 121–83, in Chicago. Dennis was in top form: 13 points, 21 rebounds. Luc was outstanding as well, with 14 points (7 of 9) in just thirteen minutes.

The game itself wasn't the only loss for the Magic.

Late in the third quarter, Horace collided with Shaq. If there's one person on planet Earth one does not want to collide with, it would be Shaquille O'Neal. Horace hyperextended his left elbow and would be out for the rest of the series.

In Game 2, they managed to do fine without him. For the first half, that is.

The Magic were on top, 53–38, Shaq his usual dominant self, with 26 points. In the third quarter, Shaq, who was doubled, took only 3 shots, allowing us to get back in the game. Heading into the fourth, we were down by just 2.

With under three minutes to go, Steve Kerr nailed a jumper to give us the lead, 83–81. We didn't trail again. The final: 93–88.

The Magic were done whether they realized it or not. In Orlando, we took Game 3, 86–67, and Game 4, 106–101. In the clincher, Michael was the leading scorer, with 45 points.

What a difference a year makes. No Nick Anderson stealing the ball. No Horace Grant being carried off by his teammates. The Bulls were back where they belonged, in the NBA Finals, to take on the Seattle SuperSonics.

Seattle won 64 games in the regular season. The Sonics, too, suffered from any comparisons to a team that won 72 games. Also similar to the Magic, they were led by two colorful stars: Shawn Kemp and Gary Payton.

No doubt the fans in the Pacific Northwest were relieved the owner had changed his mind about shipping the six-foot-ten, 230-pound Kemp to the Bulls in the summer of 1994. In each of the two seasons since then, he had averaged a shade under 20 points and roughly 11 rebounds. Once Kemp parked himself in the block, he was almost impossible to stop.

Payton, the point guard, could do everything.

He could score 20 points. He could hit the big shot. He could get the ball to his teammates in their favorite spots. Then there was his defense. That's what truly set him apart from his peers. Known as the Glove, Payton was the league's Defensive Player of the Year in the 1995–96 season.

The Sonics were far from a two-man team. Hersey Hawkins, their shooting guard, was a handful, as was small forward Detlef Schrempf. The bench was solid, as well: guards Vincent Askew and Nate McMillan, and forward Sam Perkins. Their coach, George Karl, was among the brightest in the game.

When you boiled it down, the Sonics had nothing to lose. The pressure was on us, the team that made history. If we were to fail, the 1995–96 Bulls would be remembered for losing in the Finals. Not for winning 72 games.

One possible concern: rust.

By the time we took the court for Game 1 at the United Center on June 5, we hadn't played in nine days. Practices didn't count. Nothing matches the energy of an actual game.

The Sonics, needing the full seven to knock off the Utah Jazz, had been off for only two days. That could make a huge difference.

Or not.

In Game 1, we crushed them, 107–90. MJ was our leading scorer with 28 points. A lot of guys contributed, including Toni, who poured in 18, and Harp, who finished with 15 points, 7 assists, and 5 rebounds. Luc added 14 and 4 blocks.

Two nights later, we prevailed, 92–88. Dennis was . . . Dennis, with 20 rebounds, a Finals record–tying 11 on the offensive end. The only sour note was when Harp reinjured his left knee. He was on the floor for thirty-three minutes but would be healthy enough to give us only fifteen over the next three games.

Good thing we didn't need him for Game 3 in Seattle.

The outcome was never in doubt. We were up by 24 at the half. The closest the Sonics came in the second half was 12. The final: 108–86. Toni filled in nicely for Harp, while Luc had another solid effort, with 19 points on 8 of 13 from the field.

Put the champagne on ice. Make sure the plane has enough fuel. Book the rally in Grant Park. This baby is over. Chicago, your beloved Bulls are coming home to party for the first time in three long years.

Not so fast.

Seattle took the next two games. Sorry, Chicago, you're going to have to wait a little longer.

In the first three games, the Sonics chose not to put Payton, their best defender, on Michael, because they wanted to conserve his energy so he could be more of a threat on the other end. Michael scored a total of 93 points. Down 3–0, they changed their mind.

The move paid off.

In Game 4, which Seattle won, 107–86, the Glove held Michael to 23 points on 6 of 19 from the floor, while Payton scored 21 points and dished out 11 assists. I couldn't find the basket, either, converting only 4 of 17 attempts. Two nights later, my shooting woes continued (5 of 20), as the Sonics prevailed, 89–78. I was far from alone. In one stretch, we missed 20 three-pointers in a row.

Give the other team credit. During the regular season, we averaged a league-best 105.2 points and hadn't dropped back-to-back games since February. Not having Harp didn't help. He went in and practically came right out. His knee was giving him too much trouble.

Back to Chicago we went. If not in the mood we expected, home nonetheless.

Game 6 was set for Father's Day. Michael would be dealing with a lot of emotions. I felt for him. He was Michael Jordan. He was also a son who missed his dad.

We received a big boost when Harp, who was still in a great deal of pain, walked onto the court for the opening tip. I scored the first basket, an underhanded scoop, and finished the quarter with 7 points and 2 steals. Our lead was 24–18.

From then on, we were in control. Toni hit a couple of threes. Dennis snatched every rebound. Michael and I were aggressive on both ends. And Ron Harper, bless his heart, gave us everything he had, scoring 10 points and keeping Payton from having a big game. Harp was one of our unsung heroes. In that championship season and the two to come.

Bulls, 87; Sonics, 75.

The Chicago Bulls were the best basketball team in the world. Boy, I missed saying that.

The fans were ecstatic. They were seeing something many thought, when Michael retired, they would never see again. Harp and I jumped on the scorer's table. Others joined us. Just like the scene at the Stadium in 1992 after we beat the Blazers in Game 6.

As the celebration was going on, Michael went to the locker room. He couldn't hold his emotions in any longer. He lay on the ground by the training tables, a ball cradled in his arms, sobbing. This was the first title he won without being able to share it with his dad.

Forget about the 72-10 record. Winning this one was, in some ways, harder than the others.

Consider where this team was when Michael came back in March of 1995, trying to develop the right chemistry with individuals who hadn't been around for the first three championships. The first group took years to find that chemistry. And with one of the new players—you know who—we had to learn how to bring out his best while doing everything we could to avoid bringing out his worst.

Several days later, at the celebration in Grant Park, Dennis said something that blew me away:

"I'd really like to thank one individual on this team that has accepted me and he didn't have to. And I apologize for what happened five years ago."

He was referring to the shove during Game 4 of the 1991 playoffs.

Apology accepted.

Before long, I was back in the gym, ready to represent my country again at the 1996 Olympic Games in Atlanta.

I wasn't sold on the idea at first. My mind and body needed the rest. Neither was getting any younger. Besides, nothing could possibly match being a member of the original Dream Team. In my opinion, the only Dream Team.

The folks putting the '96 squad together kept after me, explaining how the younger guys could benefit from my leadership. In the end, I couldn't say no.

Thank God I didn't.

No, playing in Atlanta didn't match Barcelona. Still, the experience was rewarding in a whole different manner.

I was one of the team's elder statesmen, as Larry and Magic were in 1992. Players such as Grant Hill and Penny Hardaway looked up to me. I was glad to help show them the way. I've always believed it is the responsibility of every veteran player to look out for the next generation, to leave the game in a better place.

Also on the squad from the Dream Team were Karl Malone, Charles Barkley, David Robinson, and John Stockton. The rest of the roster included Shaq, Reggie Miller, Gary Payton, Mitch Richmond, and Hakeem Olajuwon. The coach was Lenny Wilkens.

The United States was expected to cruise again, and it did. Not without a few struggles along the way, usually in the first half—and some anxious moments toward the end. The other teams weren't in awe of us as they were in Barcelona.

In the gold medal game against Yugoslavia, our lead with fourteen minutes to go was 1 point.

One point!

Team Yugoslavia had plenty of outstanding players, including Vlade Divac. That was no excuse.

Fortunately, with Vlade having fouled out, they had no one to stop us in the paint, leading to one dunk after another. We won going away, 95–69. David Robinson was the leading scorer with 28 points, while Reggie Miller added 20, including 3 three-pointers.

Standing on the podium with my teammates, listening to the national anthem, I was as moved as I was the first time. If I had been a part of ten Dream Teams, the feeling would have always been the same. Celebrating on American soil, seeing everyone in red, white, and blue, made it even more special.

The '96 Games, unfortunately, were memorable for another reason.

I was in my hotel room on July 27 when I heard a loud sound. When I looked out my window, I saw people running everywhere. The sound, we learned, was of a bomb exploding in Centennial Olympic Park. One person died and more than a hundred were injured. From that moment on, everything changed. We went into lockdown. Nothing happened the whole time we were in Barcelona. Now this.

I was relieved when the Games were over. Between the regular season, the playoffs, and the Olympics, I'd played in 103 games since early November.

. . . .

The Bulls got off to another tremendous start in the '96–97 season, winning their first 12 games—82-0, anyone?

The streaks kept coming, one after another:

Eight straight from December 11 to 26. Nine straight from December 28 to January 19. Eight straight from January 21 to February 5. Seven straight from February 11 to 27. At 69-13, we again finished with the best record in the league.

In the playoffs, one by one, they fell.

The Bullets in three.

The Hawks in five.

The Heat in five.

Come early June, we found ourselves in a familiar spot: the NBA Finals. This time we would face Karl Malone, John Stockton, and the Utah Jazz.

Game 1 at the United Center could have gone either way.

That's the game where Karl, who edged out Michael for the MVP that season, stepped to the free throw line with 9.2 seconds left with the score tied, and I made the comment about the mailman not delivering on Sundays.

The comment, totally spontaneous, struck the perfect tone, something that might rattle him yet not jeopardize our friendship. The friendship had meant a lot to me ever since Barcelona. I often had dinner at his beautiful house in Salt Lake City. What wonderful times they were, shooting the breeze, two poor kids from the South who had made something of themselves.

That didn't mean I felt sorry for Karl when he missed both free throws. Not a chance. He wouldn't have felt sorry for me. We were both competitors, first and foremost, after the ultimate prize in our sport.

On the next possession, the ball was in Michael's hands, the seconds ticking toward zero. The Jazz chose to cover him straight up instead of bringing in another defender to help out. Michael made them pay by nailing a 20-foot jumper over Byron Russell as the horn sounded.

Michael Jordan delivered *every* day.

Game 2 wasn't nearly as close.

We were in command from the opening tip. The final: 97–85. In the second quarter, the Jazz scored only 11 points. Michael had one of those games that he almost made routine: 38 points, 13 rebounds, 9 assists.

Even so, the series was far from over. On two occasions that season, the Jazz won 15 games in a row, and now they were going home, where their record at the Delta Center was 38-3.

Far from over, indeed.

In Game 3, Karl, bouncing back from an off night (6 for 20) showed why he was the MVP. He scored 37 points, pulled down 10 rebounds, and had 4 steals. Stockton was as efficient as usual with 17 points and 12 assists. The Jazz were better on the glass (47 to 35) and outscored us (48 to 26) in the paint. They won, 104–93.

In Game 4, played on Sunday, June 8, Utah was in trouble, trailing by 5 points with a little under three minutes left after a Michael slam capped a 12–4 run.

Stockton bailed his team out, first hitting a three from several feet behind the arc. After we scored, he followed with a huge steal from MJ and a free throw. Stockton converted two free throws on the next possession and then made an unbelievable length-of-the-court pass to Karl, who laid it in with 44.5 seconds left.

With 18 seconds to go, the Jazz ahead by 1, Karl stepped to the line. He hit both free throws.

Apparently I'd been mistaken. The mailman *can* deliver on Sundays. In Salt Lake City, at least.

Utah went on to win, 78–73, to even the series.

In four previous trips to the Finals, not once had we trailed in a series except for being down 1–0 to the Lakers in 1991. Drop a third straight game in Utah and we would suddenly be on the brink of elimination.

Of all the games the Bulls played in the nineties, Game 5 of the 1997 Finals is right up there. Everyone remembers it as the Flu Game. Or, if you believe Michael and his trainer, Tim Grover, the Food Poisoning Game.

Here are the facts as best we know them:

Michael orders a pizza around ten thirty the night before. About 2:30 a.m., he starts throwing up and can't get back to sleep. He calls Grover, who comes to his room. Michael stays in bed until it's time to leave for the arena.

Fast-forward to hours later at the Delta Center. Michael, still feeling miserable, decides he is going to give it a shot.

Early on, it didn't look good. They were making their shots (11 of 19). We were missing ours (5 of 15). Worse yet, we were committing one turnover after another. Utah went up by 16 in the second quarter.

Michael got on a roll to keep us within 4 at the half. The game went back and forth the rest of the way.

With 46.5 seconds to go, Michael stepped to the line. The Jazz were ahead, 85–84. He made the first free throw, and then came a most fortunate sequence.

After missing the second, he came up with the loose ball and took a few dribbles before getting it to me. I threw it to Toni, who tossed it to Michael, near the top of the key. Michael threw it to me near the foul line, where I was guarded by Jeff Hornacek. Russell came over, leaving Michael open behind the arc. Bad idea.

I threw it back to him. Tie game. Tie series. Michael Jordan with the basketball. The clock ticking away. Doesn't get any better than this.

Oh, yes, it does.

Bingo!

We went up 3, and won the game, 90–88. In forty-four minutes, Michael finished with 38 points, 7 rebounds, 5 assists, and 3 steals.

Many in the press ranked it as his greatest performance ever, given what was at stake and the condition he was in.

I don't necessarily disagree. However, I have a problem with how Michael was made out to be some kind of superhuman. We are professional athletes who get paid an incredible amount of money. We are supposed to perform at no less than 100 percent.

The press wasn't fully to blame. So was Michael. I'm not suggesting he wasn't sick. He obviously was. Just that he played up his role that night. The way he played up his role in almost every drama he found himself in. People made a big deal of Michael collapsing in my arms toward the end of the game. As if it showed how inseparable we were.

Sorry to spoil the script. The hug was a moment in time. Nothing more.

Making Michael too much of the story also took away for about the billionth time from what we accomplished as a team. Michael didn't hold Karl Malone to 19 points or John Stockton to 5 assists.

Anyway, the Jazz weren't done yet. They had come back before in the series. They could come back again.

Game 6 in Chicago went down to the wire.

With a little under two minutes to go, Russell nailed a three, his fifth of the evening, to tie the game at 86. The score was the same when we called time with twenty-eight seconds remaining.

Here we go again. Everyone expecting Michael to take the last shot.

Everyone except Michael, who had a feeling the Jazz might double-team him. He told Steve Kerr to be ready.

The Jazz doubled him, all right, with Stockton coming over to help out. Michael drove toward the hoop and then threw the ball to Steve, who let it go from 17 feet.

Swish.

I was thrilled for Steve, and to again see a member of the "supporting cast" come through in the clutch. We were a *team*. That's what made us great, and the point can't be emphasized enough.

With five seconds left, the Jazz had one last chance. Russell was set to throw the ball in bounds. As everyone jockeyed for position, I stayed near the free throw line. My main priority was to keep the ball from going to Karl. He was their most dangerous option.

Five . . . four . . .

The pass was headed to Shandon Anderson, their gifted rookie guard. I saw the whole play before it happened. Anticipation. Just as Coach Ireland taught us in Hamburg. I got a piece of the ball and deflected it toward Toni, who went in for the slam. Ball game.

Another championship for the Chicago Bulls. Another where nothing came easily.

That season, Dennis behaved worse than the first season. I suppose that was to be expected. A man will reveal his true colors (and

I'm not talking about his hair) eventually, no matter how much peer pressure might be applied.

He claimed he was bored. So he livened things up the way only he could.

In December, during a TV interview after a loss to the Raptors in Toronto, he used profanity while speaking about the officials. The Bulls suspended him for two games.

That was nothing compared to the events in Minneapolis on the evening of Wednesday, January 15.

After failing to secure a rebound in the third quarter against the Timberwolves, Dennis kicked a cameraman in the groin. The man was taken to the hospital and later released. The league suspended him this time, and it was for eleven games.

There was enough uncertainty in those days without having to deal with his act.

I'm referring to the future of the whole team, which was more up in the air than ever.

That's always the case in the NBA. Players move around so frequently, it's almost impossible to keep track. This was different. This wasn't just the prospect of one or two players being traded or signing with another team. The sense as the months dragged on was that much of our core group, and our head coach, might very well go their separate ways when the season ended.

Whether there was another gathering in Grant Park or not.

Every day brought further speculation: Would Michael come back? Would Phil? Would Dennis? Would I?

In any case, I didn't spend much time thinking about it. I had a wedding to attend.

My own.

CHAPTER 16: **THE LAST DANCE**

Harp called one night in August of 1996, a few days after I returned from the Olympics.

"Hey, you remember the girl I introduced you to?"

I sure did.

"She will be at this club a bunch of us are headed to in a few minutes. You should stop by."

I left right away.

The girl was a friend of someone Harp was seeing. She and I had spoken on the phone once or twice earlier that summer. She seemed pleasant enough. With my tight schedule after we beat the Jazz, the two of us couldn't find the time to meet in person.

I went to Atlanta and forgot about her.

Until Harp called.

When I got to the club, I stayed in my car. Someone, I'm guessing Harp, told her where I was parked. We talked for a while and then drove to another bar to talk some more. I found myself opening up to her about anything that came to mind. Which was unusual with someone I barely knew.

Her name was Larsa Younan. Larsa was half-Syrian, half-Lebanese. One hundred percent breathtaking.

She and I spent a great deal of time together that fall as I prepared for the '97–98 season. That was even more the case once another brutal Chicago winter descended upon us.

Being in a cold climate has its advantages. By staying indoors for hours and hours, one learns a lot about another human being. What are their virtues? What are their vices? What can I live with? What can't I live with? Do I see myself starting a family with this person? If you are lucky, as I was, you fall in love.

On July 20, 1997, Larsa and I got married at the First United Methodist Temple in Chicago.

Over the next decade, we would welcome four beautiful children into this world: Scotty Jr., in 2000; Preston, in 2002; Justin, in 2005; and Sophia, in 2008. The two of us shared a lot of wonderful times together, and like most couples, some not as wonderful. Through it all, we always put our children first. I couldn't feel more blessed.

. . . .

Meanwhile, when it came to the Bulls, one could get dizzy trying to keep track of the latest plot developments. Was this a professional basketball franchise or a daytime soap opera?

Both, if you want to know the truth.

In late June, after we defeated the Jazz, the Bulls looked once more into trading—surprise, surprise—yours truly. The offer on the table was me and Luc Longley to the Celtics for the No. 3 and No. 6 selections in the upcoming draft, along with a first-round pick in 1999.

The thinking from Jerry Krause went something like this:

Pippen will be a free agent after the coming season. Since we aren't willing to pay him what he will demand (and likely be offered in the open market), we might as well part ways with him now while we can still get something in return to help us rebuild for the future. Other teams waited too long to unload their aging stars and the rebuilding took forever.

The deal was basically done.

Until the other Jerry decided against it.

Jerry Reinsdorf believed the Bulls stood a better chance of winning one more championship with me than without me, and he couldn't be certain whether Michael, who had yet to sign a new contract, would come back for another season if I was gone. If keeping me meant the rebuild would be delayed and probably take longer, so be it.

I wasn't the only person Jerry Krause wanted out of his life. The other was Phil Jackson. Jerry had been eager to get rid of Phil for years.

Jerry brought Phil to the Bulls in 1987 when he was a nobody. Sure, Phil played in the league. A lot of guys played in the league. That didn't guarantee them a future living in basketball. Jerry felt Phil owed him big-time. Especially after he fired Doug two years later and handed Phil the job. Not just any job, mind you. A job coaching the premier player in the game and a team coming off an appearance in the Eastern Conference Finals.

For the first four or five years, Jerry and Phil got along spectacularly. Phil, unlike Doug, listened to Tex and believed in the triangle. Phil, unlike Doug, won championships.

The relationship changed in 1995 when Michael came back from his hiatus.

Phil was forced to a make a choice: Do I side with Michael, or do I side with Jerry? He couldn't side with both. Michael despised Jerry, and vice versa. Phil chose Michael.

He trusted Michael. He didn't trust Jerry.

Phil tried to keep Jerry away from the team as much as he could, sometimes asking him to leave the locker room to talk to us privately. He saw the locker room as a sacred place for the players, coaches, and trainers, who were part of *the circle*. Jerry responded like a jilted lover, pining for the day when Phil would no longer be around.

Even when the Bulls captured the NBA title in 1996 and 1997, Jerry wasn't entirely pleased. Winning meant he couldn't get rid of

Phil. Reinsdorf wouldn't let him. Jerry Krause would have to wait for the right moment. The moment finally arrived in the fall of 1997.

The two Jerrys came to an understanding:

Phil would be allowed to coach for another season but that would be it. That's when Jerry Krause told him he could go 82-0 and it wouldn't make any difference.

Jerry used to constantly claim there was a better coach out there than Phil. There wasn't a better coach out there, and that definitely included Tim Floyd, the Iowa State coach, whom Jerry was grooming for the job. He wanted to find a coach he could control, someone who would be loyal to him. Simple as that.

So what did these twists and turns have to do with me?

Plenty. Just as they had an enormous effect on Michael, who made it clear on numerous occasions he wouldn't play for any coach except Phil. The news confirmed what I had suspected for the longest time, and I was far from alone:

The 1997–98 season would be, as Phil put on the front page of a handbook he gave to the players at training camp, the *last dance.*

Once Phil signed on, Michael came aboard for another year, and then, eventually, so did Dennis. The Bulls, an old team, looked like a rock group preparing to go on a farewell tour.

Except there was one jaded member who was interested in joining a different band.

Care to guess who?

I know, I'm the guy who claimed he never really wanted to leave, that he loved Chicago, the neighborhoods, the clubs, the restaurants, etc., etc., etc. All of that was true, I swear.

However, the fall of 1997 was another of those periods in which I'd simply had enough of the lying and the disrespect and was convinced my only chance for happiness—and the payday I deserved as one of the game's elite players—was somewhere else. Anywhere else.

It started with the near trade to the Celtics.

The Bulls had just won another title—a title, if I might be so bold, like the four before, the team would have never won without me. Except, instead of being allowed to savor the moment, I soon found out I was likely headed to a franchise that won only 15 games the year before. The whole experience was demeaning beyond belief. Just like the near trade to the Sonics in 1994.

Then, in September, I got a letter from Jerry Krause threatening, if I'm not mistaken, to fine me if I appeared in my upcoming annual charity game, the Scottie Pippen Ameritech All-Star Classic. A charity game! The nerve of that guy.

Ultimately, I didn't play, although it wasn't because I was afraid of Jerry and his attorneys. My left foot, which I had injured in the conference finals against the Heat, was still giving me a lot of trouble. In early October, I underwent surgery. The initial estimate was I would be out two to three months.

The Bulls weren't pleased. If I'd had the operation in July, I would have been ready for the start of preseason. Now I wouldn't return until December, at the earliest.

Some in the organization and the media thought I delayed the surgery on purpose to get back at Jerry Krause.

Add that lie to the countless others that were spread about me over the years. I took my time because I didn't want to risk another operation and ruin a whole summer by hobbling around on crutches while there was a chance that if I got enough rest, I might be good to go by the time training camp rolled around.

. . . .

I did a lot of thinking in those first weeks after the surgery.

Of how fortunate I was to be part of a dynasty that won five championships in seven years and how sad it was our time together would soon be coming to an end. And how, when the right opportunity presented itself, I would express my appreciation to the people of Chicago, many of whom stuck by me during some difficult days.

It came at the United Center on the night of November 1.

Ring night.

Addressing the crowd in street clothes, I found myself getting choked up:

"Thank you for all the wonderful moments that the fans in this city have shown me and my teammates for ten long seasons. I've had a wonderful career here, and if I never have the opportunity to say this again, thank you."

I meant every word.

The Bulls beat the Sixers that night, 94–74. Harp led the way with 17 points and 8 assists. Jason Caffey scored 14 (7 of 8) and pulled down 6 rebounds, while Dennis, coming off the bench, added 13 boards. After that, we knocked off the Spurs in double overtime, 87–83, and the Magic, 94–81.

Maybe the guys would manage just fine without me.

Maybe not.

On November 20, we lost to the Suns in Phoenix, 89–85, to drop to 6-5. During the previous two seasons, our record after 11 games was 10-1 and 11-0. Both times, we didn't suffer our fifth defeat until January or February.

The next night, we needed two overtimes and 49 points from Michael to get by the Clippers.

Ladies and gentlemen, these are not your Chicago Bulls.

I was sitting in the locker room prior to the Clippers game when Kent McDill, a reporter from the *Daily Herald*, a paper in the Chicago suburbs, stopped by for a chat. Kent was one of the few members of his profession who was fair to me. He wanted to know if I had a good idea of when I would be back on the court. Almost two months had gone by since the foot operation.

Funny you should ask, Kent. I definitely have some thoughts on the matter. Got your notebook out? Great.

Safe to say it wasn't the answer he expected:

"I'm done playing for the Chicago Bulls. I want to go where I can get paid."

This was not some off-the-cuff response delivered in a moment of anger. I was quite calm and knew precisely what I was saying.

And the audience I was trying to reach.

Here's a hint: the initials were JK.

Only Kent didn't quote me in the next day's paper, which was unusual, to say the least. Reporters were always in a hurry to put out anything, true or false, that would generate controversy.

When I ran into Kent a couple of days later in Sacramento, I asked him what happened. Apparently he didn't believe I was serious.

I told him again. He believed me this time.

The story ran the next day. It was big news in Chicago, and around the league. When other reporters asked if it was true, I didn't back down for a second.

The near trade to the Celtics. The threatening letter from Jerry. The certainty I didn't fit into their long-range plans.

Enough was enough.

I caught some heat, as I anticipated, from fans who were sick of my complaining. Phil and Michael weren't thrilled, either. Both thought my decision to delay the surgery had harmed the whole group, and now I was causing more trouble.

They could believe whatever they wanted. I said what I needed to say and felt good about it.

If only I stopped there.

After the game against the Sonics, I had a little too much to drink. While we were on the bus, I lost my temper and went after Jerry Krause, who was accompanying the team.

"When are you going to stop taking credit for drafting me and for my career?" I shouted.

I became such a distraction during the trip that Phil suggested I return to Chicago and get therapy on my foot instead of going with the guys to the next stop, Indianapolis. I didn't argue with him. As frustrated as I was, if I hung around Jerry much longer, I was liable to say something a lot worse.

The team, meanwhile, had finally started to develop a nice rhythm.

Beginning in mid-December, the Bulls won 8 in a row to reach a record of 20-9, best in the East. In 6 of the 8, we held our opponent to 92 or fewer points.

A lot of the credit went to Dennis.

Without me around, he embraced the opportunity to be the No. 2 guy to Michael. In back-to-back games versus the Hawks and the Mavericks, Dennis pulled down a total of 56 rebounds, and in the month of December, he had at least 15 rebounds on eight different occasions (five games of 20 or more).

Meanwhile, as we rang in the New Year, one thing was becoming increasingly clear:

I wasn't going anywhere.

Believe it or not, I was okay with that. I'd had some time to cool off since the episode on the bus in Seattle. I missed playing with the guys. I missed the magic we created when everyone was on the same page. Asking for a trade never had anything to do with them.

Only my recovery wasn't going as smoothly as I had hoped. The target date for my return was sometime around Christmas. Three months had now passed since the operation. In early January, Phil told the press I was still two weeks away from even being able to participate in a full practice.

The season was passing me by.

Yet I didn't lose faith. I kept working hard with Al Vermeil while the rest of the team practiced.

The work finally paid off.

On January 10, I made my return after missing 35 games. When I took the court for warm-ups before our game at the United Center against the Warriors, the fans gave me a standing ovation, and another when I was introduced as one of the starters. I knew I missed being out there. I didn't know how much.

I scored the first two baskets and finished with 12 points, 4 rebounds, and a team-high 5 assists in thirty-one minutes. We won, 87–82. I didn't shoot the ball particularly well (4 of 11), as one would expect after such a long layoff.

Three nights later, against Seattle, I was off again: 3 of 15. No matter. I was feeding the guys in their favorite spots and forcing teams to stop double-teaming Michael. Without me in the lineup, the Bulls averaged 22.5 assists per game. Against the Sonics, whom we defeated, 101–91, the team registered 26 assists.

At the halfway mark, our record was 29-12. The only setback was when Steve Kerr fractured his collarbone against the Sixers. The estimate was he would be out for eight weeks.

All things considered, there was no reason to complain.

Except if you are Dennis Rodman and you are no longer the No. 2 guy.

Two weeks after my season debut, Dennis skipped a morning shootaround. His reason for not being there: he didn't "feel like it."

Phil, as a result, didn't feel like having Dennis around when we took on New Jersey. He sent him home.

Dennis missed another shootaround several weeks later. The excuse this time: he couldn't find the keys to his truck. I'm not making this up. I wish I were.

That winter, Dennis took off on his infamous vacation to Las Vegas. Only Dennis Rodman would ask for a vacation in the middle of a season, and only Phil Jackson would give it to him. In the end, however, the time away from basketball was what Dennis needed.

And we needed Dennis.

On February 19, another trade deadline passed and I was still a member of the Chicago Bulls. Everyone was relieved, me included. We were on track to win another championship.

After my return, the Bulls went 38-9 the rest of the season to finish with 62 victories, once again entering the playoffs as the No. 1 seed in the East.

. . . .

The first two series went pretty much according to plan. The Nets fell in three, the Hornets in five. The fewer games in those early rounds, the better. There was a lot of mileage on those legs of ours.

Next, in the conference finals, were the Indiana Pacers, who won 58 games that season.

Talk about a tough out.

The starting lineup was most formidable: Reggie Miller (shooting guard), Chris Mullin (small forward), Mark Jackson (point guard), Rik Smits (center), and Dale Davis (power forward). Miller, an incredible shooter, and Mullin, my teammate on the Dream Team, would be bound for Springfield.

The bench, with Jalen Rose, Antonio Davis, Travis Best, and Derrick McKey, was also exceptional. When the Pacers played us in March, their subs outscored our subs, 32–0. Needless to say, we would need a lot more production from Steve Kerr, Bill Wennington, Randy Brown, and Scott Burrell, a swingman we acquired from the Warriors.

Containing Jackson, who had 35 assists in the 4 games against us during the regular season, was our top priority.

Only how?

By having me guard him, that's how.

Harp, Michael, and I came up with the idea during a Breakfast Club workout. We mentioned it to Phil, who was on board 100 percent. Phil was always open to suggestions from his players, which we greatly appreciated. Not every coach is like that. If the idea came from us, Phil knew we would be committed to making it work.

Mark Jackson was the head of the snake. Not Reggie Miller.

It was Jackson who got the ball to Reggie when he came off screens. Or found Smits, a force at seven foot four, in the lane. Or threw perfectly timed lob passes to Antonio and Dale Davis (not related). Jackson saw the entire court like Magic Johnson. He just happened to be eight inches shorter. I would defend him the same way I defended Magic in the 1991 Finals. Pick him up close to half-court and make him work as hard as possible before he could get his teammates into the flow of the offense.

The strategy couldn't have worked any better.

In Game 1, which we won, 85–79, he finished with more turnovers (7) than assists (6).

My size—I had Jackson by six inches and roughly forty pounds—was too much for him to handle. The Pacers committed 25 turnovers. That was the difference in the game. Michael finished with 5 steals, while I had 4.

Ditto for Game 2: 7 more turnovers for Jackson, 19 for the team. Michael poured in 41 points in a 104–98 triumph. This time, I had 5 steals, while he had 4. I also blocked 3 shots.

Time for Larry Bird, the rookie coach for Indiana, to attempt a little gamesmanship.

Why not? Nothing else was working.

Larry complained the refs were letting me get away with too much contact. He said that would never happen if I were guarding Michael.

The gamesmanship worked. I picked up 2 fouls in the first quarter of Game 3 in Indianapolis and could not be nearly as aggressive. Jackson ended up with just 2 turnovers while sharing the point guard duties with his backup, Travis Best. Reggie was on fire, hitting 4 threes, as the Pacers beat us, 107–105.

No problem. As Michael explained to the press afterward, the loss was nothing more than a "bump in the road."

In that case, Game 4, to apply the same metaphor, felt like getting involved in a fender bender, and I had myself to blame.

With 4.7 seconds to go, I was on the line for two free throws. If I made both, we would enjoy a 3-point lead.

I missed both.

The Pacers won the game on a Reggie three-pointer with 0.7 seconds left. I was steamed. It wasn't just those two missed free throws. For the night, I was 2 for 7 from the line. I couldn't wait to redeem myself. Which I did, fortunately, in Game 5 (20 points, 8 rebounds, 7 assists) as we blew the Pacers out in Chicago, 106–87, to assume a 3–2 lead.

Two nights later, back in Indy for Game 6, I was steamed once again. Not with myself. With Hue Hollins.

You remember Hue. And the outrageous foul he called on me in the waning seconds of Game 5 against the Knicks in 1994.

He did it again.

This time, with about a minute and a half to go and the Bulls up by 1, he cited me for an illegal defense. You don't make that call at this stage of a game—especially a playoff game. What did this guy have against me? Reggie hit the free throw and the Pacers wound up winning, 92–89, to even the series. Their bench again played a pivotal role, outscoring our reserves, 25–8. Over the six games, the margin was 197–100.

The last dance was suddenly on its last legs. Was this where it was all going to come to an end? In the conference finals?

It seemed entirely possible.

Especially, early in Game 7, after the Pacers, who made their first 8 field goal attempts, seized a 13-point lead. Of our first 19 field goal attempts, we converted only 5. Indiana was up by 8 at the end of the quarter.

Enter, stage right, Steve Kerr.

Steve had 8 points in the second quarter as we outscored them 29–18 to take a 3-point advantage into the locker room. I can't overstate how critical those points were. The Pacers had been in control of the game.

Same goes for the speech MJ delivered at halftime. He never brought up the possibility that we might lose. So it didn't occur to us, either.

Enter, stage left, Toni Kukoc, who, like Harp and Horace, has never received enough credit for our success.

Maybe not being an American hurt him. Or maybe, because of Michael, Dennis, and me, there was no room on the stage for anybody else. Whatever the reason, Toni, who was elected this year to the Basketball Hall of Fame, came up big in one of the biggest games we ever played. In the third quarter, when the team extended the lead to 4, he scored 14 of our 21 points.

Even so, with about six and a half minutes remaining, the Pacers were back on top, 77–74. When Michael drove toward the basket, the ball was knocked loose, resulting in the most important jump ball of the game. And the season. Michael, at six foot six, was matched up against the seven-foot-four Smits.

Smits won the tip, but somehow the ball ended up in my hands.

After Michael missed a midrange jumper, it was batted out to where I could again retrieve it.

A new 24-second clock. A new life.

On the other side of the court, I spotted Steve, who was wide-open behind the arc.

Swish. Chicago, 77, Indiana, 77.

A new game.

About a minute later, I grabbed another rebound after Luc missed a jumper. I soon hit from the outside to put us ahead, 81–79. We wouldn't trail again. The final: 88–83.

Looking back at Game 7, the basketball gods were definitely on our side. If the jump ball between Michael and Smits had gone the other way and the Pacers had taken a 5-point lead late in a game in which both teams were struggling to score, who knows how it would have turned out?

. . . .

From one tough test to another. Next up: the Utah Jazz.

The Utah Jazz, with the same record as the Bulls, 62-20, would be well rested after sweeping the Shaq/Kobe Not-Ready-for-Prime-Time Lakers in four games. And because they had beaten us in both meetings during the regular season, the series would open in Salt Lake City. The Jazz would be the first team we'd face in the Finals for a second time, and that would surely be to their benefit. They'd know what to expect.

At least, like us, there was a lot of mileage on those legs of theirs.

Stockton was thirty-six years old, Karl Malone was thirty-four, and Jeff Hornacek, their starting shooting guard, was thirty-five. One of the keys obviously was to keep Karl in check. He was coming off another superb season, averaging 27.0 points and 10.3 rebounds per game. The assignment fell to Luc and Dennis. Brian Williams, who defended Karl well in the 1997 Finals, had signed with the Pistons.

Similar to the Pacers, the Jazz had a strong bench: along with Russell and Anderson, forward Antoine Carr, guard Howard Eisley, and centers Adam Keefe and Greg Ostertag. Our bench needed to play better than it did in the Indiana series.

In Game 1, we certainly had our chances.

With about two and a half minutes to go, I nailed a three to tie the score at 75. After Dennis blocked a jumper from Karl, I tried another three. I missed this time.

Karl scored on the next possession, and the possession after that, to put the Jazz ahead by 4. Luc made a late jumper to get us into overtime, but Stockton took over from there. He fed Karl for a layup and followed with a 3-point play. Stockton scored 7 of his 24 points in the extra session. Utah won, 88–85.

A missed opportunity, without question. No matter. Gaining the split we came to Salt Lake City for was still within reach.

And soon a reality.

In Game 2, Michael scored 37 points, including several baskets in the last few minutes to propel us to a 93–88 victory. Our defense held the Jazz to 15 points in the fourth quarter. The Jazz committed 19 turnovers, 4 by Karl, who was 5 for 16 from the field.

Then, out of nowhere, came a Game 3 in Chicago that is still hard to believe.

The final was 96–54, Bulls. Yes, final.

The 54 points (23 in the second half) were the fewest in any game since the shot clock came into effect in the 1950s. The Jazz shot 30 percent from the floor, committed 26 turnovers, and were outrebounded, 50–38. No one on their team, except Karl (22), scored more than 8 points.

If the game itself didn't any provide any drama, what took place the next day off the court made up for it. Thanks to Dennis.

Who else could it be?

First, he skipped a team meeting and a mandatory media session. The Bulls fined him $10,000 for missing the meeting. The league fined him the same amount for blowing off the media. Then he had the audacity to fly to Detroit to appear on a cable-TV wrestling show with Hulk Hogan . . . *in the middle of the NBA Finals.*

Dennis was at practice the next day. In Game 4, which we won, 86–82, he finished with 14 rebounds and 6 points, including two critical free throws to give us a 4-point lead with 43.8 seconds left.

That was Dennis Rodman in a nutshell.

One day, he acts like someone who should be committed. The next, he chases down every loose ball as if the future of mankind depended on it. Who were any of us to question the man's, shall I say, eccentricities? Maybe Dennis needed those other outlets to be at his best on the basketball court.

I was at my best, that's for sure.

In Game 4, I scored 28 points (hitting 5 of 10 three-pointers), grabbed 9 rebounds, and had 5 assists. On the defensive end, I used my size and quickness to make things difficult for Stockton, while helping out when the Jazz went to the screen-and-roll with Karl. I was building a strong case to be, for the first time, the MVP of the NBA Finals. I could think of no better way to end my eleven years with the Bulls.

Unfortunately, that's not what happened.

Despite 30 points from Toni, we dropped Game 5, 83–81. Karl was magnificent with 39 points and 9 rebounds. He hit a jumper over Dennis to give the Jazz a 4-point cushion with 53.3 seconds remaining.

I was far from magnificent, going 2 for 16, including 0 for 7 from beyond the arc. MJ wasn't much better: 9 for 26. As a team, we shot 39 percent. The Jazz shot 51 percent.

As in 1993, when we failed to clinch the title at home against the Suns, we now had to take a long plane ride we didn't expect. This time to Salt Lake City.

It was the last place in the world we wanted to be. I thought the old Stadium was the loudest arena I ever played in. The Stadium was nothing compared to the decibel level at the Delta Center. I felt as if I were sitting in the front row of a rock concert.

If the final 1.8 seconds against the Knicks is considered by others (not me) to be the lowest moment of my career, the evening of Sunday, June 14, 1998, has to go down as the exact opposite.

The day didn't start out very promising.

The problem had plagued me so many times I'd lost count—my back. I first noticed a little soreness after Game 3. Such was the price for taking a few too many charges, including two from Karl. The back bothered me in Games 4 and 5, yet I was able to play through it. Only, the pain kept getting worse. On the flight to Utah, I couldn't wait for the plane to land.

I received a cortisone injection, which helped—to a point. I was still in agony when I arrived at the arena on Sunday afternoon.

The elbow from Laimbeer in 1989. The migraine in 1990. Were the basketball gods messing with me again?

If so, I wasn't about to let them have their way.

Not this time.

When I dunked the ball on the first possession of the game, it felt as if someone had stabbed me in the back. The shock of the landing pinched my nerve. Every time I ran, I got a spasm. I tried to gut it out. I couldn't. With us leading 17–8, I went to the locker room for electrical stimulation and some stretching. I remained there the rest of the half.

While I was gone, the Jazz took advantage. They led by 3 at the end of the quarter and by 4 at halftime. Karl was on a roll. So, thank goodness, was Michael, who scored 23 of our 45 points. He kept us in the game.

I felt awful, and it wasn't just my back. I was letting the guys down. I hadn't felt that way in a long time. I told Chip Schaefer, our trainer:

Do whatever you have to do. Just get me out there as fast as you can.

I returned in time to start the third quarter.

However, with about three minutes to go in the quarter, I went to the locker room again for further therapy. We stayed within reach, trailing by 5 points heading to the fourth.

Early in the quarter, I checked back in. I wasn't my usual self. Not even close. I'll never forget this one play earlier in the game where I would normally have slammed it home. I could barely get off the floor. I didn't want to get off the floor. Every time I did, I was compressing a disc that was on my nerve.

I thought to myself, *Don't the Jazz see me hobbling around the court? What game are they watching? Why are they even putting a man on me?*

I couldn't go to the paint. I couldn't shoot from the perimeter. I couldn't do anything except tell guys how to defend Karl. If this were any other game—hell, any other playoff game—I would have been in street clothes.

Yet, with a little over five minutes to go, I somehow managed to hit a turnaround jumper in the lane to cut the Utah lead to 1, 77–76.

It was a big basket. Every basket down the stretch was big.

None seemed bigger than the three-pointer Stockton made with forty-two seconds left, putting his team ahead, 86–83.

The Delta Center exploded. Time-out, Bulls.

The goal was to get a quick bucket so we wouldn't have to commit a foul.

We scored in less than five seconds. I'd say that was pretty quick. Michael caught the inbounds pass near half-court and drove by Byron Russell for an easy layup.

The next goal was to get a stop.

That, too, happened fast: Michael stripped the ball from Karl, who had caught the pass from Stockton on the baseline. Having seen the Jazz run the same play earlier in the game, Michael figured that Karl wouldn't be expecting him to leave his man and be there.

Now we needed a basket. Every coach would call a time-out in that situation.

Every coach except Phil Jackson.

Phil didn't want to give the Jazz a chance to set up their defense. The seconds ticked away. I knew my role without anyone having to tell me: get the hell out of the way. John Paxson nailed the winning shot in the 1993 Finals. Steve Kerr nailed the winning shot in the 1997 Finals. This was Michael's turn.

The last Finals. The last dance. The last shot. Who else?

If you follow the sport at all, you know what happened next. If you don't, I'm happy to fill you in.

Michael is covered tightly by Russell behind the three-point line, the Jazz deciding not to double-team him.

The crowd is standing. Time is standing still.

Michael drives toward the top of the key, then comes to a sudden stop. Russell slips. Michael rises. He lets it go from 18 feet. Nothing but net. The Bulls take the lead, 87–86. The Jazz call time with 5.2 seconds left. The Delta Center has never been this quiet. You can almost hear a dream drop.

The ball is thrown in bounds to Stockton, who misses a long jumper. The horn goes off. It's over. The game. The series. The dynasty.

As the celebration began, I was in a daze, too many feelings to juggle. Exhilaration for winning another championship. Exhaustion for putting my body through hell. Sadness for the end of something no one might ever see again.

Thank God we won Game 6. I couldn't have played in a Game 7.

Before we knew it, the guys and I were back on the stage at Grant Park, the fans more enthusiastic than ever.

"One more year!" they shouted.

CHAPTER 17: **GO WEST, OLD MAN**

Phil was headed to his home in Flathead Lake, Montana, for some rest and relaxation. Which he desperately needed.

In his own, if more detached, way, he cared about winning (and hated to lose) as much as Doug Collins did, perhaps more, and that took quite a toll, year after year. Even so, everyone knew he would be back coaching in the league before too long. The game was in his blood. He was only fifty-two.

Michael was headed to his second retirement. Who knew, one day, there would be a third. In the meantime, he would play more golf and film more commercials. And be Michael Jordan, a full-time job in itself.

Myself, where was I headed?

Good question.

Somewhere out West, in all likelihood, where I could look forward to a warmer climate. Any place was warmer than Chicago.

I also preferred the more free-flowing, and less physical, brand of basketball they played in the Western Conference. Especially as I approached my midthirties and the bumps and bruises didn't heal as quickly. I'd had enough of being pushed around by the Oakleys and Mournings of the world. There had to be an easier way to make a living.

The Lakers were my first choice.

With Shaq, twenty-six, and Kobe, only twenty, they were the team of the future—perhaps, with me providing veteran leadership, the team of the present. None of the Lakers, except for Robert Horry, had earned a ring. Los Angeles seemed perfect for me.

Phoenix was another possible destination.

Except the Suns, while extremely talented, weren't on the verge of winning a championship. After the success I enjoyed in Chicago, even in the year without Michael, I couldn't imagine settling for anything less.

In the end, I joined the Houston Rockets. They *were* on the verge. Or so I assumed.

I didn't come aboard until January of 1999. That's due to the NBA lockout that had threatened to cancel the whole season. Once the players and owners finally reached an agreement, it was decided each team would play just 50 games. That was fine with me. I'd had another operation on my back in July. It turned out that I had played the final three games against the Jazz with two bulging discs.

The deal was for five years and $67 million. The payday I waited for my whole career had finally arrived.

For that, I had someone I never expected to thank, Jerry Krause.

By agreeing to a sign-and-trade with the Rockets, the Bulls made it possible under league rules for the deal to be worth at least $20 million more than it would have been. Perhaps Jerry wasn't such a bad guy, after all.

I called him shortly after everything was finalized. The conversation went well.

Despite everything, I never forgot the chance he took on me. What if I had been a bust? Who knows if the Bulls would have become . . . the Bulls? If not for Jerry, I would probably have ended up with a franchise that was hoping to rebuild.

That didn't have Michael Jordan.

Maybe it would have worked out, regardless, and I would still have been one of the Greatest 50 Players ever, as I was named by the league in 1996, prior to its fiftieth-anniversary season. And maybe I would still have picked up my share of rings.

Maybe not.

I looked forward to working out with my new teammates in Houston. Such as the future Hall of Famer Hakeem Olajuwon, who had just turned thirty-six years old. The Bulls never had a big man close to his caliber.

So Hakeem was not the player he was in his prime? Neither was I.

One guy, unfortunately, wasn't at practice. He was playing golf at the Bob Hope tournament in Palm Springs, California, where the amateurs, including celebrities, compete with the pros from the PGA Tour. I'm referring to my teammate from the Olympics, Charles Barkley.

I remembered reading some article where Michael said Charles wasn't dedicated enough to win a championship.

I didn't agree. Charles worked as hard in practice as anyone else on the Dream Team and, in the games themselves, left everything on the floor. On the other hand, his decision to play golf—with Michael, of all people—after the lockout ended wasn't a good sign. We needed to be on the floor, all of us, together, as soon as possible to see how we meshed as a unit and what we needed to work on.

The new, condensed 1998–99 season would be here in no time. Where every game would take on greater significance.

He showed up, eventually, and when he did, he was the same old Charles. At thirty-five, Charles was still one of the best players in the league.

Hakeem, Charles, me—a Big Three before Big Threes became the trend in the NBA. What could go wrong?

Plenty.

A month into the season, despite playing more than forty minutes a game (with the Bulls, I had never averaged more than 38.6), my scoring was way down, and there was a reason.

Two reasons, to be precise: Charles and Hakeem. I kept feeding the ball to them in the low post. That was my whole job.

Which meant a lot of standing around and watching them play one-on-one. I was used to the triangle, to the ball moving from one player to the next on every possession until we found the best scoring opportunity. I felt as if I were back in the late eighties, watching Michael throw up a million shots night after night. The game wasn't much fun anymore. I wondered, Why did the Rockets want me in the first place? Anyone could throw the ball into the post.

Just then, we started to win. A lot. Nine in a row over the final two weeks of March, 5 of them on the road. Gaining the No. 1 seed in the ultracompetitive West was a real possibility.

Unfortunately, we managed no better than about .500 ball down the stretch. Still, the team finished a more than respectable 31-19, third in the Midwest Division behind the Spurs and Jazz.

Our opponent in the first round of the playoffs, a best three-of-five, would be the Lakers.

These weren't the Lakers who would soon become the NBA's next dynasty. They started the season coached by Del Harris. He was fired after 12 games (they were 6-6), replaced by Kurt Rambis. Yet with Shaq and Kobe, and a cast that included forwards Glen Rice, Robert Horry, and Rick Fox, and point guard Derek Fisher, the Lakers finished with the same record as us. Notice I didn't say *supporting* cast.

Anyway, in Game 1 in Los Angeles, we had the ball and a 1-point lead with less than thirty seconds to go.

One more basket and we might be on our way.

I then lost my balance in the lane, the loose ball grabbed by a diving Fisher, who wisely called time with 7.6 seconds left. Horry threw it in bounds to Kobe, who was fouled by one of our guards, Sam Mack. Kobe made both free throws.

The Lakers were now up, 101–100. Time-out, Rockets; 5.3 seconds to go.

After catching the inbounds pass, Cuttino Mobley, a talented rookie, drove toward the hoop. The ball was swatted away from behind by Shaq. The buzzer sounded.

Gone was a wonderful opportunity to steal one on the road. We didn't get another.

The Lakers took Game 2, 110–98, and won the series in four. I couldn't recall the last time I was this disappointed. Perhaps the migraine game in 1990. Or the Hue Hollins fiasco in 1994. I thought this team had a chance to go to the Finals.

For the season, I averaged 14.5 points, my lowest output since 1988–89. The offense installed by our coach, Rudy Tomjanovich, wasn't fully to blame. So was the man in the mirror. That man wasn't the same. Whether it was any lingering damage from the two bulging discs or Father Time—I would turn thirty-four in September—or both, I couldn't go all out on every possession as I did in Chicago. I needed to pick my spots and rely more on my basketball IQ.

The story was the same in the playoffs. Except for Game 3, when I scored 37 points, a postseason high, I was pathetic. I scored 36 in the other three games *combined*. In Game 2, I was 0 for 7 from the field. In Game 4, I was 6 for 23. For the series, I shot 33 percent.

I let my teammates, the organization, and the city of Houston down.

Unfortunately, I wasn't the only one.

Michael was correct. Charles wasn't dedicated enough to win a championship. Not even close.

Before the season got under way, Tim Grover, Michael's trainer, came to town to work out with Charles and me. Charles didn't last one week. Michael could get away with playing golf and a hectic lifestyle. Charles could not. Something had to give, and that was basketball. He was a lot like Shaq. As great as he was, he should have been greater.

In any case, that summer, I spread the word that I wanted out of Houston—if possible, to hook up with the Lakers, who had recently hired a new coach I was a little familiar with, Phil Jackson.

Believe me, I hadn't forgotten about Phil having Toni Kukoc take the last shot. That I would never forget. At least I knew Phil wouldn't tolerate players showing up out of shape or not working hard enough, and he, as well as Tex, one of L.A.'s assistant coaches, would make sure everyone got involved in the offense. There would be no more standing around, watching guys go one-and-one. The game would be fun again.

Once Charles learned of my intentions, he opened that big mouth of his. He said I owed the Rockets and him an apology.

Okay, Chuck, if that's how you want to play it.

"I wouldn't give Charles Barkley an apology at gunpoint," I told the press. "He can never expect an apology from me. If anything, he owes me an apology for coming to play with his sorry fat butt."

I would never have said anything against him if he hadn't gone after me first. What gave him the right? When he did, it brought out the frustration I had kept bottled up for months. I didn't have many years left in my career. I had just wasted one of them.

Charles and I are cool now. That was a long time ago. The two of us simply had different approaches to the game, and there was only one way to resolve them.

Yes, I was soon on the move again.

Not to Los Angeles. The owner, Dr. Jerry Buss, wasn't willing to pick up the last year of my deal. I couldn't blame him. He was already paying Shaq a fortune. I'll always wonder what it would have been like to play with Shaquille O'Neal and Kobe Bryant. I might have been a Laker until I was forty.

Instead, I was headed to Portland in exchange for six players: Kelvin Cato, Stacey Augmon, Walt Williams, Ed Gray, Brian Shaw, and Carlos Rogers.

Talk about a soft landing. The Blazers, coming off a loss to the Spurs in the 1999 Western Conference Finals, were loaded.

Besides myself, they had recently added Atlanta guard Steve Smith and Seattle forward Detlef Schrempf to a roster that included Rasheed Wallace, Damon Stoudamire, Arvydas Sabonis, Greg Anthony, Brian Grant, Bonzi Wells, and a promising center who had come straight out of high school, Jermaine O'Neal. I could not wait to get to work.

Me in Portland. Phil in Los Angeles. Wouldn't it be something if we were to meet in the Western Conference Finals?

Slow down, Pip. You had high expectations with the Rockets and look how that turned out.

Portland isn't a big city like Los Angeles. I didn't care. What matters when you are a professional basketball player is where you spend your time—and the people you spend your time with.

Your teammates.

The neighborhood.

The organization.

Check. Check. Check.

＝＝＝＝

I was used to fast starts with the Bulls, and here was another:

Four in a row. Ten of 11. Thirteen of 15. Come early December, we were leading our division, a game and a half ahead of the Lakers and the Kings. We cooled off a bit, then regrouped to win 6 straight on two occasions.

The team was as formidable as I thought it would be. If not more.

One game on the schedule in those early months stood out. How could it not? I was going home. That's how I felt about Chicago. Home. No matter how much I had been disrespected. No matter how many times I'd asked the Bulls to trade me.

So much had changed since my last appearance at the United Center in Game 5 of the 1998 Finals. For myself, on my third team in three years, and for the Bulls, coached by Tim Floyd, who were 2-25 (they would finish the season 17-65). In case you're wondering, I didn't feel sorry for Jerry Reinsdorf or Jerry Krause. They were getting exactly what they deserved.

The organization was another matter entirely. It didn't deserve this. By the organization, I'm referring to the ticket sellers, the security officials, the maintenance workers, the PR guys, etc., etc. Everyone I ran into told me the same thing:

"It certainly ain't what it used to be."

Prior to the opening tip, the Bulls showed a video of my highlights on the big screen. The ovation I received couldn't have been more generous. For a moment, the fans had something to celebrate.

As for the game itself, it was as lopsided as expected.

The Bulls committed 31 turnovers in dropping their eleventh in a row, 88–63. Damon Stoudamire led us with 16 points and 5 steals. I added 11 points and 6 assists.

I felt bad for former teammates who had been left behind, such as Randy Brown, Dickey Simpkins, and Toni Kukoc, who was out with back spasms (luckily, for him, he would be traded a month later to Philadelphia). Same for Will Perdue and B. J. Armstrong, in his final season, who were back where they began their careers in the late eighties. I couldn't begin to imagine what they were going through.

In late February, we took on the Lakers in Portland. This wasn't a typical regular season game. Both teams stood at 45-11, the best record in the league. Both had won 11 straight. Something had to give.

Us, as it turned out.

The Lakers prevailed, 90–87, Shaq leading the way with 23 points and 10 boards. Kobe had 22 points.

The night wasn't a total loss. Our guys showed a lot of resiliency in coming back from an 11-point deficit in the fourth quarter and had a chance to tie the game near the end. I walked out of the Rose Garden with my head held high.

Wait until May. We can beat this team. No doubt about it.

If only we could beat the other teams on our schedule.

From March 1 through the end of the regular season, our record was a lackluster 14-11. With the playoffs about to get under way, there was definitely cause for concern. We didn't have a leader, someone to get on guys when they weren't doing their jobs. Someone, I dare say, like Michael Jordan, even if he went too far on more than a few occasions. Better too far than not far enough.

Why not me?

I have asked myself the same question many times over the past twenty years. I wish I had a good answer.

Being new to the team, I was concerned with fitting in with players who had been around for a while, such as Damon and Rasheed. I should have been concerned with doing whatever was necessary to win a championship.

Our first opponent, in a best-of-five series, was the Minnesota Timberwolves, led by a young star, Kevin Garnett. They went down in four.

Next was the Utah Jazz, led by two stars who were not young. Stockton was thirty-eight and Karl was about to turn thirty-seven. Yet the Jazz were as gritty as ever, staying alive with an 88–85 victory in Game 4 after losing each of the first three by 18 points or more. The end came in Game 5.

Watching those two future Hall of Famers, and Hornacek, who

was about to retire, reminded me of the memorable duels with the Bulls in 1997 and 1998.

I was about to take part in another.

I had asked for the Lakers, and here they were, with the winner headed to the Finals.

With so much on the line, Phil was up to his usual mind games. A year in the Montana woods hadn't mellowed him one bit.

The target on this occasion was someone he knew well.

"I personally think that if Scottie doesn't lead this basketball club and take this team by the horns," Phil told the press, "they're not going to get by us."

It was my turn to be the snake, and he was looking for a way to cut off my head.

This time, however, the Zen Master had met his match. I knew him as well as he knew me. Certainly enough not to take his bait.

I also knew the triangle. I knew it better than the Lakers players themselves. Whenever I saw how they were set up, I yelled to our guys what was coming next. That had to tick off Phil to no end.

Shaq, on the other hand, hadn't met his match.

I could yell until doomsday the play they were running and it would make no difference. In Game 1, which the Lakers won, 109–94, he had 41 points, 11 rebounds, 7 assists, and 5 blocks. I played well (19 points, 11 rebounds, 5 assists) but we were never really in it.

Most disappointing was Rasheed Wallace, who was ejected in the third quarter when he received a second technical. Rasheed was our best player, by far. His one fault, and it was a big one, was he couldn't control his anger. He made Dennis Rodman look like a Boy Scout. During the regular season, Rasheed committed 38 technicals, the most in the league.

He assured me it wouldn't be a problem in the playoffs. He was wrong.

I didn't realize his trouble with the refs went back a ways, and once you have a bad reputation, it follows you the rest of your career. You can forget about getting the benefit of the doubt on any close calls.

Rasheed was the Kevin Durant of his day, able to get off a high-percentage shot anytime he wanted, with his left or right hand. He was one of the first bigs to run to the three-point line. He could make it from Steph Curry range. Rasheed would need to be at his best for us to win the series.

In Game 2, he was (29 points, including 3 of 3 from behind the arc, 12 boards, and 2 steals), as we cruised to a 106–77 victory to get the split in L.A.

Heading to Portland, we felt good about our situation. Leaving Portland, we felt horrible.

The Lakers took both games to go up 3–1.

In Game 3, a 93–91 win, Ron Harper, who had signed with the Lakers as a free agent, nailed a 19-foot jumper from the corner with 29.9 seconds remaining to put them on top. Kobe stripped the ball away from Rasheed on the next possession and blocked a shot from Sabonis at the end.

In Game 4, the Lakers didn't need any late heroics in prevailing, 103–91. They outscored us, 34–19, in the third quarter. Shaq was 9 for 9 from the line. What were the odds of that happening?

Everyone figured the Blazers were finished. We had other ideas.

In Game 5, we jumped out to an early lead on the road and held them off the rest of the way. The final: 96–88. I scored 22 points, including 12 in the first quarter. The win would mean nothing unless we could back it up, which we did, capturing Game 6 in Portland, 103–93. Bonzi Wells was terrific off the bench with 20 points.

Which brings us to the Staples Center in Los Angeles, California, on the evening of June 4, 2000. Of all the games in my career, this is the one that keeps me up at night. Not the migraine game. Not the 1.8 seconds game. Not the Hue Hollins game. This game.

What if I had done this? What if our coach, Mike Dunleavy, had done that? What if . . .

I drive myself crazy thinking of all the what-ifs.

I will explain what took place as best I can. If I can't bear it any longer, I hope you'll understand.

At halftime, the score was 42–39 in our favor. Both offenses continued to struggle early in the third. A 19-foot jump shot by Glen Rice put the Lakers on top, 51–50, with under six minutes remaining in the quarter.

Then it happened. We turned into the 1995–96 Bulls. Over the next five minutes or so, we outscored the Lakers, 21–4.

In that stretch, Steve Smith made 4 field goals, including 2 threes. Rasheed also hit a few baskets, while I nailed a three-pointer of my own with twenty seconds left to give us a 16-point advantage. Up to that point of the quarter, the Lakers had scored only 16 points. Kobe had 4, while Shaq took 2 shots and missed both of them.

The fans were in shock.

During his team's final possession, Kobe, drawing a double, passed it to Brian Shaw, who banked in a three with a couple seconds to go.

A bank? Are you serious? He didn't call bank.

I was worried the Shaw prayer might get the Lakers, and their fans, back in the game.

It didn't. Smith hit a bucket early in the fourth to extend the lead to 15, and it was still 15 around the ten-minute mark.

Nothing could stop us now.

Nothing except an inability to make a basket and that no one on the Portland Trail Blazers, including me, a six-time NBA champion, and Dunleavy, a veteran coach, took charge when everything began to fall apart.

Where was Phil Jackson when you needed him? Coaching the other team, that's where.

Shaq kicked off the Lakers rally with an easy one in the lane. On the next possession, Brian Shaw, that man again, hit another three. No bank this time.

Suddenly, alarmingly, the Lakers were only 10 back. We called time. The fans were into it now. Over the next six and a half minutes, we missed 11 shots in a row (13 overall), allowing the Lakers to tie the game at 75. Six of the 13 misses were from Rasheed.

Missing shots wasn't our only problem. So was our attitude. It was horrible.

During an earlier time-out, Dunleavy had drawn up a play to throw the ball inside to Rasheed. The Lakers couldn't guard him in the block. He was almost as automatic as Shaq. Yet as we broke the huddle and walked onto the court, Rasheed explained he had a different play in mind.

"Smitty [Steve Smith], fuck what that bitch [Dunleavy] just said," Rasheed told us. "I'm going to kick that bitch [the ball] out to you, and you shoot the three."

I was beside myself. I had been around the game a long time, and I figured I'd heard it all.

Guess again, Pip.

I'd never heard a player defy a coach so blatantly, and on such a big stage. I should have said something to Rasheed before the ref blew the whistle and play resumed. I don't know why I didn't.

And it wasn't as if this were a onetime occurrence. Heavens, no. The players disrespected Dunleavy all the time, and worse yet, he let them get away with it. He raised his arms in frustration when guys executed a different play from the one he called, but there were never any consequences. He had lost control of the team long ago.

Yet, despite missing shot after shot and defying our coach, here we were, still with an opportunity to reach the Finals. Remarkable, really.

With just under three minutes to go, Rasheed scored in the lane over Robert Horry to end the drought and put us ahead, 77–75. Then, after Shaq converted two free throws—he always seemed to hit them when they mattered most—and made a basket, Rasheed secured good position again. Shaq blocked his shot but was called for goaltending.

The score was tied at 79.

On the next possession, Kobe was fouled by Rasheed. He made both free throws. When we got the ball, Shaq fouled Rasheed. He missed both free throws. The second wasn't close. After Kobe hit a jumper, the lead was 4.

Then, with about a minute left, I took a three, my third shot of the quarter. No good. All three were no good.

That's it. I can't bear to go on with any more play-by-play. I told you that might happen.

Lakers, 89; Blazers, 84.

Here's the worst part: the game was for more than the Western Conference title. The game was for the whole thing. The Indiana Pacers, who defeated the Knicks in the Eastern Conference finals, would be a heavy underdog to whoever emerged from the West. (The Lakers won it in six.) To top it off, this was my second—and final—chance to win a championship without Michael.

The first time, Hue Hollins got in the way. This time, there was no one to blame but ourselves.

The Lakers didn't win Game 7. We lost it.

Too often that season, guys bickered with one another and with Coach Dunleavy instead of remembering who the real enemy was, the other team.

It didn't kill us against everyone else. We had too much talent.

It killed us against the Lakers. Especially in the fourth quarter when everything began to unravel. When we needed to stick together. When we needed a leader.

. . . .

I spent three more seasons in Portland. Three forgettable seasons. I was always nursing one injury or another.

Not once did the Blazers advance past the first round of the playoffs. In 2001 and 2002, the Lakers, on the path to two more championships, swept us in a best-of-five series. Only once in the six games was the margin of victory less than 7 points. Dunleavy was fired in May of 2001. I felt bad for him, as I'd felt bad for Doug. Truth is, though, he should probably have been let go a lot sooner.

Replacing him was Mo Cheeks, who had been an assistant coach in Philadelphia. Mo's honeymoon lasted about five minutes. Guys weren't crazy about his substitution patterns and the way he utilized the roster.

The players in that generation were different from the players in my generation. Tex would have had a heart attack if he had to coach this group.

There was, however, one night that brought back a lot of memories.

It was December 10, 2002, when we played the Wizards in the nation's capital. Neither team was going anywhere. Surely just another game in an 82-game grind.

Not quite.

On the Washington roster was a player wearing number 23. Yup, that number 23.

How strange, indeed, for Michael and me to be on opposite sides after all these years, both of us long past our prime. He was in his second season with the Wizards. We didn't go against each other his first season because he was hurt both times our teams squared off.

Many people thought Michael was tarnishing his legacy by coming back at the age of thirty-eight. I was not one of them. He wanted to play the game he loves, and there was nothing wrong with that. If he felt he could still compete today, I guarantee you he would be out there.

Neither of us put up great numbers that night. I had 14 points and 7 rebounds. He had 14 points and 5 rebounds. My team won 98–79.

Michael retired for good after the 2002–2003 season.

For me, there was one act to go.

On July 1, 2003, I officially became a free agent for the second time.

One of the first calls I received was from a former teammate, John Paxson, the general manager for the Bulls. Jerry Krause had resigned in April after eighteen years with the organization.

Pax didn't waste any time:

"Scottie, we would like you to come here and play for us this year. We need you. Bill [Cartwright, the coach] needs you."

Safe to say, ending my career in Chicago wasn't something I'd ever thought of during the five years in Houston and Portland. In addition to the guys being young and not very good (the Bulls finished 30-52 in the 2002–03 season), I hadn't, if you recall, exactly left town on the best of terms.

Besides, now that the end was near, I wanted to go out on top. What athlete doesn't?

Pat Riley's Miami Heat, one possible destination, wasn't willing to offer more than the veteran's minimum of $1.5 million per season. After the lack of respect I endured year after year in Chicago, I told myself I would never accept being underpaid again.

Which left the Memphis Grizzlies as perhaps the most attractive option, and not due to the salary alone, which would be for the same amount the Bulls would offer. Michael Heisley, the owner, brought up the possibility of me purchasing a piece of the team once my playing days were over.

Here was one time I did want to be like Mike. (Michael Jordan became a minority owner with the Wizards after his second retirement and today owns the Charlotte Hornets.)

One place I wasn't headed back to was the Pacific Northwest.

The Blazers had recently laid off nearly a third of their front office and arena employees, and clearly weren't about to pay me enough. I felt sorry for the fans in Portland, perhaps the most rabid in the NBA, and will always feel bad I didn't bring them a championship.

We came so close. If not for that final quarter against the Lakers in 2000.

In the end, I chose the Bulls because I was familiar with the situation: the city, the building, the coach, all of it. I was eager to help Bill, whom I had tremendous respect for, any way I could. He wasn't given the greatest hand to play with when he took over in December of 2001.

So much, by the way, for Jerry Krause's faith in Tim Floyd. Floyd's record in a little more than three seasons with the Bulls: 49-190.

Having family around—Larsa was from Chicago—as she and I, in 2000, had started a family of our own, was another important factor in the decision.

I signed a two-year contract for $10.3 million, for what is referred to in the league as the mid-level exception. I was never good at math but I knew that mid-level beat minimum.

The role the Bulls had in mind was perfect for an old fogy such as me.

I would play maybe twenty to twenty-five minutes a game, helping youngsters such as bigs Eddy Curry and Tyson Chandler, and guards Jamal Crawford and Kirk Hinrich. I was impressed by how gifted they were and the passion they showed for the game. Yet being as raw as Eddy and Tyson were—both went from high school to the NBA before the "one-and-done" rule went into effect in 2005—they had a great deal to learn.

Due to the usual nemesis, my back, I missed the first five preseason games. Finally, on October 18 at the United Center, I put on a Bulls uniform for the first time since Game 6 of the 1998 Finals in Salt Lake City. I scored 4 points and collected 3 rebounds and 3 assists.

I figured the team was in for a long season—perhaps longer than I thought after what happened on opening night.

We lost at home to the Wizards, who, let's face it, weren't exactly the Shaq/Kobe Lakers. Lost? Try slaughtered. The score: 99–74. The guys shot 32 percent from the floor and finished with more turnovers (18) than assists (16). We also missed 12 of our 31 free throws. Other than that . . .

Two nights later, the Hawks came to town. We played much better, our bigs showing why their future was bright. Tyson pulled down 22 rebounds (9 offensive) and blocked 4 shots. Eddy scored 22 points, including a thunderous dunk to put us up by 4 with about a minute to go.

From the future to the past. During halftime, the Bulls unveiled a banner, which read: GENERAL MANAGER, JERRY KRAUSE, 6 NBA TITLES.

Once the ceremony honoring Jerry was over, I shook his hand and wished him well. Same for his wife, Thelma.

I realize now that plenty of times when Michael and I were critical of Jerry Krause, we should probably have pointed the blame at Jerry Reinsdorf. Reinsdorf made the important business decisions, not Krause. Reinsdorf refused to renegotiate my contract year after year, not Krause.

Reinsdorf owned the Chicago Bulls. Not Krause.

I was on the court for thirty-one minutes against Washington and twenty-seven against Atlanta. Bad back or not, I was holding up pretty well for a man of my advanced age.

Guess again.

My left knee, which had been operated on in March, was acting up again. The following night in Milwaukee, I played only thirteen and a half minutes and not very well: 0 for 6 from the field. The Bucks destroyed us, 98–68. After undergoing an MRI, I missed the next four games.

On November 10, we fell to the Nuggets, 105–97, our fourth loss in five games at the United Center. So much for home-court advantage. Worse yet, a few guys were complaining about being removed from the starting lineup.

I thought I was back in Portland.

We'd held a team meeting earlier that day, where I spoke longer than anyone else. That was the reason they brought me here, to teach the kids how to behave like professionals. I backed Bill 100 percent, and not because he was my friend. Because he was my coach. He had a right to play whomever he wanted. Afterward, everyone appeared to be on the same page.

Two days later, we defeated the Celtics in Boston, 89–82. I finished with 12 points, 5 rebounds, and 2 steals. Our record was 4-5.

Maybe this wouldn't be a long season after all. Maybe we could surprise some people.

Not a chance.

After two more losses at home, to Minnesota and Seattle, the team hit the road. The change in scenery didn't do us any good.

On November 23, we dropped our fifth game in a row, 110–99, to the Kings in Sacramento.

On November 24, Bill was fired. Our record: 4-10.

When I heard the news, it all hit me at once:

Here we go again. Even without Jerry Krause, this franchise is as dys-

functional as ever. I should never have come back. I should have taken the Memphis offer, played for a couple of years, and then become one of the owners. What was I thinking?

Pax got rid of Bill way too quickly. Bill wasn't the reason we were losing. He didn't pick the players.

I deserved some of the blame. I had let Bill down. As a mentor, and as a player.

In those last five losses, I scored a total of 35 points and had 17 rebounds. If we had won two or three of those games, he might have kept his job.

Anyway, once he was let go, I checked out. I started looking for the exit signs. If the Bulls had brought in a good coach to replace him, I might have gotten fired up again.

They didn't. They brought in Scott Skiles.

I didn't like Skiles, who had coached several seasons for the Suns, from day one. He acted as if he were a tremendous winner with a tremendous work ethic because he'd played with Shaq in Orlando.

Give me a break. All he did was pass the ball to Shaq. Anyone could have done that.

Skiles couldn't stand Eddy being out of shape. I wasn't crazy about it, either. Only his answer was to run everyone to death. I was old-school. You don't punish the whole team because one guy is out of shape.

My knee, meanwhile, wasn't getting any better. I kept getting the fluid drained. The fluid kept coming back.

There was no mystery here. My body was going to break down at some point, and that point had finally arrived. Since the fall of 1987, I'd played a total of more than forty-nine thousand minutes, including the playoffs, and undergone nine surgeries. I was lucky it hadn't broken down before.

Make that ten.

After having an operation to clean up some cartilage, I was out for about a month, returning in mid-January against the Pistons. I didn't score a single point. In my next eight games, I reached double figures only once. The team lost each one of those eight.

On January 31, we took on the Blazers in Portland. The fans were on my side that night, giving me a standing ovation during the introductions. I was quite touched.

The basketball gods were also on my side:

Pip, we know you are very close to the end of your career so, for old times' sake, we have decided to give you one last chance to shine. Make the most of it.

I did just that, with 17 points, 7 rebounds, and 4 assists in thirty-five minutes. I hadn't scored 17 points in a game the whole season or played longer than thirty minutes since November 21. We lost in overtime, 102–95.

Two nights later, with 9:53 to go in the first quarter against the Sonics, I caught a pass from Kirk Hinrich and hit a 21-foot jumper.

Nothing special about the basket.

Nothing and everything.

The basket was my last ever in the NBA. Ironic that it came in Seattle, the franchise that, technically, drafted me. And almost traded for me in 1994.

I soon was back on the injured list and didn't play another game. I finished the season averaging 5.9 points, 3 rebounds, and 2.2 assists.

All that was left now was when I would officially announce my retirement. I would wait for the fall when training camp got under way. No player retires during the off-season. You never know what might change your mind.

One day, I received a call from a financial guy with the Bulls. The team still owed me a little more than $5 million for the second year of the contract. I was wondering when we might get around to that.

"We would like to spread the money out over a few years," he said. "You okay with that?"

Absolutely not.

I got my way, which caused more bad blood between me and the organization. As if there hadn't been enough bad blood to last a lifetime.

■ ■ ■ ■

The October 5 press conference at the Berto Center was nothing like the press conference on that unforgettable October day in 1993. When Tom Brokaw was there, and David Stern, and every cameraman and reporter in America. When fans were in shock that Michael Jordan was leaving the game in the prime of his career.

I didn't wear No. 23, and people had seen my retirement coming for months.

"I'll miss the camaraderie of being around the players and competing each and every day," I told the press. "That's going to be the hardest thing to deal with."

I thanked the fans, Jerry Reinsdorf, and John Paxson.

"It's a tough day for me," I said, "but I also understand the game of basketball has been so great to me for so long."

Before I knew it, no more pictures were being taken and no more questions were being asked.

Walking out of the Berto Center with Larsa and my two boys, I felt the way I did after finishing high school and college.

Now what?

One possibility was coaching. Working with the young players in Chicago, I realized I still had a lot to give to the game I loved.

The game that changed my life. The game that gave me everything.

I knew how to draw up plays and set defenses. I knew how to put the right people in the right positions. I knew how to motivate a group of individuals to act as one.

Another possibility was to work for the Bulls in some capacity.

Despite how things ended with management, I was still a member of six championship teams, and no one could ever take that away from me. I fell in love with the city in the summer of 1986 when I went to visit my sister and played hoops on Lake Shore Drive with Dwyane Wade's father.

I never fell out of love.

Anyway, after the sacrifices I'd made to get to the NBA, and stay there, I was in no rush to figure out the next move. I had a family to raise. With the arrival of another son, Justin, in 2005, there were five of us now.

A new team to nurture.

. . . .

On December 9, 2005, the Bulls retired my jersey during halftime of a game against the Lakers.

The fans were tremendous. The ovation I received when Johnny "Red" Kerr, the longtime TV commentator, introduced me is something I'll always cherish. I was hard on them, and vice versa, but more often than not, they were in my corner. In the good, and the bad, times.

Having ex-teammates such as Oak, Dennis, Horace, Toni, and others on the stage meant more than I could ever describe. I appreciated, as well, the kind words from Phil and Michael. Hard to believe seven years had gone by since the last dance.

In March of 2011, the group got together at the United Center to mark the twentieth anniversary of our first championship.

Michael didn't want to come. I had to convince him and it wasn't easy. That's one of the reasons the Bulls put me on the payroll as an "ambassador" in 2010. To get Michael back into the fold. To show the fans and media we were one big happy family.

I was playing the same role I did on the court: bringing everyone together.

"Do it this one time," I told MJ, "and I promise I will never ask you again."

He was still angry with the organization for not giving us an opportunity to win another championship. Seriously, who else but the Bulls would break up a team after winning it all?

Winning not just once, mind you. Three years in a row! Six out of eight!

On the other hand, I have always felt it was fitting our reign ended when it did. Everything must end at some point, in basketball and in life. We should celebrate change, wherever it might lead us.

I'm beginning to sound like the Zen Master.

Could we have won another title? Without a doubt. The shorter, 50-game season would have been perfect for our old legs. Nothing against the Spurs, who, with David Robinson, Tim Duncan, Avery Johnson, and Sean Elliott, defeated the Knicks in the 1999 Finals. Only that we were better.

That's true, as well, for the two dynasties that came later: the Los Angeles Lakers of the early 2000s and the Golden State Warriors of recent years. I'll stack our roster against the Warriors any day—especially our second three-peat teams.

Let's go through the matchups:

Dennis Rodman or Draymond Green at power forward? Dennis.

Luc Longley or Andrew Bogut / JaVale McGee at center? Luc.

Michael Jordan or Klay Thompson at shooting guard? Michael.

Me or Kevin Durant at small forward? You could go either way.

The only matchup clearly in Golden State's favor would be Steph Curry over Ron Harper at point guard.

One more thing: the Warriors had nobody off the bench as skilled as Toni Kukoc.

Prediction: Bulls in six. (The series couldn't go seven. After all, we were never extended to a Game 7 in the Finals.)

As long as we are comparing dynasties, I'm happy I played in my era and not today. Back then, the game was officiated evenly for the offensive and defensive player. Now the offensive player has a distinct advantage.

Today, by halftime, teams sometimes have 70 points. We used to have plenty of games with the final scores in the 80s.

Anyway, when the guys reunited in 2011, it didn't go well. Michael wasn't alone. Everyone felt bad about the way things came to an end.

We're still not one big happy family, and that's on the Bulls. They have done very little to honor any of the other five championship teams, including the 1995–96 group that won 72 games. They act as if those teams never existed.

Believe me, if this had been the Lakers or the Celtics, and we had won six titles in eight years, we would be treated like royalty. Those are first-class franchises. The Bulls are not. It's no coincidence they haven't been in the Finals since 1998.

Even the Cubs have won a championship since then.

In the spring of 2010, on the weekend of the Final Four in Indianapolis, I was elected to the Naismith Memorial Basketball Hall of Fame.

Though I had no doubt that the announcement was coming, I was blown away. In the one-on-one games at Pine Street, when Ronnie Martin and I talked about our dreams for the future, neither of us ever brought up the Hall of Fame.

Some dreams are too big to imagine.

How, then, did it happen? How was I able to join this incredibly exclusive club with the likes of Wilt, Kareem, Magic, Michael, and Larry?

Luck played a huge role. The right people kept finding a way into my life, and thank God I was wise enough (most of the time) to learn from them. Michael Ireland, Donald Wayne, Don Dyer, Arch Jones, Phil Jackson, etc.

Hard work played a huge role, as well. I treated every setback as an opportunity. Starting with those damn bleachers.

The hard work didn't start with me. Heavens, no. The hard work started with Ethel Pippen.

I saw the effort Mom made every day with my brother, my father— with all of us. There was no limit to the amount of love in that woman's heart. She passed away in February of 2016 at the age of ninety-two. I miss her more than words can possibly describe.

. . . .

For the Hall of Fame ceremony, I needed to choose an official presenter, a person to stand on the stage with me as I delivered my remarks. That individual is required to be a member of the Hall.

I thought about asking Dr. J, since he was the player I idolized growing up. Except I barely knew him.

Instead I picked someone I knew quite well, whose greatness I observed up close, day after day, year after year. There really was no other choice.

So what if Michael and I weren't best friends?

The two of us will forever be linked together, the best duo in NBA history. He helped make my dreams come true, as I helped make his. He said yes right away and I was extremely grateful.

The ceremony in Springfield, Massachusetts, was held on August 13, 2010. What a night. In addition to being honored for my individual accomplishments, the 1992 Dream Team was also inducted. Seeing the group together again brought back a lot of wonderful memories.

In my speech, I thanked my parents; my brother Billy; Ronnie Martin; the Bulls organization; my former coaches and teammates; and, of course, Larsa.

"I played this game that I love so much, and everything I had, I laid it out there," I told the audience. "I've also tried to live my life in the way that will make the people I love and care about proud of me. . . . I have been able to live my dream of playing basketball surrounded by people I love and being cheered on by the best fans in the world. It was a great ride."

■ ■ ■ ■

Every so often, since my retirement, I explored the idea of coaching. I missed the game terribly.

In 2008, to show how interested I was, I asked Michael for a job. I prided myself on asking him for as little as possible. He had recently hired Larry Brown to be the head coach of his team in Charlotte, then known as the Bobcats.

"Talk to Larry," Michael said.

I wasn't offended in the least. Brown was one of the most highly regarded coaches in the game, winning titles in college (Kansas) and the pros (the Pistons). He had a right to pick his assistants and not have one of the owners interfere. No matter who that owner happened to be.

Brown didn't seem interested.

"I have the staff I need," he told me.

I didn't ask Michael, or Brown, for a job ever again.

On several occasions, I brought up the idea with people in the Bulls organization. They told me Tom Thibodeau, who coached the team from 2010 to 2015, didn't want me around. I never found out why.

Not long after Thibodeau was let go and the Bulls hired Fred Hoiberg, who had been the coach at Iowa State, I realized that I would never be offered a meaningful role in the organization. I moved the family to Florida.

One person who gave me a chance to do some coaching early on was Phil Jackson, who was back with the Lakers after a year away from the game.

"Come to training camp in Hawaii," Phil said, "and we'll talk after that."

This was in the fall of 2005. I worked with the players on different aspects of the triangle. I enjoyed the experience immensely. Working with Kobe was a special thrill. For years, from a distance, I had observed his growth both as a player and a man. To watch him up close, on and off the court, I was even more impressed. His death in late January of 2020 hit me hard.

The audition, if that's what it was, couldn't have gone better. However, after it ended, Phil never said another word about any coaching position. I suspect Brian Shaw, one of his assistants, viewed me as a threat, which kept Phil away.

I once received an offer from my alma mater, Central Arkansas. I turned it down. I didn't feel it would have been fair to uproot my family.

Looking back, my not being a coach worked out for the best.

I'd already lived a life where basketball was No. 1, and No. 2 was far behind. I lived that life my *whole* life.

Instead, I was able to lead a different group of youngsters, my kids. I couldn't be prouder of them. They include Antron, Taylor, Sierra, Scotty Jr., Preston, Justin, and Sophia.

I think about Antron every day. He passed away a few months ago from complications related to asthma. He was only thirty-three.

Antron was one of my best friends. The courage he displayed in dealing with his health problems reminded me a lot of my brother Ronnie. He never saw himself as a victim. I will forever wonder what amazing things he would have accomplished.

Speaking of amazing things, I'm excited about the future for Scotty

Jr., twenty-one, the eldest of the four children I had with Larsa. He is quite a player in his own right.

Last season, as a six-foot-three starting point guard for Vanderbilt, he averaged 20.8 points and 4.9 assists. In one game, against Cincinnati, he scored 36 points and had 4 steals. Now in his junior year, he has a chance to play in the NBA.

Scotty Jr. is a different kind of player from what I was, and the game has changed dramatically since I was his age.

Yet, as I watch him in his journey, I think of my own.

Of how we finally got past Isiah, Laimbeer, and the rest of the Bad Boys.

Of the incredible joy I felt after we beat the Lakers for our first championship.

Of the gold medal around my neck in Barcelona as they played "The Star-Spangled Banner."

Of gutting it out in Game 6 of the 1998 Finals when I could barely get off the ground.

Of the coaches who taught me so much about the game—and about life.

Mostly, I think of the skinny boy from Hamburg, Arkansas, who had nothing going for him but a dream. I think of Pine Street and Grandma's dirt court. And of the day in high school I almost quit running the bleachers.

While I gasped for air on those steps, I heard an inner voice speaking to me with more urgency than ever before. The voice was saying the same thing my teammates were saying—a message I would carry from that day forward, from one challenge to the next.

"Come on, Pip. You can make it."

ACKNOWLEDGMENTS

For the longest time, friends and family members told me that I should write my life story. That the journey I took could be a source of inspiration, to young people especially, proof that your dreams can come true if you work hard and never stop believing in yourself.

The idea of digging into my past was tempting, to be sure. Still, I always resisted. I was too busy living my life to take the time to talk about it.

A few years ago, as I approached my midfifties, I stopped resisting. I realized that I had better tell my story before I came up with more excuses and it became too late.

Not long afterward, in the early weeks of the pandemic, I watched the first episode of *The Last Dance*. I became more convinced than ever that I was making the right decision. If I didn't tell my story, no one else would.

Or they would tell a distorted version of it.

I soon learned that writing a book isn't much different than playing on a basketball team. Many people, not just the ones who occupy center stage, have an important role to fulfill, and if they don't do their job properly, the final product has no chance of success.

Fortunately, from day one, the team at Atria Books was full of talent and dedication. I couldn't be more fortunate.

I'll start with the editor, Amar Deol. It wasn't just his vision of the project that was so impressive. It was also his boundless energy. Whatever the task, whatever the issue might be, he was always there with an encouraging word.

I owe a lot, as well, to many others at Atria: publisher Libby McGuire; associate publisher Dana Trocker; editorial director Lindsay Sagnette; editorial assistant Jade Hui; marketing specialist Maudee Genao; deputy director of publicity David Brown; managing editor Paige Lytle; assistant managing editor Jessie McNiel; production manager Vanessa Silverio; production editor Al Madocs, and designers Dana Sloan and Renato Stanisic.

Of course, none of this would be possible without my co-writer, Michael Arkush.

Michael pushed me where I needed to be pushed, even to some places I didn't want to go. I will always be grateful for the dedication he showed to his craft, to making sure my story was accurate and authentic. I want to thank his wife, Pauletta Walsh, and agent, Jay Mandel. Michael is also blessed to have a great team.

During my playing career, from junior high through the pros, I was surrounded by incredible teammates. I'm still very close to many of them. It's a long list and I can't name everyone, but wanted to mention the following:

From Hamburg High: David Dennis, Darrell Griggs, Lee Nimmer, LeTroy Ware, Steven White.

From the University of Central Arkansas: Jamie Beavers, Robbie Davis, Mickey Parish.

From the Chicago Bulls: B.J. Armstrong, Randy Brown, Corie Blount, Jud Buechler, Scott Burrell, Jason Caffey, Bill Cartwright, Dave Corzine, Horace Grant, Ron Harper, Craig Hodges, Michael Jordan, Steve Kerr,

Stacey King, Joe Kleine, Toni Kukoc, Cliff Levingston, Luc Longley, Pete Myers, Charles Oakley, John Paxson, Will Perdue, Dennis Rodman, Brad Sellers, Rory Sparrow, Sedale Threatt, Darrell Walker, Bill Wennington, Scott Williams.

From the Houston Rockets: Charles Barkley and Hakeem Olajuwon. (I'd also like to acknowledge the late Moses Malone, who was a star in Houston in the late 1970s and early '80s.)

From the Portland Trail Blazers: Greg Anthony, Stacey Augmon, Brian Grant, Shawn Kemp, Jermaine O'Neal, Arvydas Sabonis, Detlef Schrempf, Steve Smith, Rasheed Wallace, Bonzi Wells.

I can't say enough for the coaches I've been around. They taught me about so much more than basketball. They include Johnny Bach, Ronnie Blake, Maurice Cheeks, Jim Cleamons, Doug Collins, Mike Dunleavy, Don Dyer, Angel Evans, Michael Ireland, Phil Jackson, Arch Jones, Rudy Tomjanovich and Donald Wayne.

I want to give special attention to the late, great Tex Winter. While Tex was my biggest critic, at the end of the day, he was also my biggest fan and he helped me play the game the right way.

Many other people were helpful in this book coming together: Ryan Blake, Muggsy Bogues, P. J. Carlesimo, Franklin Davis, Don Paul Dyer, Steve East, Frankie Frisco, Arch Jones Jr., Artie Jones, Billy McKinney, Chip Schaefer, and Phyllis Speidell.

I want to thank some in the media for their support over the years. They include: the late Lacy Banks, Melissa Isaacson, K. C. Johnson, Kent McDill, Rachel Nichols, Bill Smith, and Michael Wilbon.

Countless others have been there for me over the years, and I want to let them know how much I appreciate it.

They include Julie Brown, Jeff Chown, Matt Delzell, Peter Grant, Tim Grover, Jeff Katz, Tim Hallam, Kamal Hotchandani, Lynn and Debron Merritt, Michael Okun, Joe O'Neil, Jerry Reinsdorf, Michael and Nancy Reinsdorf, J.R. and Loren Ridinger, Wes Sutton, William Wesley, and

Jeff and Deb Wineman. I can't forget Antwan "Snake" Peters, rest in peace, my brother.

I want to thank a few people from my team:

My agent, Sloane Cavitt Logue at WME, has been a tremendous champion of mine over the past few years. I couldn't be more appreciative of her drive, passion and positivity.

The same goes for my close friend, Adam Fluck. No one in my camp has been more devoted. He's a trusted confidant and I look forward to taking on many more projects together in the coming years.

I owe a special thanks to my best friend, Ronnie Martin. Ronnie and I became friends in junior high and have been close ever since. His support, and wise counsel, have gotten me through many difficult times. Ronnie is more than a friend. He is family.

Family, of course, is everything to me. When you're the youngest of 12 children, you have too many relatives to name everyone. But I can't leave any of my siblings out: Barbara Kendricks, Billy Pippen, Faye Tucker, Ray Robinson, Ronnie Pippen, Sharon Pippen, Jimmy Pippen (deceased), Donald Pippen, Dorothy Pippen (deceased), Carl Pippen, Kim Pippen.

I'll forever be grateful to my parents, Preston and Ethel, for raising me right and providing me with the tools I needed to succeed. They are the ones who helped me understand what it means to be accountable and work hard. They also stressed the importance of being compassionate and kind. I wouldn't be where I am today without their love and support.

ABOUT THE AUTHORS

SCOTTIE PIPPEN played seventeen seasons in the NBA, winning six championships and two Olympic gold medals. He was honored as one of the 50 Greatest Players in NBA History in 1996. Pippen is the only person ever to win an NBA championship and Olympic gold medal in the same year twice and was inducted into the Naismith Memorial Basketball Hall of Fame in 2010. He lives in the Los Angeles area, and you can follow him on Facebook, Instagram, and Twitter @ScottiePippen.

MICHAEL ARKUSH has written or co-written fifteen books, including *New York Times* bestsellers *From the Outside* by Ray Allen and *The Big Fight* with Sugar Ray Leonard. Arkush previously served as a staff writer at the *Los Angeles Times*. He lives with his wife, Pauletta Walsh, in Oak View, California.